EXPRESSIONS OF ETHNOGRAPHY

EXPRESSIONS OF ETHNOGRAPHY

Novel Approaches to Qualitative Methods

Robin Patric Clair

STATE UNIVERSITY OF NEW YORK PRESS

Published by
State University of New York Press, Albany

For information, address State University of New York Press,
194 Washington Avenue, Suite 305, Albany, NY 12210-2384

Production by Kelli Williams
Marketing by Fran Keneston

Library of Congress Cataloging in Publication Data

Expressions of ethnography : novel approaches to qualitative methods / Robin Patric
    Clair, editor.
      p. cm.
    Includes bibliographical references and index.
      ISBN-13 978-0-7914-5823-5 (hc: alk. paper) — 978-0-7914-5824-2 (pbk: alk. paper)
      ISBN 0-7914-5823-7 (alk. paper) — ISBN 0-7914-5824-5 (pbk. : alk. paper)
        1. Ethnology—Methodology. 2. Ethnology—Research. 3. Qualitative research. I.
    Clair, Robin Patric.

GN33.E97 2003
305.8'007'2—dc21

                                            2002045258

                    10 9 8 7 6 5 4 3 2 1

Contents

Acknowledgments

It is an honor to have worked with the contributing authors of this edited collection. Each has brought unique insights to the topic and expression of ethnography. At the close of individual chapters many of the contributors, including myself, have acknowledged the assistance of those who have helped them in one way or another with their specific chapter. With respect to the book in its entirety, I would like to acknowledge the professional and ever so pleasant assistance I received from both Diana Cable and Kim Sole in the word processing of this collection. I am also indebted to Lani Blackman, copyeditor and Kelli M. Williams, production editor. Finally, I would like to thank my editor at State University of New York, Priscilla Ross.

Prologue
Introduction

Expressions of Ethnography is an edited collection of essays that demonstrate the creative potential for novel forms of expression to speak of cultural experiences. Ethnography has a rich history replete with both political and aesthetic undertones. In Part one, chapter 1 of this book, I provide an overview of ethnography, which takes to task the colonial underpinnings of ethnographic practices. I also develop an overview of the changing story of ethnography. Ethnography has metamorphosed over the years so that varying strains of ethnography have developed. These different perspectives may vary with respect to the guiding theory, the style of engagement, or the way the ethnographer expresses the cultural practices under study.

Part two or *Ethnographic Perspectives* offers the reader an overview of several different ethnographic perspectives from individual contributors. In chapter 2, Pamela Chapman Sanger provides a review of feminist ethnography that puts past criticism of feminist ethnographic contributions to rest, once and for all. Feminist ethnographers have given us not only new theoretical insights, but also new methods as well as new forms of representation. In chapter 3, Jim Thomas expertly describes critical theory as a guiding theory for ethnographers. H. L. Goodall, Jr., discusses a new interpretive ethnography, in chapter 4. This new approach derives from interpretive ethnography and draws on more current perspectives such as postmodernism. Bryan C. Taylor, questions the blurring of theoretical positions and argues that a more reflective and careful look at the theoretical distinctions between postmodern and other perspectives is needed. Taylor provides an overview of the guiding principles of postmodernism before offering the voices of 9–11, in chapter 5. Maria Cristina González provides an eloquent discussion of the de-colonial ways of knowing culture, in chapter 6. Through the four seasons of ethnography, an alternative approach to engaging and representing culture, González challenges traditional, colonialized forms of ethnography and offers alternative ways of being an ethnographer. Finally, in chapter 7, I write of the beauty and logic involved in ethnography. I ask ethnographers to consider taking an aesthetic approach—"a rigorous and creative manner, a vulnerable, sensitive, dynamic and pulsating engagement with cultural ways of being in the world" in hopes that "poignant portrayals and mesmerizing images of cultural practices" might touch all our lives.

Part three, *Dialogue and Interview as Expressions of Ethnography* focuses on dialogue. Traditional ethnographies relied in large part on interviewing individuals. The vibrant meaning of the term, interview, has faded over the years. It has been relegated to mean a systematic and formulated way of asking questions of another person. Yet, "inter," which means with each other, together, between, or mutual, and "view," which means to look and consider, deserve further attention. Marifran Mattson and Christina W. Stage breathe new life into an old term, while William K. Rawlins provides not only new terminology, but also new ways of engaging and expressing the inter-view as dialogue. Elaine B. Jenks brings dialogue and inter-viewing to new heights with her story. After I read it, I thought to myself, "I would like to meet her." Then I realized that I already have met Elaine, perhaps not in-person, which relied on my old bias of "seeing" her, but rather I have met her through this phenomenal chapter.

Part four, *Personal Narrative as an Expression of Ethnography,* highlights the personal narrative in bas relief from the traditional ethnography. In short the authors provide chapters that espouse rigorous ethnographic principles and practices while telling their own stories within a framework of "others'" stories. Bob Krizek sets the stage for understanding the personal narrative as both a means and expression of ethnography. This approach demands that the personal narrative move beyond the individual and develop connections with the culture. Paaige K. Turner does just that in her moving story of birth, continuing her award-winning research on midwifery. Sarah J. Tracy relies on traditional methods of observation and interviewing. Based on her award-winning work, Tracey's personal narrative as a researcher is woven within the chapter.

Part five, *Short Stories as Expressions of Ethnography,* demonstrates how the short story can act as a means of expressing cultural phenomenon. These chapters are less concerned with showing the rigors of their practice or linking the narrative to cultural background and more concerned with creating an image that speaks of struggle, of people, of relationships, of love, of loss, of tragedy, and of hope. Lisa M. Tilmann-Healy, Christina E. Kiesinger, and Particia Geist-Martin each offer compelling stories. Following Tolstoy's dictate these authors infect others, stir emotion and sometimes, as in the chapter by Julie M. Crandall and Mary Helen Brown, simply offer us a cultural "moment in time" which allows us to reflect on who we are as cultural beings.

Part six, *Novels as Expressions of Ethnography*, suggests that our cultural selves can be portrayed rather expressively through the genre of the novel. Frederick C. Corey and Catherine Becker, each, provide the reader with excerpts from their in-progress novels. Each one draws the reader into unique cultural circumstances, yet in this chapter the two novelists weave their different "places" in the world into a compelling chapter about ethnography.

Part seven, *Artifacts as Expressions of Ethnography,* tells us that it is not only the place, but also the artifacts found in those places that create cultural experiences as well as express it. In chapters 20 and 21, Dean Scheibel and Amardo Rodriguez, respectively, write about the expressiveness of artifacts. Each tells of how artifacts create a reality beyond any surface interpretation. They each offer rich and compelling interpretations of graffiti as cultural expression.

Part eight, *Genealogy and Post-colonial Identities as Expressions of Ethnography,* brings together four authors who each work in the area of genealogy and cultural construction of identity. Jason E. Combs sets the stage by offering theoretical insights that give way to the conclusion that the study and practice of genealogy lends itself to the expression of identity and culture. Nick Trujillo uses his genealogical research to tell the story of his grandmother's ethnicity. In telling Naunny's story, he is in part telling his own story of cultural identity. Devika Chawla uses family history to guide her own reflexive study of personal identity in a postcolonial era. The short story is without a doubt a wonderful portrayal of how so many people find themselves walking in two worlds as a result of colonial influences. Finally, in chapter 25, I tell the story of my trip to the Qualla Boundary (a.k.a. the Cherokee Reservation). The trip was part of a larger ethnographic project to write a novel—*Echoes of Silence*—about my great-great-great-grandmother's life. She was a Cherokee woman who lived through what is often called the "Trail of Tears." My own story speaks of cultural identity and hints at the diaspora produced by colonization.

In the end, an epilogue is offered to address future possibilities for the study of culture through ethnography. As it becomes more apparent that cultures are not static and that colonization (past and present) has caused cultures to collide, we need to be exploring new avenues in the expression of ethnography.

PART ONE

An Overview of Ethnography

CHAPTER 1

The Changing Story of Ethnography

ROBIN PATRIC CLAIR

Ethnography is a practice and an expression with a capacious historical past that necessarily includes philosophical, political, spiritual, and aesthetic elements. These elements have at times defined cultures, named people, and told them who they are and what they might become. In short, ethnography grew out of a master discourse of colonization. Today, scholars question the legitimacy of that discourse (Ellis and Bochner, 1996; Burawoy, et al., 1991; Clair, 1998; Clifford and Marcus, 1986; Denzin, 1997; Denzin and Lincoln, 1994; Van Maanen, 1995; Wolf, 1992). These challenges have come at a time that may mean the demise of ethnography. At the very least and without a doubt, the days of naive ethnography are over; if indeed, they ever truly existed. However, it may be somewhat premature to pronounce a requiem for ethnography, as alternative forms of writing culture continue to surface. A review of the history of ethnography should help to place ethnography in its political terrain, set the stage for discussions of alternative perspectives, and provide a backdrop for the essays included in this collection.

The First Wave of Colonialism

Ethnography, the writing of culture, traces its origins to ancient Greece. Herodotus, who is also known as the father of history, traveled from one culture to another to document the traditions and sociopolitical practices among people of the ancient world during the third century B.C.

Herodotus wrote a nine volume tome, entitled *History*, which is the Greek word for *inquiry*. It focuses on two main themes: (1) expressing the culture, and (2) writing its political history. Specifically, Herodotus explored the Middle East

3

as the center of the world which he believed was being torn asunder by the tensions between two distinct civilizations: Eastern and Western; Persian and Greek. This division, among others, is revisited currently by postcolonial scholars (see Ashcroft, Griffiths, Tiffin, 1995; Castle, 2001) as well as postmodern scholars (see Clifford and Marcus, 1986) or both (see Denzin, 1997).

The *History* is also considered a creative work, because Herodotus chose prose to express his discoveries. "Critics have paid tribute to its grandeur of design and to its frank, lucid, and delightfully anecdotal style" (Bram and Dickey, 1986, p. 83). Herodotus traveled the ancient world in order to collect the artifacts that expressed the uniqueness of cultures. To view ethnography as travel (Neumann, 1992) or as a means of collecting not just the stories of other cultures, but of collecting ourselves, in a sense, in order to define who we are (Neumann, 1996), speaks to the heart of ethnography: the interest in self, others, and the world. However, that interest is not always pure; sometimes, it is unjustifiably self-righteous.

Ethnographers have been known to create or construct the Other as primitive. Certain Western scholars evidenced arrogance through their judgmental interpretations of Others.[1]

The Second Wave of Colonialism

The second wave of colonization spawned renewed interest in ethnography, mostly as a means of *saving* cultures that were being virtually annihilated. It began during the mercantilist period in Europe and continued through the 1800s. Exploration and trade increased as did the lust for land and the greed for gold. European conquistadors ravaged what came to be known as North and South America, Latin America, and Africa. Slavery, which had all but died out during the Middle Ages, resurfaced with a vengeance.

Spain and Portugal took the lead in colonizing what came to be known as the "Americas" (North, South, and Central). The French and British followed close behind. Historians, poets, explorers and missionaries kept careful diaries that detailed the conquests of these *strange* cultures. And, indeed, the New World cultures were strange to the Europeans. These cultures evidenced such curious customs that Europeans were forced to question what could be deemed *natural* to humankind and what was culturally specific. For example,

> Bernard Romans, traveling in the Southeast [United States] in the late eighteenth century, informed his European readers that "a savage man discharges his urine in a sitting posture, and a savage woman standing. . . . I need not tell you how opposite this is to our common practice" (White, 1993, p. 248)

Ethnographers and historians working from the late fifteenth to the mid-nineteenth centuries lived during tumultuous times and provided accounts of cultural annihilation, slavery, and torture. Friar Bartolome de Las Casas, who wrote the *History of the Indies* in 1552, reported the following account:

> [The Spaniards] made bets as to who would slit a man in two, or cut off his head at one blow; or they opened up his bowels. They tore the babies from their mother's breast by their feet, and dashed their heads against the rocks. . . . They spitted the bodies of other babes, . . . on their swords. . . . [They hanged Indians] by thirteens, in honor and reverence for our Redeemer and the twelve Apostles, . . . All this did my own eyes witness. (Las Casas as cited in Josephy Jr. 1994, p. 114)

Historical accounts speak volumes not only of the conquered culture, in this case, *Native Americans* of the *West Indies*, but also of the European conquerors, as well. Revisionist history is a part of the contemporary postcolonial concern about the representation of culture. Postcolonial scholars ask that alternative views be written into textbooks. For example, the general notion that Christopher Columbus was a hero to be emulated takes a different turn with respect to the following accounts:

> Columbus, who . . . began shipping Indians in chains to the slave markets . . . stopped briefly at the island now known as St. Croix, where without provocation members of his expedition attacked four Indian men and two women in a canoe, cutting off the head of one of the men with an ax and taking the other Indians aboard ship as captives. (Josepy Jr., 1994, p. 123)

All of this he did to people whom he described as:

> generous with what they have, to such a degree as no one would believe but he who had seen it. (Columbus' diaries, see Josephy Jr., 1994, p. 115)

Columbus gave one of these Arawak women to a colonist at St. Croix who without shame or remorse reports:

> I took a most beautiful Carib woman, whom the lord Admiral [Columbus] made a gift of to me; and having her in my berth, with her being nude . . . . the desire to enjoy myself with her came over me; and wishing to put my desire to work, she resisting, she scratched me with her fingernails to such a degree that I would not have wished then that I had

begun; but with that seen . . . I grabbed a leather strap and gave her a
good chastisement of lashes, so that she hurled such unheard of shouts
that you could not believe. Finally, we reached an agreement in such a
manner that I can tell you that in fact she seemed to have been taught
in the school of whores. (see Josephy, Jr., 1994, p. 123)

The atrocities were so extensive that "by 1552, the Indians of Hispaniola had
become extinct" and the Spanish had to replace the Indian slave labor with captured Africans (Josephy Jr., 1994, p. 129).

Disruption of African cultures created a diasporic condition. Slaves taken to
America lost most of the knowledge of their cultural heritage as their language
and customs were stolen from them. Treated as brutally as the Indians, captured
Africans died at a rate of seven out of every ten brought to America. Although the
impact upon their cultures was devastating, ethnographic studies of African cultures would not surface for several decades. Instead, American anthropologists
focused their *salvage* efforts on painting cultural portraits of the decimated
Native American cultures.

Henry Lewis Morgan, the founding father of American anthropology, has
been praised for his insights and severely critiqued for his bias. Morgan studied
the Ho-de'-no-sau-nee or Iroquois during the mid-1800s. Influenced by Darwin's
theories of evolution, Morgan developed a framework for studying disparate cultures. He believed that cultures evidenced different stages of development
moving from savage to barbaric to civilized. He believed four factors influenced
the level of sophistication that a culture attained. These include: (1) material
invention and scientific discoveries, (2) establishment of government, (3) kinship
system, and (4) economic or material practices related to property (see Moore,
1997).

Supported by the Smithsonian Institution, Morgan conducted extensive
cross-cultural studies using over three hundred societies (Cohen and Eames,
1982). Yet, his own cultural background led him to draw erroneous conclusions
about different cultures. For example, in many Native American societies, both
the mother and her sister are called "mother" by the children. Morgan determined
that the people were promiscuous and uncivilized, because the children did not
seem to know who was their rightful biological mother. To the contrary, in the
Native American society, the children simply demonstrated respect for the
women who raised them. Furthermore, it could be argued that Euro-American
culture encourages distance and separation rather than closeness among relatives.
Euro-Americans dissect relationships (e.g., half-brother, step-mother), delineate
relationships (great-great-grandmother instead of grandmother, second cousin or
cousin once-removed instead of cousin as in the Native American tradition.)

Although Morgan's discussion of kinship systems were influential, his
"materialist basis of cultural evolution has been considered his principal legacy

by subsequent evolutionists like Marx, Engels, [and others]" (Moore, 1997, p. 36). Scholars today might take notice of the continuing assumption that technology is progress, private property inevitable, bureaucratic government denotes organization, and a patriarchal family superior to a matriarchal family—all of which invites cultural analyses of the biases of Euro-American cultures.

Although Morgan was influential, his British counterpart, Edward Tyler, had a stronger effect on American anthropologists. Tyler's most enduring contribution to the field of anthropology was his definition of culture:

> Culture or civilization, taken in its wide ethnographic sense, is that complex whole which includes knowledge, belief, art, law, custom, and any other capabilities and habits acquired by man [sic] as a member of society (Tyler, 1871/1958, as cited in Moore, 1997, p. 17)

Tyler's intellectual travel guides of Mexican culture were supported by anthropological and archeological studies. Like Morgan, he also conducted comparative ethnography by sifting "through missionaries' accounts, explorers' journals, ancient texts, and ethnological reports to search for similarities in human cultures" (Moore, 1997, p. 19). Tyler believed that the ethnographer played a key role in classifying cultural creations. However, his classifications included the theme of progress and like Morgan fell into the trap of self-aggrandizement. Tyler arranged cultures in order (e.g., Australian [aborigine], Tahitian, Aztec, Chinese, Italian) with Europeans situated at the zenith of civilization (Moore, 1997).

One of the most influential American anthropologists was German born, Franz Boas (Cohen and Eames, 1982). Boas challenged the evolutionary approach to the study of culture arguing that it might be the case that "fire must precede pottery making . . . but there is no ethnographic evidence indicating that matrilineal kin systems preceded patrilineal kin systems or that religions based on animism developed before polytheistic religions" (Moore, 1997, p. 49). Thus, he fervently attacked academic anthropological racism.

Boas is probably most famous for expanding the study of anthropology to place emphasis on linguistics, archeology, sociocultural considerations and physical anthropology. His studies of the Kwakiutl people of northwestern America are highly praised for attention to linguistics, the vigilant collection of artifacts, photographic documentation, and a more holistic approach to understanding individual cultures. His career took him from university teaching to museum directing and back again. He probably influenced more American anthropologists than either Tyler or Morgan and contributed to the development of anthropological societies, magazines, and university curriculum. Some of his student protégées include Alfred Kroeber, Ruth Benedict, Edward Sapir, and Margaret Mead, to name a few. "Boas' personal contacts with his students extended his intellectual influence and shaped the institutions of American anthropology" (Moore, 1997, p. 42).

Recognizing that colonization threatened cultures across the globe, anthropologists like Boas, began serious efforts to document endangered cultural practices (Cohen and Eames, 1982). The presence of a dominant culture that intended to exterminate, assimilate or control the subordinate culture placed cultural survival as an anthropological priority. Of course, anthropologists did not literally try to save cultures or people except in rare instances. Rather,

> the main motif that ethnography as a science developed was that of salvaging cultural diversity. The ethnographer would capture in writing the authenticity of the changing cultures, so they could be entered into the record for the great comparative project of anthropology (Clifford and Marcus, 1986, p. 24).

Some of these scholars intended to have the cultural legends, myths, history, language and medicines safeguarded for future generations (e.g., James Mooney's, 1891, 1900/1992 work among the Tsaragi—Cherokee). Others, including Ruth Benedict (1934), and Margaret Mead (1928) took a more theoretical stance by asking questions about culture and humanity as they documented their cultural discoveries. Alfred Kroeber's studies of Arapaho; Ruth Benedict's studies of the Serrano, Zuni, Coachiti, O'otam, and the Apache; Edward Sapir's (see Moore, 1997) interest in Yana, Puite, Shashone, Nootka languages and combined work with Benjamin Whorf (1956) on the Hopi language and culture, all contributed to documenting cultures, salvaging them, perhaps, but saving them, I think not. Ironically, the winds have shifted dramatically. Currently, Native Americans are conducting ethnographic studies of archaeologists, if not anthropologists (see Peters, 2000).

The second wave of colonization contributed to the preponderance of studies of Native American cultures. The third wave of colonization brought with it a change in perspective concerning who constituted the *Other* and which cultures would or should be documented.

The Third Wave of Colonization

The third wave of colonization is characterized by a resolve on the part of dominating countries to tighten their colonial grip. Noting that the sun never sets on the British Empire, the English both extended their rule and enforced it with great vigor. The British were not alone in these colonizing efforts. France and Portugal continued their exploitation. The Dutch had taken the Muslim center of learning in Aceh, Indonesia. Italy attempted to take Ethiopia, but failed. Germany took small portions of Africa. Russia extended her boundaries. Japan entered the game of expansion, as well. And, the United States of America all but completed its imperial expansion based on manifest destiny at home and extended its colonial grasp beyond its current domestic borders.

The early 1900s were a scramble for control that ended in jealous rivalries between European nations. But more lurked beneath the surface than simply land acquisition. No one recognized this better than W. E. B. DuBois (1914) who wrote:

> The present war in Europe is one of the great disasters due to race and color prejudice and it but foreshadows greater disasters in the future. . . . It is not merely national jealousy, or the so called "race" rivalry. . . . It is rather a wild quest for Imperial expansion. . . . between Germany, England, and France primarily and Belgium, Italy, Russia, and Austria-Hungry to a lesser degree. (DuBois, 1914—as cited in Lester, 1971, p. 68)

For DuBois, colonization was intricately interwoven with race prejudice:

> A theory of the inferiority of the darker peoples and a contempt for their rights and aspirations has become all but universal in the greatest centers of modern culture. . . . civilized nations are fighting like mad dogs over the right to own and exploit these darker peoples. (DuBois, 1914 as cited in Lester, 1971, p. 68)

DuBois's ethnographic work, which revealed the "Souls of Black Folks" in America and his political activism at the both domestic and international levels, bravely attacked imperialism and its inherent prejudice against dark-skinned people.

DuBois was not alone as an activist and writer of the times who understood the ravages of imperialism. James Joyce, the novelist, produced two works prior to World War II—*The Dubliners* (1914) and *A Portrait of the Artist as a Young Man* (1916) which provide auto-ethnographic accounts of economic, ideological, and personal struggles in British occupied Ireland. Joyce's work is praised by contemporary postcolonial and postmodern writers as fundamental to the new movements in ethnography (Denzin, 1997; Wolcott, 1995)

This third wave of colonization triggered both World War I and World War II (DuBois, 1914/1971). During this time, ethnographers found themselves in precarious and unique situations that ranged from unexpected studies of the Other to atypical ethnographies of the colonizers. For example, Austrian born, Bronislaw Malinowski traveled to Australia with a British contingent in the early 1900s. He arrived as World War I began and was arrested as an enemy by Australian forces, but was allowed to conduct field work in New Guinea during his period of incarceration (Moore, 1997).

World War I shattered Émile Durkheim's school of sociology as many of his students, including his son, were killed on the battlefield (Moore, 1997). Only Marcel Mauss, Durkheim's nephew, was left to carry on the sociological ethnographic tradition, which he did with great vigor until World War II. Maus' (1925/1967) greatest contribution is his cross-cultural comparison of *exchanges* as *total phenomenon* that reflect the prescribed nature of giving. His work entitled, *The Gift* exposed exchange as a phenomenon that stretched well beyond economics and pointed to interrelationships with other cultural institutions including religion. Maus' work has been described as "economic ethnography" as well as "structural" ethnography as the type practiced by Claude Levi-Strauss (1963, see Moore, 1997, p. 124). Mauss also influenced the highly respected work of Mary Douglas (1966) who posed "dirt" as a total phenomenon of cultural and cross-cultural interest (see Wuthnow, Hunter, Bergesen, and Kurzweil, 1984 for a discussion of Douglas' contributions). Mauss was forced into retirement during the Nazi occupation of France (Moore, 1997).

Between World War I and World War II, George Orwell provided a moving account of his own experience with poverty through the novel, *Down and Out in Paris and London* (1933/1961). Described as autobiographical, this work may be considered an auto-ethnography or personal ethnography, as well. The novel extends beyond an autobiography by capturing the sordid conditions of poverty as a cultural phenomenon. Orwell's second book, *Burmese Days* (1934) is also autobiographical with cultural insights on imperialism.

World War II affected ethnography in other ways as well. For example, Ruth Benedict (1946) found herself conducting an ethnography via archival documents of Japanese culture for the American government during World War II. However, more common ethnographies of this time period included, Gregory Bateson and Margaret Mead's (1942) study of the Balinese, and E. Evans-Pritchard's (1940) studies of the Nuer. Although classical or traditional ethnography continued to flourish, alternative forms surfaced in response to World War II.

During the Great Depression era and continuing through World War II and beyond, sociologists began to study the plight of the urban poor. Field work in the cities of London, Chicago, and Philadelphia eventually developed into schools of urban ethnography, specifically the Chicago School. Outstanding contributors to urban ethnography include Robert Park, W. E. B. DuBois, Sidney and Beatrice Potter Webb (see Van Maanen, 1988) and W. F. Whyte (1955). A more recent example of urban ethnography is Dwight Conquergood's (1994) study of the South Chicago street gangs. Contemporary urban ethnographers represent different fields of study including sociology, communication, and anthropology.

In addition, World War II gave rise to the ethnographic study of organizations. W. F. Whyte's (1948) studies of *Human Relations in the Restaurant Industry* were undertaken to address the cultural impact of World War II on industry. Whyte discovered that with work populations shifting cultural norms were being challenged. Whyte's work in organizations initiated a new ethnographic contextual setting. Numerous scholars have undertaken organizational ethnographies and have done so using different perspectives as well as different styles of presentation (also see e.g., Goffman, 1956, 1959, 1963). For example, Donald Roy's (1959) study of factory workers does not use the same perspective as Michael Burawoy and colleagues' (1991) micro-macro critical ethnographies. Even when organizational ethnographers use the same line of work their approaches vary. For example, John Van Maanen's (1988) studies of police work are quite different from Nick O'Donnell-Trujillo and Michael Pacanowsky's (1983), and Nick Trujillo and George Dionisopoulos' (1987) studies of police work. Today, organizational ethnographies are broad based and proliferative.

Gregory Bateson (1972) introduced a third approach to ethnographic work following World War II. Focusing on patterns, interactions and communication, Bateson noted early on that communication is *framed*. For example, people have the ability to recognize the difference between real fighting and playful fighting because they have ways of framing or commenting upon the behavior. That is to say, people communicate about their communication—they meta-communicate. Further, Bateson promoted the idea that certain expressions were more salient than others in determining cultural distinction—what constitutes *the difference that makes a difference* is worthy of ethnographic exploration. He also took great pains to explore the connectedness of life. Bateson's work stimulated discussions in psychology, communication, sociology, and anthropology.

Mary Catherine Bateson, the daughter of Gregory Bateson and Margaret Mead, extended her parents' work and contributed to interpersonal ethnography. For example, her book, *Composing a Life*, (1990) allows the ethnographer to look at herself in relation to others as well as the wider cultural framework. Contemporary interpersonal ethnographers often highlight interpersonal relationships and personal struggles. That is, they explore subjectivity through reflexivity (Ellis and Flaherty, 1992). Ways of expressing these personal and interpersonal cultural experiences include dialogue, short story, and performance (Ellis and Bochner, 1996).

Fourth, during World War II, the Frankfurt School of critical scholars recognized that in addition to the economic orientation of previous Marxist-driven research, the cultural aspects of domination and exploitation needed to be discussed. Antonio Gramsci (1971), famous for the *Prison Notebooks*, wrote on the concepts of power, politics, and hegemony from his prison cell after the Fascists incarcerated him. Other critical theorists exiled from Germany, some of whom made their way to the United States, promoted cultural studies of power. Kenneth Burke who was influenced by Émile Durkheim, Sigmund Freud, and Karl Marx contributed significant philosophical insights that promoted understanding of identification, alienation, and symbolization. Out of these traditions, a new form of ethnography developed—critical ethnography. A contemporary and classic example of critical ethnography has been provided by Paul E. Willis (1977) in his study of working-class lads in England.

Yet another stream of cultural studies surfaced during World War II. Like Joyce and Orwell, Simone de Beauvoir and other French existentialists felt the genre most conducive to expressing philosophical and cultural commentaries is the novel. For de Beauvoir, the novel provided an expressive means of convey-ing rich philosophical and political ideas. The threat of Nazi occupation of France exists at the shadowy edges of her classic existential novel, *She Came To Stay* (1954/1990).

Simone de Beauvoir (1961) also presented her ideas in scholarly format. French existentialists struggled with the issues of 'being' and 'otherness.' De Beauvoir (1961), developed feminist existentialism which gave rise to a sophis-ticated understanding of women as cultural beings defined as the Other in rela-tion to men. Her work challenges biological and psychological explanations of gender difference and argues that patriarchal constructions of women and men have placed women in a position of existence that names them as the Other.

Following World War II, American feminists used ethnographic methods to further expose the patriarchal construction of the world. Specifically, feminist ethnographers combined feminist theory, critical theory and postcolonial theory to explore cultural issues. Eleanor Burke Lealock's (1954, as cited in Moore, 1997) work provides a leading example of this blending of perspectives.

Eleanor Burke Lealock, the daughter of Kenneth Burke, and "the leading Marxist feminist in American anthropology" (Moore, 1997, p. 201) successfully blended Marxist insights with Boas' position that argued against the evolutionary progression model for its inherent prejudice. In addition, she took a feminist per-spective to advance these notions into a unique critique of past cultural theories. Her work on the fur trading industry suggests that prior to infusion of European colonization trade patterns among the Montagnais-Naskapi were dynamic and changing. Primitive societies are not stagnate, she argued. They did not depend on Europeans to advance. However, colonization did indeed have a monumental impact on their culture. Colonization, capitalism, and Christianity, especially that of the Jesuits, redefined the culture especially for women. Women's economic independence was curtailed, divorce was made illegal, promiscuity was called a sin, monogamy was instituted, and patriarchy enforced. Writing during the McCarthy era, Lealock's Marxist's insights would have been considered unpatri-otic, at best. Furthermore, her feminist leanings would have been dismissed by a sexist society (see Moore, 1997).

Following World War II, Betty Friedan (1963) used ethnographic methods to interview women (mostly middle- to upper-middle-class white women) to paint a portrait of a despondent group whose depression could be traced to patri-archy. In so doing, Friedan offered a unique ethnographic form and a political commentary that set off a tinderbox of opinions about feminism and patriarchy.

At the same time, Gloria Steinem undertook a journalistic ethnography of a sexist institution—the Playboy Club—where she participated as a playboy bunny (Steinem, 1963/1983). Elizabeth Boyer, one of the founder's of National Organization for Women (NOW) and the leading founder of Women's Equity Action League (WEAL), used ethnographic and historical methods to uncover the story of one strong woman. Both a novel and scholarly books provide archival evidence of the life experiences of Demoiselle Marguerite (1975, 1983).

The economic, social, and political connection of most white women including the above mentioned feminists, to the imperializing white Euro-American male did not go unnoticed. African American women challenged the white middle-class bias of these studies (hooks, 1984) as well as the heterosexual focus (Lorde, 1984). During the 1980s and 1990s voices from the colonized began to (re)surface.[2] But before they did (at least in a manner loud enough to be heard by white academic audiences), ethnography took a turn toward the interpretive direction.

The Fourth Wave of Colonization

The fourth wave of colonization moved from capitalist development in *Third World* countries through extended globalization of capitalist engagement around the world, via policies such as the North American Free Trade Agreement (NAFTA) and practices such as the employment of offshore (meaning off American and European shores) labor pools. Neocolonialism has been criticized as the Americanization of the world or capitalist globalization. This new form of colonization led to new forms of ethnography. Each of these new forms highlighted the linguistic and eventually the political aspect of culture. As colonized subjects pursued, explored, or recovered from Euro-American educational systems, their voices reached academic and popular audiences. The colonized began speaking for themselves, albeit with altered voices (Clair, 1997). And an era of postcolonialism emerged with an emphasis on the linguistic turn.

The Linguistic Turn in Ethnography

The linguistic turn refers to the emphasis on language to create culture as well as to understand culture, to guide inquiry, and to express discoveries. Several schools of thought exist as part of the linguistic turn. They include the interpretivist, the critical, particular feminist theories, the postmodernist, and the postcolonial perspectives. Each of these schools of thought has some unique aspects as well as similarities.

The Linguistic Interpretive Turn

Following World War II, ethnographers continued the colonial project in a new world order. Clifford Geertz, for example, working for the Ford Foundation, explored "Third World development, with the explicit goal of improving economic growth" (Moore, 1997, p. 239). Geertz (1973, 1977) ushered in a new era for ethnography. Geertz is most famous for viewing ethnography as a textual undertaking that requires *thick descriptions* and searches out *webs of significance*. His focus on symbols, text, and language gave birth to what is sometimes called "interpretive ethnography."

Interpretive ethnography placed meaning at the center of its enterprise and encouraged scholars to conduct ethnographies of communication (Hymes, 1964). Politics and power were not completely dismissed, but signification and symbol systems were highlighted. Cultures were clearly labeled and the idea that the ethnographer could represent the Other still permeated much of the research. The idea that one specific truthful interpretation and representation could be garnered still acted as the basic assumption of ethnography.

John Van Maanen (1988) describes interpretive ethnography as a rhetorical practice that represents the "social reality of others through the analysis of one's own experience in the world of these others" (p. ix). He sees ethnography as "hauntingly personal" (p. ix) and yet at the same time a "portrait of diversity" (p. xiii). Although always evocative and self-transformative, ethnography can take different forms of presentation including a realist form, a confessional form, or an impressionistic form (Van Maanen, 1988). These three forms are detailed through examples of his and other ethnographer's work. Sometimes these three forms of presentation may overlap within one work (see Van Maanen, 1988, or Hayano, 1982). No matter what style of representation is chosen, the focal point for the interpretive ethnographer is understanding the *meaning* of certain phenomenon. For example, Nick O'Donnell-Trujillo and Michael Pacanowsky's (1983) search for the meaning of *tough talk* among police officers was grounded in Clifford Geertz' (1973) interpretive notions, which were based on Max Weber's insights, that webs of significance exist in the symbolism, in this case, in the everyday talk of the members. When Nick Trujillo and George Dionisopoulos (1987) are faced with the odd and seemingly unexplainable act of a police officer shooting a pigeon, they are able to interpret this act based on Victor Turner's (1981) social drama theory. In this case, the social drama serves the purpose of alleviating the routine boredom of police work in a small town. In short, interpretive ethnographers are looking for the meaning of cultural practices—what is the meaning of tough talk; what is the meaning of shooting pigeons?

Critical and Radical Feminist's Linguistic Turn

Although numerous political differences exist between critical scholars and radical, socialist, or Marxist feminist scholars, their views on communication are somewhat similar. Communication and language are never neutral. Communication can be oppressive and act as a means of silencing different groups of people. However, communication also carries with it the possibilities for emancipation.

Earlier, I suggested that Paul E. Willis' (1977) ethnography of working-class lads is an excellent example of critical ethnography. However, Angela McRobbie (1981) also clearly points out that Willis' ethnography marginalizes women. Nevertheless, both radical feminist ethnography and critical ethnography seek to uncover oppressive practices (see Burawoy et al., 1991 for other examples).

A unique example of uncovering sexist language and oppressive practices is found in the work of Mary Daly (1973). Using ethnographic methods (reviewing historical documents and hermeneutics), Daly exposes the patriarchal construction of Christian cultural institutions (e.g., the Roman Catholic Church), especially through myths (e.g., stories of Adam and Eve, the Virgin Mary). Furthermore, Daly deconstructs and plays with language in order to offer a new liberated set of meanings for old terminology (e.g., crones and hags as positive). Thus, Daly critiques culture, exposes oppression, highlights the political nature of language, and offers forms of resistance. In short, she provides a unique ethnographic expression.

The Postmodern Linguistic Turn

Postmodernists diverged from these three schools of thought (i.e., interpretive, critical, and radical feminist) in several ways. They criticized interpretivists for not being political enough; they rarely mentioned contributions by critical scholars (for an exception see Marcus, 1986); and, they blatantly ignored feminist contributions (see Clifford, 1986). Separating themselves from these schools of thought went beyond neglecting or criticizing others. Postmodernists also set their own agenda. First, postmodern ethnographers positioned language, discourse, text, or symbol systems in a privileged position beyond that of previous schools of ethnography. Discourse is not only a means to understand culture but is culture itself. Second, they argued that past ethnographies were couched in colonial constructions thus presenting Westernized views of the Other. Third, they suggested that more than one truth could be garnered from an ethnography and that a single interpretation taken to be Truth merely contributed to the hegemonic order. Thus, the political nature of ethnography, according to postmodernists, resurfaced with a new vengeance and new perspective. Marcus for instance, writes: "ethnographers of an interpretive bent—more interested in problems of cultural meaning than in social action—have not generally represented the ways in which closely observed cultural worlds are embedded in larger, more impersonal systems" (pp. 165–166). However, this can be debated.

Jerry Moore (1997) argues that politics was always embedded in ethnographies and that Boas for one recognized and argued openly these implications. In short, the postmodern claim to exposing the political nature of ethnography is not new. Claims to new ethnographic genres may also be stretching the truth/Truth a bit since all of the varied forms existed prior to postmodernism. They quite simply had not been labeled under a coherent rubric.

In spite of these oversights, postmodernists can be credited with offering a new and valuable conceptualization of culture:

> If "culture" is not an object to be described, neither is it a unified corpus of symbols and meanings that can be definitively interpreted. Culture is contested, temporal, and emergent. Representation and explanation— both by insiders and outsiders—is implicated in this emergence. (Clifford, 1986, p. 19)

James Clifford and George Marcus (1986) provide a notable series of essays that pointedly criticize the tenets of modernist ethnography including the interpretivist mode. Clifford Geertz' work is challenged for establishing an artificial authority and a representation that tells no lies, but does not tell the whole truth (Crapanzano, 1986). Additional criticism includes Clifford's meta-communicative critique of ethnography. In his critique, Clifford (1986) uses Victor Turner's notion of social drama to explain modernist ethnography, and although it is interesting, one is hard pressed to understand how postmodern ethnography will not be yet another chapter in the social dramas of ethnography. Stephan A. Tyler's (1986) eloquent essay moves beyond critique of the modernist enterprise and attempts to define postmodern ethnography:

> A postmodern ethnography is a cooperatively evolved text consisting of fragments of discourse intended to evoke in the minds of both reader and writer an emergent fantasy of a possible world of common sense reality, and thus provoke an aesthetic integration that will have a therapeutic effect. (p. 125)

The therapeutic effect is reminiscent of interpersonal ethnography as suggested by Gregory Bateson and at a more macro-level links with feminist and critical calls for consciousness raising. But extends beyond either of these schools of thought by arguing that realities are constructed of fragments and the ethnographer is complicit in writing the culture into what it is, so to speak.

Postmodern ethnography has both strengths and weaknesses, like any other ethnographic model. The main weakness of postmodern ethnography is that its theoretical foundation is plagued with paradoxes. For example, although the postmodern school of thought encourages the elimination of bifurcations (see e.g., Derrida's work), they are firmly grounded in bifurcations. As J. D. Moore (1997) points out "one attempt to distinguish modernism and postmodernism was a schematic list of thirty-two paired opposites describing *modernism* and *postmodernism* respectively: purpose/play, design/chance, hierarchy/anarchy, selection/combination, and so on (Hassan, 1985 as cited in Moore, 1997, p. 261). A second paradox that confronts postmodernism and in turn postmodern ethnographies is the issue of truth/Truth. Although postmodernists argue against one *Truth* (Foucault, 1972, 1973, 1976/1990) their firm grounding as a school of thought has become legitimized as *The Answer* to modernist frailties. The only postmodernist to actually confront postmodernism with its own inflated sense of self-importance is Jean Baudrillard (1977/1987). Third, they cannot help but to create a limited picture of cultural phenomenon based upon their own sense of truth as they select out the fragments of discourse meant to represent, if not create, their version of the world. Thus, the ethnographer maintains cultural control. Fourth, the development of postmodern concerns with oppression, hegemony, and resistance rest primarily on the shoulders of European males (e.g., Foucault, Derrida, Lacan, Baudrillard). Thus, their cultural analyses are still guided by European philosophy. Finally, a number of postmodern ethnographies are still very much couched in modernist views of who and what constitutes ethnographic inquisition. James Fernandez's work in Gabon, "a Francophone nation on the Atlantic coast of Africa," has been highly praised for capturing the discursive focus of postmodern ethnography (Moore, 1997, p. 263). He studies the tropes, especially metaphors, of the Fang culture. True to a postmodern stance he studies how metaphors create a way of being in the world. But one cannot help but note that his subjects are Africans who have relentlessly been viewed as "Other."

An example of postmodern feminist ethnography by Margery Wolf (1992) also uses the life story of the Other (in this case a woman from China). Wolf tells the woman's story through different tales including fiction, field notes, and scholarly commentary. Nevertheless, it is Wolf who is speaking on behalf of the woman. As such, Wolf notes that Edward Said (1978) pointed out that ethnography may be an act of colonial dominance. Yet, she suggests that Said was referring to ethnographies that were used blatantly to control the colonized and that she hopes her work addresses the more subtle forms of domination that all women have faced. Thus, postmodernists are not blind to these criticisms.

Additionally, the definition of the Other has taken a turn with the help of postmodernism. Postmodernists readily complicate the concept of other. They suggest that the Other is not simple and cannot be defined in opposition to one dominant group. Instead, the Other is seen as holding multiple subject positions which shift and slip into each Other (Laclau and Mouffe, 1985). Although postmodernists are generally credited with refining the concept of multiple subject positions, its origin might be traced to the classic and eloquent speech, "Ain't I A Woman" by Sojourner Truth, who points out that she is both a woman and a person of African descent who was once a slave. Gender, race, and class collide in a moment that evidences both discursive and materialist evidence of the plurality of subject positions for a colonized individual.

The Postcolonial Turn

With the advent of postmodernism another school of thought—post-colonialism—which had been lying dormant for some years, emerged with renewed strength. Postcolonialism, as a field of study, is not easily defined. As Bill Ashcroft, Gareth Griffiths, and Helen Tiffin (1995) suggest the "field itself has become so heterogeneous that no collection of readings could encompass every theoretical position now giving itself the name *postcolonial/post-colonial*" (p. xv). Debates continue as to whether postcolonialism/postcolonialism should be understood as "an amorphous set of discursive practices, akin to postmodernism" or to a more *"historically* located set of strategies," (p. xv). Nevertheless, we know that "postcolonial theory has existed for a long time before that particular name was given to it" (Ashcroft, Griffiths, and Tiffin, 1995, p. 1) and that it necessarily speaks of "migration, slavery, suppression, resistance, representation, difference, race, gender, place, and response to the influential master discourses of imperial Europe" (Ashcroft, Griffiths, and Tiffin, 1995, p. 2).

Second, the conceptualization of postcolonial thinking is not limited to literature and literary criticism. There are a wide variety of issues and genres, respectively: issues of migration, identity, diaspora, representation, hegemony, resistance, and artificial decolonization; as well as genres such as the novel, revisionist history, poetry, dialogue, short story, cultural reclamation, and performance. Writing about the "effects," the "responses," or the "process" of colonization are all part of the postcolonial dialogue (Ashcroft, Griffiths, and Tiffin, 1995, p. 3).

Third, postcolonialism is political. It challenges the master discourses of European imperialism. Postcolonial writings span diverse cultures, races, and gender; yet, sustain a connection through a shared sense of history and contemporary struggle to expose the ravages of colonization as they existed in the past and continue today. Challenging master discourses means to uncover the artificial bifurcations of the world, the presumed inferiority of the Other, the violently assumed privileged position of European culture and the continuing discursive practices that sustain the world order in an unquestioned way (Said, 1993). Ethnography is founded on one such master discourse. It is the study of the Other.

Subsequently, one might give pause to consider whether the concept *postcolonial ethnography* should be considered an oxymoron. Postcolonial theory, challenges the very existence of ethnography as an imperial endeavor. Yet, some postcolonialists have found a way to write ethnography in such a way as to *unveil* the complexities of colonization (Vivian, 1999) or to rewrite ethnographic practices to suit the cultural ways of the colonized (see González, 2000) or portray self in a self-reflective manner that captures the complexities of both the colonized culture and the practices of imperialism (Hall, 1985, 1995/2001; Lamming, 1960/1995, 1991/2001; Uchendu, 1973; also for edited collections see Ashcroft, Griffiths, and Tiffin, 1995; Castle, 2001). Ethnography is taking a turn from expressing a one-sided view of the Other to expressing its own possibilities as a language of resistance and emancipation.

However, postcolonial studies, like postmodern studies, are entrenched in what may be inescapable ironies. For the most part, postcolonial writers are colonized people who have been well-trained in the educational system of the colonizer. As I have written elsewhere, colonization has produced *altered natives* or *alter-natives* by intermarriage, rape, colonial education, and/or other forms of assimilation (see Clair, 1997). The alter-natives may not be able to speak for anyone other than themselves. On the other hand, I have suggested that these alter-natives might provide *alternatives* to previous discourses about the Other. Nevertheless, being an alter-native presents paradoxes for the postcolonial scholar. As George Lamming (1960/1995, 1991/2001) pointed out, he sought acceptance as a novelist among the European, and especially English critics; thus, still buying into British elitism. Or they may be directing much of their discourse to an elite academic audience (as in the writings of Hall, 1996; Spivack, 1988/1995 — see e.g., criticisms by Parry, 1987/1995).

Postcolonial ethnographers must grapple with the idea that novel forms of expression may be required to portray the past, the present, and the future of culture. From James Joyce to George Lamme, the artists' voice may be the most freeing from the academically based paradoxes. Hear the voice of Bob Marley and then ask, what is the role of academic intervention?

Freeing one's aesthetic sensibilities may help ethnographers to create "untold, unheard, unseen, and heretofore unimagined possibilities" (Clair, 1998, p. 186). In order to do this, I have suggested that we seek out aesthetic ways of being and give up restraints intended to limit ethnography; and instead, recognize and relish its complexities, subtleties, and ironies. After all, ethnography is not simply the methodological expression of anthropological field trips; it is the expression of history, politics, culture, and the essence of being. Ethnography necessarily implicates the ethnographer in the creation of an expression of who and what a culture is all about (Clair, 1998). It concomitantly describes the ethnographer as s/he describes the Other. Contemporary aesthetic ethnographers highlight these points (e.g., Clair, 1998).

Many traditional anthropologists seemed unaware of their own assumptions and biases. Contemporary scholars are attempting to unveil not only the biases of the past, but also add reflexive interpretations that speak to their own cultural assumptions and prejudices. Today, several forms of alternative ethnography exist. The following chapters, found in part one of this book, detail a variety of ethnographic perspectives. They include feminist, critical, interpretive, postmodern, postcolonial, and aesthetic perspectives. In part two, these perspectives, are elaborated further through philosophical discussion and exemplars from different schools of thought.[3]

Notes

1. It is important to note that:

I set off the word "western" in quotes because it is another example of linguistic limitations that have been driven by political, imperialist and patriarchal agendas. This language functions to split the world in half — eastern from western. It then labels western as white European so that every time someone invokes western traditions as a description, it further erases Native Americans. (Clair, 1998, p. 216)

And these are not the only cultures that are affected by this artificial bifurcation. For example, this discourse marginalizes African Americans because, they have a distinct cultural heritage that is neither eastern nor western per se and yet contains elements of both. It leaves the cultural contribution of South American cultures in question. Spanish, Hispanic, Latino, Mexican identities are placed in a precarious position. There is no clear place for the Irish who have suffered the throes of colonization for generations. Geopoliticizing under the term "western" further erases marginalized groups like people who are bi-homo or a-sexuals as British rule mandated sexual laws. Furthermore, American feminists trace their oppression to colonial rule. Elizabeth Cady Stanton argued that the *civil death* of American women in the mid-1800s was "a throwback to British Colonial days" (Banner, 1986, p. 91). Thus, it would seem that even women of "western" origin have been constrained by colonization. Finally, I do not intend to imply that the second wave of colonization was any more turbulent than the first wave of colonization. Slavery, torture, diaspora, paterarchy and a host of other ills existed during the first wave of colonization also, but it is simply beyond the scope of this chapter to detail that history.

2. Harriet Jacobs, *Incidents in the Life a Slave Girl* (1861; reprint, New York: Oxford University Press), is one example of the writings of the colonized appearing in print long before the acceptance of the term postcolonial.

3. The author would like to thank Patricia Geist Martin for her editorial comments.

References

Ashcroft, B., Griffiths, G., Tiffin, H. (Eds.). (1995). *The post-colonial studies reader*. London and New York: Routledge and Kegan Paul.

Banner, L. W. (1986). Act One. *Wilson Quarterly, 10*: 90–98.

Bateson, G. (1972). *Steps to an ecology of the mind*. New York: Ballantine.

Bateson, M.C. (1990). *Composing a life*. New York: Plume.

Bateson, G. and Mead, M. (1942). *Balinese character: A photographic analysis*. New York: New York Academy of Sciences

Baudrillard, J. (1987). *Forget Foucault*. New York: semiotexte. (Original work published 1977)

Benedict, R. (1934). *Patterns of culture*. Boston: Houghton Mifflin.

— — —. (1946). *The chrysanthemum and the sword: Patterns of Japanese culture*. Boston: Houghton Mifflin.

Boyer, E. (1975). *Marguerite de la Roque: A story of survival*. New York: Popular Library.

— — —. (1983). *A colony of one: The history of a brave woman*. Novelty, OH: Veritie Press.

Bram, L. L. and Dickey, N. H. (Eds.) (1986). *Herodotus*. New York: Funk and Wagnalls.

Burawoy, M., Burton, A., Ferguson, A. A., Fox, K. J., Gamson, J., Gartrell, N., Hurst, L., Kurzman, C., Salzinger, L., Schiffman, J. and Ui, S. (1991). *Ethnography unbound: Power and resistance in the modern metropolis*. Berkeley, CA: University of California Press.

Castle, G. (2001). *Postcolonial discourses: An anthology*. Malden, MA: Blackwell.

Clair, R. P. (1997). Organizing silence: Silence as voice and voice as silence in the narrative exploration of the Treaty of New Echota. *Western Journal of Communication, 61*: 315–337.

— — —. (1998). *Organizing silence: A world of possibilities*. Albany: State University of New York Press.

Clifford, J. and Marcus, G. E. (1986). *Writing culture: The poetics and politics of ethnography*. Berkeley, CA: University of California Press.

Clifford, J. (1986). Introduction: Partial truths. In J. Clifford and G. E. Marcus (Eds.), *Writing culture: The poetics and politics of ethnography* (pp. 1–26). Berkeley, CA: University of California Press.

Cohen, E. A. and Eames, E. (1982). *Cultural anthropology*. Boston: Little, Brown and Company.

Conquergood, D., (1994). Homeboys and hoods: Gang communication and cultural space. In L. R.Frey (Ed.), *Group communication in context: Studies of natural groups* (pp. 23–55). Hillsdale, NJ: Lawrence Erlbaum.

Crapanzano, V. (1986). Herme's dilemma: The masking of subversion in ethnographic description. In J. Clifford and G. E. Marcus (Eds.), *Writing culture: The poetics and politics of ethnography* (pp. 51–76). Berkeley, CA: University of California Press.

Daly, M. (1973). *Beyond God the father: Toward a philosophy of women's liberation*. Boston: Beacon Press.

de Beauvoir, S. (1961). *The second sex*. (H. M. Parshley, Trans. and Ed.). New York: Bantam Books.

———. (1990). *She came to stay*. New York: W. W. Norton. (Original work published 1954)

Deetz, S. A. (1992). *Democracy in an age of corporate colonization: Developments in communication and the politics of everyday life*. Albany: State University of New York Press.

Denzin, N. K. (1997). *Interpretive ethnography: Ethnographic practices for the 21st century*. Thousand Oaks, CA: Sage Publications, Inc.

Denzin, N. K., and Lincoln, Y. S. (Eds.). (1994). *The handbook of qualitative research*. Thousand Oaks, CA: Sage Publications, Inc.

Douglas, M. (1966). *Purity and danger: An analysis of the concepts of pollution and taboo*. New York: Pantheon.

DuBois, W. E. B. (1914). *The crisis*. In *The seventh son: thoughts and writings of W. E. B. Du Bois*. Vol 1. New York: Vintage Books.

Ellis, C., and Bochner, A. P. (Eds.). (1996). *Composing ethnography: Alternative forms of qualitative writing*. Walnut Creek, CA: Alta Mira Press.

Ellis, C., and Flaherty, M. G. (Eds.). (1992). *Investigating subjectivity: Research on lived experience*. Newbury Park, CA: Sage Publications, Inc.

Evans-Pritchard, E. (1940). *The Nuer: A description of the modes of livelihood and political institutions of Nilotic people*. Oxford: Clarendon Press.

Friedan, B. (1963). *The feminine mystique*. New York: Norton.

Foucault, M. (1972). *The archeology of knowledge* (A. Sheriden Smith, Trans.). New York: Pantheon.

———. (1973). *The order of things.: An archeology of the human sciences*. New York: Vintage Books. (Original work published 1966)

———. (1990). *The history of sexuality: An introduction, Vol. I* (R. Hurley, Trans.). New York: Vintage Books (Original work published 1976, English translation 1978)

Geertz, C. (1973). *The interpretation of cultures*. New York: Basic Books, Inc. Publishers.

Geertz, C. (1977). "From the native's point of view": On the nature of anthropological understanding. In Janet L. Dolgin, David S. Kemnitzer, and David M. Schneider (Eds.), *Symbolic anthropology: A reader in the study of symbols and meanings* (pp. 480–492). New York: Columbia University Press. (Original published in 1974 in *Bulletin* of the American Academy)

Goffman, E. (1956). Embarrassment and social organization. *American Journal of Sociology, 62*: 264–274.

— — —. (1959). *Presentation of self in everyday life*. New York: Doubleday Anchor.

— — —. (1963). *Behavior in public places: Notes on the social organization of gatherings*. Glencoe, IL: Free Press.

— — —. (1974). *Frame analysis: An essay on the organization of experience*. Cambridge, MA: Harvard University Press.

González, M. C. (2000). The four seasons of ethnography: A creation-centered ontology for ethnography. *International Journal of Intercultural Relations, 24*: 623–650.

Gramsci, A. (1971). *Selections from the Prison Notebooks of Antonio Gramsci*. Quintin Hoare and Geoffrey Nowell Smith, Eds. and Trans. New York: International Publishers

Hall, S. (1985). Signification, representation, ideology: Althusser and the post-structuralist debate. *Critical Studies in Mass Communication, 2*: 91–114.

— — —. (1996). When was 'the post-colonial'? Thinking at the limit. In Iain Chambers and Lidia Curti (Eds.), *The post-colonial question: Common skies, divided horizons* (pp. 242–260). London and New York: Routledge and Kegan Paul.

— — —. (2001). Negotiating Caribbean identities. In G. Castle (Ed.), *Postcolonial discourses: An anthology*. Malden, MA: Blackwell. (Original work published 1995)

Hassan, L. (1985). The culture of post-modernism. *Theory, Culture and Society, 2(3)*: 119–132.

Hayano, D. M. (1982). *Poker faces: The life and work of professional card players*. Berkeley, CA: University of California Press.

hooks, b. (1984). *Feminist theory: From the margin to the center*. Boston: South End Press.

Hymes, D. (1964). Introduction: Toward ethnographies of communication. *American Anthropologist, 66*: 1–33.

Jacobs, H. (1988). *Incidents in the life of a slave girl*. New York and Oxford: Oxford University Press. (Original work published in 1861)

Josephy, Jr., A.M. (1994). *500 Nations*. New York: Alfred A. Knopf.

Joyce, J. (1946). *The Dubliners*. New York: Viking Press. (Original work published 1914)

— — —. (1946). *A Portrait of the artist as a young man*. New York: Viking Press. (Original work published 1916)

Laclau, E., and Mouffe, C. (1985). *Hegemony and socialist strategy*. London: Verso.

Lamming, G. (1995). The occasion for speaking. In B. Ashcroft, G. Griffiths, H. Tiffin (Eds.), *The post-colonial studies reader* (pp. 12–17). London and New York: Routledge and Kegan Paul. (Original work published 1960)

Lamming, G. (2001). Colonialism and the Caribbean novel. In G. Castle (Ed.), *Postcolonial discourses: An anthology* (pp. 271–279). Malden, MA: Blackwell. (Original work published in 1991)

Lealock, E. Burke. (1954). The Montagnais "Hunting territory" and the fur trade. *American Anthropologist, 56(5)*: Part 2, Memoir 78. Washington D.C.: American Anthropological Association.

Lester, J. (1971). *The seventh son: The thoughts and writings of W. E. B. Du Bois. Vol. I.* New York: Vintage Books.

Levi-Strauss, C. (1963). *Structural anthropology, Vol. 1.* New York: Basic Books, Inc., Publishers.

— — —. (1969). *The elementary structures of kinships.* Boston: Beacon Press.

Lorde, A. (1984). *Sister outsider.* Trumansburg, NY: Crossing Press.

Marcus, G. E. (1986). Contemporary problems of ethnography in the modern world system. In J. Clifford and G. E. Marcus (Eds.), *Writing culture: The poetics and politics of ethnography* (pp. 165–193). Berkeley, CA: University of California Press.

Mauss, M. (1967). The gift: Forms and functions of exchange in archaic societies. (I. Cunnison, Trans.). New York: W. W. Norton. (Original work published in 1925)

McRobbie, A. (1981). Settling accounts with subcultures: A feminist critique. In T. Bennett, G. Martin, C. Mercer, and J. Woolcott (Eds.), *Culture ideology and social process: A reader* (pp. 111–123). London: The Open University.

Mead, M. (1928). *Coming of age in Samoa.* New York: Mentor Books.

Mooney, J. (1992). *James Mooney's History, Myths, and sacred formulas of the Cherokee: Myths of the Cherokee, The sacred formulas of the Cherokees.* Ashville, NC: Historical Images. (Original works published 1900 and 1891 respectively)

Moore, J. D. (1997). *Visions of culture: An introduction to anthropological theories and theorists.* Walnut Creek, CA: Alta Mira Press.

Neumann, M. (1992). The trail through experience: Finding self in the recollection of travel. In C. Ellis and M. G. Flaherty (Eds.), *Investigating subjectivity: Research on lived experience* (pp. 176–201). Newbury Park, CA: Sage Publications, Inc.

— — —. (1996). Collecting ourselves at the end of the century. In C. Ellis, and A. P. Bochner (Eds.), *Composing Ethnography: Alternative forms of qualitative writing* (pp. 172–198). Walnut Creek, CA: Alta Mira Press.

O'Donnell-Trujillo, N., and Pacanowsky, M. E. (1983). The Interpretation of organizational cultures. In Mary S. Mander (Ed.), *Communication in transition: Issues and debates in current research.* (pp. 225–241). New York: Praeger.

Orwell, G. (1961). *Down and out in Paris and London.* New York: Harcourt Brace Jovanovich. (Original work published in 1933)

— — —. (1962). *Burmese days*. Orlando, FL: Harcourt. (Original work published 1934)

Pacanowsky, M. (1988). Communication in the empowering organization. In J. A. Anderson (Ed.), *Communication yearbook II* (pp. 356–379). Newbury Park, CA: Sage Publications, Inc.

Parry, B. (1995). Problems in current theories of colonial discourse. In B. Ashcroft, G. Griffiths, and H. Tiffin (Eds.), *The post-colonial studies reader* (pp. 36–44). London and New York: Routledge and Kegan Paul.

Peters, R. (2000). *Repatriation*. Presentation given at the Atlatl Native Arts Network Conference, New York City. October.

Roy, D. F. (1959). "Banana Time" Job satisfaction and informal interaction. *Human Organization, 18*: 158–168.

Said, E. W. (1978). *Orientalism*. New York: Random House.

— — —. (1993). *Culture and Imperialism*. New York: Knopf.

Spivak,G. C. (1995). Can the subaltern speak? In B. Ashcroft, G. Griffiths, and H. Tiffin (Eds.), *The post-colonial studies reader* (pp. 24–28). London and New York: Routledge and Kegan Paul. (Original work published in 1988)

Stienem, G. (1983). *Outrageous acts and everyday rebellions*. New York: Plume (Original book published Holt, Rinehart and Winston) (Original essay published in 1963 by *Show* magazine)

Trujillo, N., and Dionisopoulos, G. (1987). Cop talk, police stories, and the social construction of organizational drama. *Central States Speech Journal, 38*: 196–209.

Turner, V. (1981). Social dramas and stories about them. In W. Mitchell (Ed.), *On Narrative* (pp. 33–44). Chicago: University of Chicago Press.

Tyler, E. (1958). *Primitive culture*. New York: Harper and Row (Original work published in 1871)

Tyler, S. A. (1986). Post-modern ethnography: From document of the occult to occult document. In J. Clifford and G. E. Marcus (Eds.), *Writing culture: The poetics and politics of ethnography* (pp. 122–140). Berkeley, CA: University of California Press.

Uchendu, V. (1973). A Navaho community. In R. Naroll and R. Cohen (Eds.), *A handbook of method in cultural anthropology* (pp. 230–237). New York: Columbia University Press.

Van Maanen, J. (1988). *Tales of the field: On writing ethnography*. Chicago and London: University of Chicago Press.

— — —. (Ed.) (1995). *Representation in Ethnography*. Thousand Oaks, CA: Sage Publications, Inc.

Vivian, B. (1999). The veil and the visible. *Western Journal of Communication, 63*: 115–139.

White, R. (1993). Expansion and exodus. In J. Miller, R. White, P. Nabokov, and P. J. Deloria (Eds.). *The Native Americans: An illustrated history* (pp. 211–300).

Whorf, B. L. (1956). *Language, thought and reality*. Boston: MIT Press.

Whyte, W. F. (1948). *Human relations in the restaurant industry*. New York: McGraw-Hill.

———. (1955) *Street corner society*. Chicago: University of Chicago Press. (Original work published in 1943)

Willis, P. E. (1977). *Learning to labour: How working class kids get working class jobs*. Farnborough, UK: Saxon House.

Wolcott, H. F. (1995). *The art of fieldwork*. Walnut Creek, CA: Alta Mira Press.

Wolf, M. (1992). *A thrice told tale: Feminism, postmodernism and ethnographic responsibility*. Stanford, CA: Stanford University Press.

Wuthnow, R., Hunter, J. D., Bergesen, A., and Kurzweil, E. (1984). *Cultural analysis: The work of Peter L. Berger, Mary Douglas, Michel Foucault, and Jurgen Habermas*. London and New York: Routledge and Kegan Paul.

PART TWO

Ethnographic Perspectives

CHAPTER 2

Living and Writing Feminist Ethnographies

Threads in a Quilt Stitched from the Heart

PAMELA CHAPMAN SANGER

In a thought-provoking essay, Stacey (1988) poses the question, "Can there be a feminist ethnography?" And, while there is no simple answer to this question, the concerns raised by it are the focus of this chapter.[1] According to Reinharz (1992), "we have been slow in weaving the connections among all the studies that exist and therefore deficient in reaching a grounded understanding of what feminist ethnography actually is" (p. 75). No single scholar, no single project can or should claim to have the final articulation of "feminist ethnography." I hope, however to add to a conversation that may shed light on a research process that holds great promise and potential for a better understanding of the human condition.

Despite contrary claims by Clifford (1986), feminists' contributions to ethnography have been documented as early as 1837 (Mascia-Lees, Sharpe and Cohen, 1989; see e.g., Mead, 1923; Parsons, 1906, 1916). Although early methods may not have been described as "feminist" in today's terms, these projects contributed to a focus on women, gender systems, and the politics of family structure, issues previously ignored by anthropologists (Visweswaren, 1997). Currently, feminist ethnographic scholarship is marked not only by its emphasis on the "centrality of women's experience" (Roseneil, 1993, p. 178), but also by a number of critical calls to enact feminist politics in the research process. Among these calls are the need to identify our biases (Wolf, 1992) and take care not to exploit the people we study (Roseneil, 1993). The central concerns raised of and by feminists' ethnographies include: the relationship between the "knower" and the "known"; for example, power, objectivity, reflexivity, and polyvocality.[2]

29

The relationship between the "knower" and the "known"

Feminists' concerns about the relationship between the researcher and the researched generally fall along four main lines of interest: the construction of the "Other," possibilities of dialogical methods, trust, and accountability. The construction of an Other is a central concern for many feminists. While holding ethnographic methods in high regard, feminists have raised serious questions about the nature of such research, especially given traditional ethnography's long history of "us" studying "them" (Stacey, 1988; Strathern, 1987; and Wolf, 1992). In general, the ethnographic process and product can be characterized by the objectifying creation of an Other, as Acker, Barry, and Esseveld (1991) note: "The act of looking at interviews, summarizing another's life, and placing it within a context is an act of objectification" (p. 142). One way in which feminists' attempt to counter the objectification of the Other is through the use of dialogic methods.

A number of researchers discuss the concept of dialogic methods. Callaway (1992) and Roseneil (1993) provide specific examples of this unique way of knowing. According to Callaway, dialogic methods are adopted with the shift from observational and empirical methods to communicative and constitutive approaches. This shift can be understood in terms of the change from visual metaphors (e.g., "seeing" and "viewing") to metaphors expressing voice ("listening" and "understanding"). Denzin (1997) opines that visual or ocular metaphors turn "the knowing subject into someone who is looked at, made a spectacle of, and the subject of the gazing ethnographer's eye" (p. 54). The voice-centered approach (Kissling, 1996) focuses on women's authorial power to speak with the researcher and reader, and is at the core of Denzin's (1997) description of the "feminist communitarian ethical model." As such, dialogic methods involve a research process that "becomes a dialogue between the researcher and researched, an effort to explore and clarify the topic under discussion, and to clarify and expand understanding; both are assumed to be individuals who reflect upon their experiences and who can communicate those experiences" (Acker, Barry and Esseveld, p. 140). While some might contend that the goals of ethnographic dialogue are not always guided by "clarification," but rather by experience, discussion, and sometimes confusion (e.g., Ellis and Bochner, 1996; Holman Jones, 1998, a, b, c), the metaphors of dialogue and voice pervade feminists' ethnographies. As Goodall (2000) notes: "Voice is the sound of the ethnographic world being called into being" (p. 140); and as Clair (1998) explains, expressing the silence of marginalized individuals is fundamental to ethnography.

Roseneil (1993) claims to have found the dialogic method to be energizing and highly significant in her overall project of describing life at the Greenham peace camps. Like Finch (1984) in her study of wives of clergy, as Roseneil began her interviews she noticed that the women were eager to talk to her once they realized that she had shared their experiences. In interviews with cannery workers in the Santa Clara Valley, Zavella (1987) noted that participants had to overcome a devalued sense of self and suspicion that arose from their beliefs that no one in power had ever cared about their thoughts. Relatedly, Bird's (1995) collection of letters and follow-up telephone calls to tabloid readers often ended with respondents thanking her for wanting to know about them.

Oakley (1981) suggests that interviewing should be a committed, egalitarian process, much as a conversation with a friend would be, if it is to be dialogic in nature. This approach was extremely useful to Trethewey (1997) who notes: "I was much more comfortable approaching the clients as friends rather than as subjects or data" (p. 286). Interviews are often conducted in the homes of participants (Kondo, 1990; Murphy, 1998, 2001; Trethewey, 1997; Zavella, 1997), a practice which attempts not only to make respondents feel more comfortable, but also can be problematic as it impinges on respondents' privacy and family relations (see especially Trethewey, 1997, and Zavella, 1997). In dialogic research premised on the "friendship" model of interviewing, there is often a great deal of give-and-take in the discussion, rather than a traditional interview that follows a strict "interview schedule" in which the researcher speaks only to ask questions and draw information from the interviewee (Kauffman, 1992). The mutual exchange of ideas and stories adds to the richness of feminists' ethnographies and allows for greater understanding of both the researched and the researcher (Roseneil, 1993).

However, the "friendship" model is often viewed as a utopian figment, as an ideal that falls far short of its potential and speaks to the issue of trust between the "knower" and the "known." Trust between researcher and researched is something vital to many feminist projects. Zavella (1987) faced the fact distrust of previous researchers' exploitative efforts could hamper her own project. She explains: "There is a long history of minority-group hostility toward Anglo researchers who are perceived as furthering their careers at the expense of people's time, trust, and privacy" (p. 21). Zavella's many and varied efforts to prove herself trustworthy led to important and fulfilling relationships, a point that is not lost on her: "I was privileged to have had my informant's confidence and trust, and I am dedicated to guarding it" (p. 29). Issues of confidentiality and consent forms are common in ethnographic research, and especially significant for the ways in which they speak to the trust between researcher and researched. Finch (1984) noted, with some surprise, how easily women spoke with her, often about intimate issues. This put her in a precarious position insofar as she had a great deal of "data," but she was quick to recognize that her "data" were the special, even sacred experiences and lives of women. She recalls: "I emerged from interviews with the feeling that interviewees need to know how to protect themselves from people like me. They have often revealed very private parts of their lives in return for what must be, in the last resort, very flimsy guarantees of confidentiality" (p. 80). Wong (1998) noticed that many participants in his study simply signed the form without reading it, and he states that this served as a constant reminder of the "differential relationship between the respondent and me" and heightened his accountability to those he researched.

For Hochschild (1983, 1989, 1997), the issue of trust is framed by an almost spiritual notion of faith. She notes in the introductions to her books that she is indebted to the flight attendants and families who relied on their "faith" in her as a researcher; "faith that I meant well" (1983, p. xii), "the faith that this research would help couples in similar situations" (1989, p. xvi).

Faith and trust, existing between knower and known, often leads to a strong feeling of accountability on the part of feminist ethnographers. Accountability marks feminist ethnography in both process and product. Studying education and popular culture in Mexico, Levinson (1998) found himself in the position of confidante and even an object of affection for several schoolgirls, and became very close with one girl and her family. As he negotiated these relationships carefully, he reflexively questioned his role in their lives, as well as how his relationships affected him, those he interviewed, and the larger politics of gender relations in Mexico. Similarly, Lengel's (1998) research in Tunis found her in the position of confidante—to a woman who had been raped by her doctor. Attempting to "afford a safe space for narrators to share intimate stories" and yet also wanting to challenge a politically gendered system that rendered rape victims powerless to speak up, left Lengel with disappointment that weighed heavily upon her. These quandaries relating to trust feature prominently in Holman Jones' (1998, a, b, c) ethnography of a club that feature's "women's music." Holman Jones recognizes her power as author to intervene in the lives of those she writes: "These are questions of the flesh—questions of the heart and soul, rather than the mind."

Such questions of the flesh are not easily reconciled. As Stacey (1988) cautions, the ethnographies of feminists, done with the presupposition of egalitarianism, can be risky. She writes: "the appearance of greater respect for and equality with research subjects in the ethnographic approach masks a deeper, more dangerous form of exploitation" (p. 22). The greater intimacy that highlights feminists' ethnographies can lead to danger and betrayal for both the researched and the researcher, as Wong (1998) discovered in his research with women in the Aid to Families with Dependent Children (AFDC). Wong admits that he "used [his] personality to strike a rapport with my respondents so that data could be obtained" and that in the apparent "friendship" he had with his respondents, he "performed heterosexuality" in order to continue to extract data. When faced with "friendly" comments about his dating life, he explains,

> When I structured my rapport as friendship, I staged my own outing. My sexual, intimate, and private life came under the scrutiny of the women's questions. However, the apparent friendship that I imagined

was rendered a mirage when I resisted their questions. There was no reciprocity nor equal exchange. My own intimate life was laminated. My privacy was retained. Meanwhile, I continued to probe their lives.

In this way, Wong's friendships with the women he interviewed seem less than genuine and led to a questioning of his very sense of self and identity. Facing a similar crisis of selfhood, Schacht (1997), a self-defined feminist, collected ethnographic data from a rugby team that repeatedly engaged in sexist, misogynistic comments and rituals. Believing that he must join the group to understand it, Schacht explains that he denied his feminist disdain for the group's practices, becoming instead a "sylph—a being without a soul"—who functioned as a participant-observer of the team. He contends that this was necessary to maintain the trust of the team members and that "doing so not only earned me the respect of many of the club members, [but] it also led to temporary friendships." While Schacht maintains that his "long-term moral commitment to doing sociological research, especially as a feminist male" demanded and enabled him to lose his soul temporarily, many feminist ethnographers would question his ethics and morals in this situation. Exploitation and betrayal of self and others is a major risk undertaken whenever an ethnographer attempts to "write a culture," and it is inextricably woven with the issue of power.

Power

Wolf (1992) argues that feminist ethnographies cannot avoid the issue of power in the process or product of ethnography. She claims: "Whether we are talking about nonexploitative methodology in field research or authority in writing ethnography, we are talking about power—who has it, how it is used, for what purposes" (p. 133). Feminists often make deliberate attempts "to expose power relations embedded in any ethnographic work" (Mascia-Lees, Sharpe and Ballerino Cohen, 1989, p. 10), and to minimize hierarchical relations, especially in processes like interviews (Kissling, 1996). Traditionally, feminists' concerns about power and the appropriation of knowledge from research subjects has taken the form of questions like, "Can I really 'give voice' to women in these communities, or am I simply taking those voices?" (Lengel, 1998). The interview is imbued with so many different and varied power relations. We ought not forget that those who participate in interviews often have their own power in the interview process (i.e., the power to refuse to speak, the power to refuse to speak accurately); they can render the researchers quite powerless (Kondo, 1990). Ultimately, though, many feminists seek to avoid the scenario of "who has power over whom" and attempt, instead, to engage in research *with* those whom they study, rather than research *about* them (Holman Jones, 1998a; Roseneil, 1993).

Nonetheless, feminist researchers struggle with the pragmatic ways in which power differentials can be acknowledged and simultaneously reckoned with in such a way that the asymmetry that most feminists work so diligently to avoid in society is not reproduced in the very research that they undertake to understand that society.

One issue that proves especially salient in discussions of power in the practices of fieldwork is that of reciprocity. Zavella (1987) reports: "I was very much aware of their kindness in spending their valued leisure time with me, and I reciprocated as best I could by bringing small gifts and giving advice when they requested it" (p. 23). When asked how her research had helped "The Club," Holman Jones (1998b) explains that she is going to donate one-half of the proceeds from her book sales to aid the music venue. And Trethewey (1997) provided the pragmatic service of babysitting to assist her respondents. Adams (1998) notes that many ethnographers "engage in reciprocity because we feel it is moral to do so. This moral obligation is particularly pressing when we study people in less fortunate economic circumstances than our own."

Offering money or other assistance, however, can often times simply serve to magnify power differentials in the research relationship. Wong (1998) offered interview subjects $20 to complete an interview session, and he soon found himself hounded by women, financially desperate and trying to survive on meager government stipends. Similarly, Adams (1998) offered to assist craftspeople in Chile, thinking that her efforts would be well received. Instead, the craftspeople were reminded of their marginality and of the class differences between them and the researcher. As Lengel (1998) asks of reciprocity, "do researchers then become the donor gods and goddesses, furthering the dependence of the powerless on the powerful?" Whether involving the commodification of experience or the magnification of status distinctions, reciprocity is an issue that exemplifies the complex web of power dimensions that pervade the ethnographies of feminists. Many feminists see efforts to break down power differentials in the research process as linked to the abandonment of a pretense of scientific "objectivity."

Objectivity

Traditional fieldwork done by anthropologists was often judged by the relative "objectivity" of the researcher. Ethnographers were expected to leave biases behind and "enter the field" free of values, beliefs, and assumptions. Ethnographers were cautioned about the danger of "going native," or becoming too close to those they study. For example, an ethnography primer warns that "the research may be contaminated by 'subjectivity' and personal feelings. . . . Research 'objectivity,' in the traditional view, is not unlike virginity: Once lost, it cannot be recovered" (Jorgensen, 1987, p. 62). Feminists, interested in the social construction of self and believing in the claim that the personal is political, have long questioned the possibility and utility of objectivity, especially in ethnographic projects. Callaway (1992) explains one of many feminists' concerns regarding objectivity: "One of the tacit rules of ethnography have been the 'neutrality' of the author in a pursuit of 'value-free science.' Among other exclusions of anthropologists' selves, 'genre' all but eliminated 'gender'" (p. 31). This point is evident in McRobbie's (1981) critique of Willis' work and in Clair's (1998) reinterpretation of Conquergood's work. Relatedly, Acker, Barry, and Esseveld (1991) argue that objectivity is a form of male bias that pervades theory and research.

In stark contrast to traditional ethnography's fetish with objectivity, Clair (1995) unites feminism, ethnography, and phenomenology in an exciting method she terms "fenomenography." She then utilized this approach to explore her own experiences while living in an urban neighborhood. Holman Jones (1998c) also invites herself fully into her research in both the process and product. In her account, she explains that, "I want to feel the artistry, the reverence, the fire of this place. I want to love it as they do" (p. 22). The passion Holman Jones feels is evident throughout her ethnographic experience as she speaks of the fear, elation, confusion, joy, frustration, and constant questioning of her "personal obligations and professional responsibilities," for both complicate and enrich her project as she learns not only about the culture of "The Club," but also about herself (1998b). Krieger's (1985) study of a Midwestern lesbian social group, of which she was a part, offers an example of how a feminist ethnographer can and must bring herself to the research project. She articulates the struggles she faced when dealing with her own inability to seek "analytic distance" from her research project. Describing a process of "reengagement" that she followed, Krieger explains that the "knower" and the "known" are interconnected in so many ways that, "We need to link our statements about those we study with statements about ourselves, for in reality, neither stands alone" (p. 321). This supports Williams' (1993) claim that one can see all ethnographies as autobiographies since the self is so completely involved in the process (also see Crawford, 1996; Ellis and Bochner, 1996). Among the many ways to "do autoethnography," journals are a means by which the researcher seeks not only to write culture, but also writes the self. For example, Lorde's (1980, 1988) journal entries about her experiences with cancer speak not only to her own journey, but also to the journeys of thousands of women who are faced with the challenges of breast cancer. Journals also figure prominently in Ross and Geist's (1997) discussion of women's experiences of miscarriage. In addition to journals, poetry also allows for autoethnographic exploration of previously marginalized experiences and emotions (Anzaldua, 1987; González, 1997).

The self also speaks as Kolker (1996) uses her own experiences with breast cancer to illumine the bureaucratic nightmare of managed care. In a different arena, Fiske (1994a) analyzes his own experiences as a "fan" of "The Newlywed Game," in addition to exploring how other audiences apprehended the gender politics of the show. The performance of autoethnographic narratives allows Calafell and Van Deman (2000) to give voice to diverse women as they work as graduate assistants, while Ronai (1995; 1996) uses her own experiences as the victim of sexual abuse and daughter of a mentally retarded woman in a layered account to explore family dynamics and self-identity. These pieces exemplify autoethnography as the authors offer their own stories, much as traditional ethnographers offered the stories of others, in an effort to further our understanding of human experience.

The offering of one's own story does not come easily, however. In his weaving of his own reflections along with family members' memories of his grandmother, Trujillo (1998) deals with ethical and emotional questions as he probes the fabric of his own family. Likewise, the series of autoethnographic pieces by Communication Studies 298 (1999) share deeply personal confessions about, among other issues, body image, divorce, and receiving welfare. These pieces reveal intimate moments experienced by the researchers in an effort to give voice to the ways in which the process of consuming shapes the (feminist) self. Sharing is a major issue in Tillman-Healy's (1996) autoethnography of living with bulimia. As she explains: "I take the emotional/professional risk of sharing the darkest, most painful secret of my life in order to expose some of the lived, felt consequences of these stories and to open dialogues aimed at writing new and better ones" (p. 81). Such risks are prevalent as feminists step from behind traditional ethnography's cloak of objectivity and lay bare their souls, however, most all autoethnographers seem to concur that the risks are worth taking (also see e.g., Holman Jones, 1998c). An issue closely related to the subjective perspective of many feminist autoethnographers is the issue of reflexivity.

Reflexivity

Insofar as all of the issues or threads discussed are interwoven in multifaceted ways, it is difficult to speak of one without referencing the others. This is especially true of the notion of reflexivity. Reflexivity involves an explicit discussion of how the self effects and is effected by the research and writing processes. As Goodall (2000) notes: "To be 'reflexive' means to turn back on our self the lens through which we are interpreting the world" (p. 137). While not limited to feminists' ethnographies, Dyck (1993) explains that reflexivity is of special interest to feminists, for it allows for the gendered nature of the research process and product. Moreover, reflexivity also allows for comments on how class (e.g., Adams, 1998); ethnicity (e.g., Zavella, 1987); sexual orientation (e.g., Krieger, 1985); and race (Trinh, 1991) create and are created by the research process. Because it "confronts the politics of representation," Callaway (1992) contends that an emphasis on reflexivity has enabled feminists to challenge the colonial and imperialists roots of ethnographic inquiry. Moreover, she explains that reflexivity is a political move, involving "opening the way to a more radical consciousness of self in facing the political dimensions of fieldwork and constructing knowledge" (p. 33).

While most feminist researchers state that they engage in self-reflexivity through an explicit acknowledgement of their feminist perspective (e.g., Trethewey, 1997, 1999; Wong, 1998), others are aware of their self-identity as feminists because they are men, engaging in feminist research in misogynistic settings (e.g., Levinson, 1998; Schacht, 1997; Wendt, 1995). In the latter exemplars, the researchers felt the prominent power of their own "masculine gaze" as they entered into situations that made them uncomfortable and put their feminist politics to the test.

One means by which many feminists have attempted to position themselves while negotiating the tension between "writing a culture" and yet not constructing that culture as "Other" is claimed by Collins's (1990) concept of "outsider within." Collins explains that black women, among others, can author from this perspective insofar as they are "outsiders" living within white society. Positioned in this fashion, outsiders within claim not only to have an ability to understand both self and the world around oneself, but also to illuminate one's positionality and the ways in which that positionality holds epistemic power.

In her highly reflexive project, Holman Jones (1998c) forces the reader to confront with her the most challenging and complex issues facing ethnographic researchers. While learning about the culture and politics of an organization, the reader is taken on the author's powerful journey of self-questioning and self-discovery. The self is always implicated in reflexive research, as Lengel (1998) aptly notes: reflexivity always involves a discussion of not only the author's position as it relates to the researched, but also of the author's position as it relates to the author's sense of self. In this way, many feminists work not only to reveal themselves, but also to allow a plurality of voices to be heard. Polyvocality serves not only the feminist political goal of providing a forum for the traditionally marginalized to be heard, but also to acknowledge the partiality of truth in the ethnographic process (Callaway, 1992).

Polyvocality

Polyvocality refers to the possibility of allowing for many voices, rather than simply that of the researcher, to speak in ethnographic texts. For many feminist scholars, polyvocality is more than a textual strategy; it is a perspective that guides praxis. Polyvocality is intertwined in infinite ways with the concerns already identified in this chapter. It speaks to the relationship between the knower and the known in the issues of dialogue and trust; to power and the "right" that one has to speak for and about another; the ways in which a text might serve to objectify (or not) the voices, lives, and experiences of those involved in the research; and the potential that reflexivity has for encouraging polyvocality. Polyvocality can occur in many ways, and feminists' interpretations of polyvocality range from attempts to ensure that the experiences of those researched are "heard" in the text (but still in the researcher's voice) to using the respondents' own words, rather than paraphrasing, to explicit attempts to coauthor a text with the researched, as well as variations and combinations of the above. For example, consistent with the dialogic approach, both Trethewey (1997, 1999), and Zavella (1987) used a "collaborative" interview style whereby women could ask her questions, in a conversational style, rather than a traditional interview, and then featured women's own words when writing her study.

Decentering her authority even further, Lather (2001) gives voice to women with HIV by presenting "the women's words on the top of the page in bigger font, and researcher narratives on the bottom in smaller font" and interrupts researcher interpretations with discussions from and about angels. Upon creating this textual format, Lather checked with the women she researched before it was published as a book, and included their conversations about the text in an article that explicated the research process. Many feminists' ethnographers offer their texts to those with whom they researched as a means of collaborating on the writing process (e.g., Clair, 1994; Levinson, 1998).

Many feminists, and ethnographers in general, find polyvocality very challenging. Acknowledging some practical matters, such as deadlines and manuscript length, makes it difficult to allow *everyone* to say *everything* that they might like to say (Reinharz, 1992). Further, there are respondents who do not wish to collaborate (see Holman Jones, 1998 a, b, c; Willis, 1977). And, ultimately, if a piece has an author, then that author must make choices and the text that results does have an element of "finality" to it, even if only temporarily final. Roseneil (1993) explains that despite her efforts to create a polyvocal text: "I have *exploited* and 'used' the women I have interviewed (and probably also unsuspecting women I have not interviewed), extracting their words to illustrate points of my choosing. . . . In the final analysis, it has been *my* analysis that has triumphed; I retain power of authorship" (p. 204, emphasis in original). The power of authorship proves to be a real challenge for feminists working to create a polyvocal text and several maintain that authorship ultimately prevents a truly polyvocal text (Stacey, 1988; Wolf, 1992). Mascia-Lees, Sharpe, and Cohen (1989) argue that claiming to be "polyvocal" masks serious concerns about power imbalances in the research process:

> Authors who experiment with point of view, presenting a seeming
> jumble of perspectives and subjectivities in a variety of voices, may
> well be writing no more open texts than classic works in which all

action is mediated by a unitary narrative voice. The literary techniques of fragmentation, metaphor, thematic and verbal echo, repetition, and juxtaposition, which the new ethnography borrows, are all devices through which an author manipulates understanding and response. They function to structure the reader's experience (p. 30).

In this way, polyvocality echoes the myriad of other issues that permeate the fiber of feminists' ethnographies—full of fruitful possibilities and wrought with challenges.

Postscript

And so the stories told by feminist ethnographers continue to be lived, written, and shared. As I hope this brief review makes clear, feminists have made incredible contributions to the writing of culture(s). While there are, no doubt, countless feminists whose positions are not presented here, I believe that this chapter does add an important voice in the dialogue about feminists' ethnographies. This chapter offers a fragment of much larger discussions about the theoretical, methodological, political, and pragmatic concerns of feminism. Feminist ethnographers have done much to challenge the traditions of ethnographic research, driving all of those who conduct ethnographic research to address some vital issues regarding the politics of their endeavors. From a sensitivity to methods used to "collect data" to attempts to "de-authorize" the textual ethnographic product, feminists ceaselessly interrogate the praxis and product of ethnography in ways that are difficult and, at the same time, incredibly rewarding. Writing from the heart, with passion, vigor, and, at the same time, rigor, feminists' ethnographies speak to us in ways that touch our souls and challenge our minds.

Notes

1. Since there are obviously multiple feminisms (Tong, 1989) and many and varied forms of ethnographic research, it follows that there is no monolithic definition of "feminist ethnography." However, I consider ethnography as a multimethod analytic process which, according to Reinharz (1992), "usually includes observation, participation, archival analysis, and interviewing, thus combining the assets and weaknesses of each method" (p. 46). Holman Jones (1998b) explains that, "Feminist ethnography, then, is the sought and written experience of women within and between cultures . . . feminist ethnographic writing is almost always done by women and takes many forms including poetry, fiction, travelogues, and songs, as well as what we consider to be more traditional anthropological formats.

Such writing is feminist because it recognizes the multiple positions women occupy within and between cultures without erasing or collapsing power relationships among women as well as power differentials between women and men. Such writing inscribes how these power differentials work to naturalize bodily, subjective, experiential, cultural, and institutional differences among many women (and between women and men) that legitimate the interests of a few." It is important to note that men certainly can and do engage in feminist ethnographic research (e.g., Gurney, 1997; Levinson, 1998; Schacht, 1997; Taylor, 1993; Trujillo, 1998; Wendt, 1995; Willis, 1977; Wong, 1998). Regardless of the gender of the researchers, feminist ethnographic studies are indeed proponents for the centrality of women's experience and "contribute to the understanding of women's oppression and to further the struggle for women's liberation" (Roseneil, 1993, p. 179). In this way, ethnographic research addresses the aims of most feminisims. Dyck (1993), however, cautions that there ought not be a totalizing notion of research for "women." Insofar as such a notion attempts to speak to oppression of all women at the expense of understanding the nuances of varied oppressions experienced in the intersection of race/class/gender/sexual orientation/religion/ethnicity, it is dangerous to feminists' political project.

2. All of these issues are inextricably linked to one another. I present them individually only as a starting point for discussion, which inevitably lead to the many other threads in this chapter and this text.

References

Acker, J., Barry, K., and Esseveld, J. (1991). Objectivity and truth: Problems in doing feminist research. In M. M. Fonow and J. A. Cook (Eds.), *Beyond methodology: Feminist scholarship as lived research* (pp. 133–153). Bloomington, IN: Indiana University Press.

Adams, J. (1998). The wrongs of reciprocity: Fieldwork among Chilean working-class women. *Journal of Contemporary Ethnography, 27* (2): 219–242. Retrieved December 17, 2001 from Infotrac online database (Expanded Academic ASAP).

Anzaldua, G. (1987). *Borderlands/la frontera: The new Mestiza*. San Francisco: Aunt Lute.

Bird, S. E. (1995). Understanding the ethnographic encounter: The need for flexibility in feminist reception studies. *Women and Language, 18* (2): 22–27. Retrieved December 17, 2001 from Infotrac online database (Expanded Academic ASAP).

Calafell, B. M., and Van Deman, F. B. (2000). Succulent women: An autoethnographic exploration of graduate assistant experiences. *Women and Language, 23* (1): 43.

Callaway, H. (1992). Ethnography and experience: Gender implications in field-work and texts. In J. Okley and H. Callaway (Eds.), *Anthropology and autobiography* (pp. 29–49). New York: Routledge and Kegan Paul.

Clair, R. P. (1993). The use of framing devices to sequester organizational narratives: Hegemony and harassment. *Communication Monographs, 60*: 113–136.

— — —. (1994). Resistance and oppression as a self-contained opposite: An organizational communication analysis of one man's story of sexual harassment. *Western Journal of Communication, 58*: 235–262.

— — —. (1995). Fenomenography (feminism, phenomenology, and ethnography) as an approach to studying narratives of an urban neighborhood. Lecture presented at Purdue University, West Lafayette, IN.

— — —. (1998). *Organizing silence: A world of possibilities*. Albany: State University of New York Press.

Clifford, J. (1986). Introduction: Partial truths. In J. Clifford and G. E. Marcus (Eds.), *Writing culture: The poetics and politics of ethnography* (pp. 1–26). Berkeley: University of California Press.

Collins, P. H. (1990). *Black feminist thought: Knowledge, consciousness, and the politics of empowerment*. London: Routledge and Kegan Paul.

— — —. (1991)

Communication Studies 298. (1999). Shopping for family. *Qualitative Inquiry, 5* (2): 147–180.

Crawford, L. (1996). Personal ethnography. *Communication Monographs, 63*: 158–170.

Denzin, N. K. (1997). *Interpretive ethnography: Ethnographic practices for the twenty-first century*. Thousand Oaks, CA: Sage Publications, Inc.

Dyck, I. (1993). Ethnography: A feminist method? *The Canadian Geographer, 37* (1): 52–57.

Ellis, C., and Bochner, A. P. (Eds.). (1996). *Composing ethnography: Alternative forms of qualitative writing*. Walnut Creek, CA: Alta Mira Press.

Finch, J. (1984). 'It's great to have someone to talk to': The ethics and politics of interviewing women. In C. Bell and H. Roberts (Eds.), *Social researching: Politics, problems, practice* (pp. 70–87). London: Routledge and Kegan Paul.

Fiske, J. (1994a). Audiencing: Cultural practice and cultural studies. In Norman K. Denzin and Yvonna S. Lincoln (Eds.), *Handbook of qualitative research* (pp. 189–198). Thousand Oaks, CA: Sage Publications, Inc.

González, M. C. (1997). Indian time; Incognito; The controversial vision; Untitled; Homecoming; That white thing; Sympathetic ailments (poems). In L. A. M. Perry, and P. Geist, *Courage of conviction: Women's words, women's wisdom* (pp. vii, 70, 102, 168, 202, 236, 266). Mountain View, CA: Mayfield Publishing Company.

Goodall, H. L. (2000). *Writing the new ethnography.* Walnut Creek, CA: Alta Mira Press.

Gurney, C. M. (1997). ". . . Half of me was satisfied": Making sense of home through episodic ethnographies. *Women's Studies International Forum, 20* (3): 373–386.

Hochschild, A. R. (1983). *The managed heart: commercialization of human feeling.* Berkeley, CA: University of California Press.

———. (1989). *The second shift: Working parents and the revolution at home.* New York: Viking.

———. (1997). *The time bind: When work becomes home and home becomes work.* New York: Metropolitan Books.

Holman Jones, S. (1998a). Kaleidoscope notes: Writing women's music and organizational culture. *Qualitative Inquiry, 4* (2): 148–178. Retrieved December 17, 2001 from Infotrac online database (Expanded Academic ASAP).

———. (1998b). Turning the kaleidoscope, re-visioning ethnography. *Qualitative Inquiry, 4* (3): 421–442. Retrieved December 17, 2001 from Infotrac online database (Expanded Academic ASAP).

———. (1998c). *Kaleidoscope notes: Writing women's music and organizational culture.* Walnut Creek, CA: Alta Mira Press.

Jorgenen, D. (1987). *Participant observation: A methodology for human studies.* Newbury Park, CA: Sage Publications, Inc.

Kauffman, B. J. (1992). Feminist facts: Interview strategies and political subjects in ethnography. *Communication Theory, 2*: 187–206.

Kissling, E. A. (1996). "That's just a basic teen-age rule: Girls' linguistic strategies for managing the menstrual communication taboo. *Journal of Applied Communication Research, 24* (4): 292–309.

Kolker, A. (1996). Thrown overboard: The human costs of health care rationing. In C. Ellis. and A. P. Bochner (Eds.), *Composing ethnography: Alternative forms of qualitative writing* (pp. 132–159). Walnut Creek, CA: Alta Mira Press.

Kondo, D. K. (1990). *Crafting selves: Power, gender, and discourses of identity in a Japanese workplace.* Chicago: University of Chicago Press.

Krieger, S. (1985). Beyond "subjectivity:" The use of the self in social science. *Qualitative Sociology, 8* (4): 309–324.

Lather, P. (2001). Postbook: Working the ruins of feminist ethnography. *Signs, 27* (1): 199. Retrieved December 17, 2001 from Infotrac online database (Expanded Academic ASAP).

Lengel, L. B. (1998). Researching the "other," transforming ourselves: Methodological considerations of feminist ethnography. *Journal of Communcation Inquiry, 22* (3): 229–251. Retrieved December 17, 2001 from Infotrac online database (Expanded Academic ASAP).

Levinson, B. A. (1998). (How) can a man do feminist ethnography of education? *Qualitative Inquiry, 4* (3): 337–369. Retrieved December 17, 2001 from Infotrac online database (Expanded Academic ASAP).

Lorde, A. (1980). *The cancer journals*. San Francisco: Aunt Lute Books.

———. (1988). *A burst of light*. Ithaca, NY: Firebrand Books.

Mascia-Lees, F. E., Sharpe, P., and Ballerino Cohen, C. (1989). The postmodern turn in anthropology: Cautions from a feminist perspective. *Signs, 15* (11): 7–33.

McRobbie, A. (1981). Settling accounts with subcultures: A feminist critique. In T. Bennett, G. Martin, C. Mercer, and J. Woolcott (Eds.), *Culture, ideology, and social processes* (pp. 111–124). London: Routledge and Kegan Paul.

Mead, M. (1923). *Coming of age in Samoa*. New York: William Morrow.

Murphy, A. G. (1998). Hidden transcripts of flight attendant resistance. *Management Communication Quarterly, 11* (4): 499–535.

———. (2001). The flight attendant dilemma: An analysis of communication and sensemaking during in-flight emergencies. *Journal of Applied Communication Research, 29* (1): 30–53.

Oakley, A. (1981). Interviewing women: A contradiction in terms. In H. Roberts (Ed.), *Doing feminist research* (pp. 30–61). London: Routledge and Kegan Paul.

Parsons, E. C. (1906). *The family: An ethnographical and historical outline*. New York: Putnam and Sons.

———. (1916). *Social rule: A study of the will to power*. New York: Putnam and Sons.

Reinharz, S. (1992). *Feminist methods in social research*. New York: Oxford University Press.

Ronai, C. R. (1995). Multiple reflections of child sex abuse: An argument for a layered account. *Journal of Contemporary Ethnography, 23*: 395–426.

———. (1996). My mother is mentally retarded. In C. Ellis and A. P. Bochner (Eds.), *Composing ethnography: Alternative forms of qualitative writing* (pp. 109–131). Walnut Creek, CA: Alta Mira Press.

Roseneil, S. (1993). Greenham revisited: Reserching myself and my sisters. In D. Hobbs and T. May (Eds.), *Interpreting the field: Accounts of ethnography* (pp. 177–208). Oxford: Clarendon Press.

Ross, J. L., and Geist, P. (1997). Elation and devastation: Women's journeys through pregnancy and miscarriage. In L. A. M. Perry, and P. Geist, *Courage of conviction: Women's words, women's wisdom* (pp. 167–184). Mountain View, CA: Mayfield Publishing Company.

Schact, S. P. (1997). Feminist fieldwork in the misogynist setting of the rugby pitch: Temporarily becoming a sylph to survive and personally grow. *Journal of Contemporary Ethnography, 26* (3): 338–364. Retrieved

December 17, 2001 from Infotrac online database (Expanded Academic ASAP).

Stacey, J. (1988). Can there be a feminist ethnography? *Women's Studies International Forum, 11* (1): 21–27.

Strathern, M. (1987). An awkward relationship: The case of feminism and anthropology. *Signs, 12* (2): 276–292.

Taylor, B. (1993). Register of the repressed: Women's voice and body in the nuclear weapons organization. *Quarterly Journal of Speech, 79* (3): 267–286.

Tillman-Healy, L. M. (1996). A secret life in a culture of thinness: Reflections on body, food, and bulemia. In C. Ellis and A. P. Bochner (Eds.), *Composing ethnography: Alternative forms of qualitative writing* (pp. 76–108). Walnut Creek, CA: Alta Mira Press.

Tong, R. (1989). *Feminist thought: A comprehensive introduction.* Boulder, CO: Westview Press.

Trethewey, A. (1997). Resistance, identity, and empowerment: A postmodern feminist analysis of clients in a human service organization. *Communication Monographs, 64*: 281–301.

Trethewey, A. (1999). Isn't it ironic: Using irony to explore the contradictions of organizational life. *Western Journal of Communication, 63* (2): 140–142.

Trinh, T. M. (1991). *When the moon waxes red: Representation, gender, and cultural politics.* New York: Routledge and Kegan Paul.

Trujillo, N. (1998). In search of Naunny's grave. *Text and Performance Quarterly, 18*: 344–368.

Visweswaran, K. (1997). Histories of feminist ethnography. *Annual Review of Anthropology, 26*: 591–621.

Wendt, R. F. (1995). Women in positions of service: The politicized body. *Communication Studies, 46*: 276–296.

Williams, A. (1993). Diversity and agreement in feminist ethnography. *Sociology, 27*, (4): 575–589.

Willis, P. (1977). *Learning to labour: How working class kids get working class jobs.* New York: Columbia University Press.

Wolf, M. (1992). *A thrice-told tale: Feminism, postmodernism, and ethnographic responsibility.* Stanford: Stanford University Press.

Wong, L. M. (1998). The ethics of rapport: Institutional safeguards, resistance, and betrayal. *Qualitative Inquiry, 4* (2): 178–200. Retrieved December 17, 2001 from Infotrac online database (Expanded Academic ASAP).

Zavella, P. (1987). *Women's work and Chicano families: Cannery workers of the Santa Clara Valley.* Ithaca, NY: Cornell University Press.

CHAPTER 3

Musings on Critical Ethnography, Meanings, and Symbolic Violence

JIM THOMAS

In the past decade, critical ethnography has moved from the periphery of scholarly attention to the forefront, spreading from the traditional social sciences into other disciplines, such as education, business, and nursing. However, the emergence of the perspective from the shadows of marginalization and the use by a broader range of scholars has created a rather variegated mosaic that often clouds the fundamental precepts shared by practitioners. This too often results in scholars labeling any form of cultural criticism as "critical ethnography." Fortunately, volumes such as this one provide the opportunity for researchers to share and compare their diverse views as a way of illustrating their common themes of social critique in order to distinguish critique from simply criticism. Here, I summarize a few core themes of critical ethnography and illustrate one (of many) ways it can be applied to address the symbolic violence of conventional research.

An Overview of Ethnographic Critique

To call critical ethnography "conventional ethnography with an attitude" is too glib (Thomas, 1992), and reducing it simply to social criticism distorts and oversimplifies the critical ethnographic project. At its simplest, critical ethnography is a way of applying a subversive world view to more conventional narratives of cultural inquiry. It does not necessarily stand in opposition to conventional ethnography, or even to conventional social science. Rather, it offers a more reflective style of thinking about the relationship between knowledge, society, and freedom from unnecessary social domination.

Recognizing that power relations and knowledge are interconnected, critical ethnography challenges the conventional ideological images inherent in all research by investigating the possibility of alternative meanings. This does not necessarily require a rejection of conventional or "common sense" meanings. But, it does demand that the researcher locate the meaning of events within the context of asymmetrical power relations.

What distinguishes critical ethnography from the other kind is not so much an act of criticism, but an act of critique. Criticism, a complaint we make when our eggs are undercooked, generally connotes dissatisfaction with a given state of affairs, but does not necessarily carry with it an obligation to dig beneath surface appearances and challenge them. Critique, by contrast, assesses "how things are" with an added premise that "things could be better" if we examine the underlying sources of conditions, including the values on which our complaints are based. Unlike criticism, critique is iterative, moving back and forth between examining the assumptions and foundations of how things are, how they got that way, how things might be changed, and why we should care in the first place. That is, critique proceeds simultaneously from the three components of epistemological and ontological reflexivity, empirical inquiry, and action. While these three components may not be, and rarely can be, elaborated in the narrative of every individual study, they remain the fundamental tasks that guide the critical inquiry process.

The Roots of Critique

Critical ethnography is not a theory, because it does not, in itself, generate a set of testable propositions or law-like statements. Rather, it is a perspective that provides fundamental images, metaphors, and understandings about our social world. It also provides value premises around which to ask questions and guide transformative action. It is a methodology that "strives to unmask hegemony and address oppressive forces" (Crotty, 1998, p. 12).

Borrowing from John Dewey's (1933, p. 9) conception of reflective thought, critical ethnography builds on "active, persistent, and careful consideration of any belief or supposed form of knowledge in the light of the grounds that support it and the further conclusions to which it tends." Yet, if critical ethnography is to be more than a reflection of the ethnographer's conscience or claims, then some conceptual unity must be placed upon it. For some, this unity remains ideological, guided by Marxian thought to justify the label of "critical." For others, a broader conception of unity, more humanist than Marxist, binds the variations. However, demand for ideological unity subverts the central project. Insistence on "correct" political thinking dissolves critique into a narrow mode of inquiry that limits thought and diminishes possibilities for action. By proffering critique rather than ideology as the primary unifying principle, we find it easier to identify other approaches that share the critical enterprise.

Social critique, by definition, is radical. Borrowed from the Greeks (*Kriticos*, to judge) by the Romans, the Latin term *criticus*, meaning to sift, denotes an evaluative judgment of meaning and method in research, policy, and human activity. Critical thinking implies freedom by recognizing that social existence, including our knowledge of it, is not simply a "given," imposed on us by powerful and mysterious forces. This recognition leads to the possibility of transcending the immediacy of existing social or ideational conditions (Thomas and O'Maolchatha, 1988). The act of critique implies that, by thinking about and then acting upon the world, we are able to change our subjective interpretations and objective conditions. Remy Quant observed that freedom, as a component of critique, connects the emancipatory, normative, and evaluative features of critical thought:

> Freedom, first of all, implies that man is not totally encompassed and submerged in that which he de facto is. The norm, secondly, is a demand made with respect to the facts. Finally, the value is a special light which must be distinguished from the light provided by the fact (Quant, 1967, p. 30).

Critical thought facilitates challenging and perhaps overcoming ideational and structural obstacles that restrict perception and discussion of, in my own field for example, crime and social control. Critique conveys freedom in that it requires the capability to explore, without constraint, alternative meanings. It denotes value because it requires a discerning rational judgment in order to choose between conceptual and existential alternatives, and it suggests norms to guide both the discourse and interpretative activity of knowing.

Conventional ethnography assumes the status quo, affirms assumed meanings when alternatives might exist, and seldom reveals the domain assumptions of research subjects or the researcher. As insightful as conventional studies can be, they rarely integrate descriptions of cultural parts into an analysis of the whole that raises the critical implications of the descriptions or challenges relations of power. This failure subverts researchers' utility as human tools of knowledge, because simply stating the cultural context is not sufficient for understanding our topic.

But how do we attain such lofty goals when doing relatively mundane research? First, we should remember that we cannot include every good idea or intention in a single study. Especially in short papers, it is rarely possible to address the full range of issues that we would like. Second, it is useful to remember that even the simplest event can raise complex issues. We can begin by focusing narrowly, and then expanding as the data allow. This provides a way to reduce the symbolic violence associated with more conventional research.

An Example

Critical researchers begin from the premise that all cultural life is in constant tension between control and resistance. This tension is reflected in behavior, interaction rituals, normative systems, and social structure, all of which are visible in the rules, communication systems, and artifacts that comprise a given culture. Critical ethnography takes seemingly mundane events, even repulsive ones, and reproduces them in a way that exposes broader social processes of control, power imbalance, and the symbolic mechanisms that impose one set of preferred meanings or behaviors over others. A seemingly insignificant fieldnote excerpt from a project on prisoner culture illustrates one way to apply a critical perspective and examine the implications of symbolic violence:

> The criminology students, 15 females and 8 males, took a field trip to Pontiac Correctional Center, a maximum security disciplinary/segregation institution where prisoners are locked in their cells 23 hours a day. They filed into an old, two-tiered concrete and limestone cell house, staying close to the wall across from the cells. About 15 feet separated the students from the prisoners' cells. The first few cells in the first tier were solid metal with only two openings. One opening was a closed slot for inserting food trays. The other was a roughly one-square-foot window-like double-mesh opening to enable prisoners to yell out and have a partial view of the corridor between the mesh's overlapping bb-sized holes.
>
> As the students entered, a few noticed a sign, "Assaultive Inmate" attached to the first cell door. As they passed by it, two loud "bangs" echoed like small explosions as the inmate inside smashed his meshed window with considerable force. Simultaneously, a nauseating odor spread among the students. The male behind me touched my shoulder and calmly said, "I think I've just been hit with shit." His neck, shoulder, shirt and pants had been splashed by a brown liquid, and the stench was nearly unbearable.
>
> The prisoner had earlier mixed urine and stale feces to make a noxious substance intended for throwing on staff. Instead, the targets were the students. To project the foul mixture through the meshed opening, he created make-shift paper cups, filled them, and then slammed each against the mesh. This primitive method of delivery virtually assured that most of the concoction would splash over himself and his cell, but enough made it through to the unfortunate victim to have the desired effect.

The incident would seem prima facie evidence of the rigors of prison, the recalcitrant nature of bad guys, and the dangers that staff face daily. So, an obvious question is: "Why should we care?" Critical ethnographers should care for several reasons. First, the incident provides a glimpse into the world of prisoners and prisoner culture not often seen by outsiders. The "common-sense" meaning of the incident would seem to reaffirm the need to impose harsh punishment on predators. Second, a closer analyses displays the complexity of prisoner behaviors and their relationship to the constraints upon them. Third, we can view the incident as symptomatic of broader problems that put both staff and prisoners at risks resulting from prison policies and conditions. Fourth, it provides some insights into how prisons might be made safer and more humane for those affected by them by challenging existing correctional ideology. Finally, it raises the broader issues of how organizational power can put some people at a disadvantage, leaving them with few, and often only extreme, ways to resist. While all of these issues cannot be addressed here, an examination of the diverse meanings signified by the incident suggest a few ways to proceed.

This incident possesses different meanings, depending on our interpretive frame. In a conventional framework, this fieldnote snippet could be an example of the violent nature of prisoners or the vulnerability of prison staff to inmate attack. Such meanings arise from the presupposition that violence is wrong, prisons and those confined in them are dangerous, or prisoners have no right to resist what they perceive to be abusive staff conduct. However, we could look beyond the immediate imagery to ask what the meaning of throwing a noxious substance might mean for the prisoner, how the incident represents a response to powerlessness, and what options exist for resisting isolation. By ignoring alternate meanings, we risk reinforcing existing social images of our subjects, prisoners, as invariably vicious predators who need more constraints and harsher treatment. Uncritically promoting such images constitutes a form of symbolic violence, not so much on the subjects of our research as on the research conceptualization itself.

Critical Ethnography, Meanings and Symbolic Violence

Smith (1987) observes that most people do not participate in the making of their culture, and our ideas about it may not arise directly from everyday lived relationships:

> Rather, they are the product of the work of specialists occupying influential positions in the ideological apparatus (the educational system, communications, etc). Our culture does not arise spontaneously; it is "manufactured" (Smith 1987, p. 19).

Yet, most of us do not perceive this manufacturing process, especially that of the research process itself, as an act of violence. In subtle ways, uncritical conventional scholarship imposes, distorts, and twists our cognition, and subsequently our actions, forcefully and with often injurious consequences. Too often, conventional ethnographies commit the violence of rupturing the researcher from the people being studied in what John Van Maanen (1988, p. 46) calls "realist tales." In realist tales, the author vanishes from the finished text, making the reader dependent on the author's experiential authority with no opportunity to reflect on the researcher-researched process. The result imposes meanings of outsiders, including researchers and the audience of the research, on the messages we hear from our data.

Henri Lefebvre (1971, p. 145) refers to the consequences of the conflict between repression of alternatives and evasion of control as the "terrorism of everyday life," by which he means the hidden and abstract forms of subtle intimidation and domination on which social existence is built. Pierre Bourdieu (1991) adds that institutions of power lie behind behavior and cultural meanings that construct and limit choices, confer legitimacy, and guide our daily routine. This power is symbolic in that it relies on shared beliefs and ways of expressing those beliefs. Symbolic power is violent because it appropriates preferred meanings and represses alternatives (Bourdieu and Passeron 1977, p. 4). Critical ethnographers resist symbolic violence by displaying how it restricts alternative meanings that conceal the deeper levels of social life, create misunderstandings, and thwart action.

Symbolic violence refers to the power of symbols to impose, devastate, attack, suppress, and distort ways of seeing, thinking, and talking. Symbolic violence often can be more devastating than physical attack to the extent that it imposes and reinforces social harms caused by class, gender, and other status differences. It strengthens social barriers and reinforces culturally embedded domination games. In describing one way that dominant groups can exert their will over others, Bourdieu (1991, p. 209–210) observes that symbolic power presupposes a misrecognition of the violence exercised through it and therefore requires some unrecognized complicity by those on whom the effect is exercised. Critical ethnography helps reduce the researcher's own complicity.

Pierre Bourdieu and Jean-Claude Passeron (1977, p. 4) observe that the power to exert symbolic violence exists in the power to impose meanings as legitimate, thus concealing the underlying power relations. In prisoner culture research, images of deviance, marginalization and stigma can constitute a form of symbolic violence. One way this occurs is through oppressive discourses. Discourses are sets of symbols that we use to communicate who we are, or who we think we are, the context in which our existence is located, and how we intend ourselves to be understood as well as how we understand our topics. Discourses impose sets of formal or informal rules about what can be said, how it can be said, and who shall say what to whom (Schwalbe, et. al., 2000, p. 435).

As a cultural artifact, conventional discourses often impose metaphors that wrench prisoners out of their shared humanity and create conditions that exacerbate qualities such as animosity, distrust, and predation. In research, the images from these discourses are violent, because they arbitrarily impose symbols in ways that may grotesquely distort the "reality" of what is seen and what is signified by what is seen. The distortions reflect oppressive power relations that promote the interests of the more powerful. The conventional discourses of prison research impose images that obscure and distort the deeper structures of the culture and limit the possibility of seeing alternative meanings and connections. Mats Alvesson and Stanley Deetz (2000) cogently argue that critical social research should contribute to emancipation by encouraging us to both emotionally and cognitively rethink repressive emotional ideas and identities:

> Critical social research is thus oriented towards challenging rather than confirming that which is established, disrupting, rather than reproducing cultural traditions and conventions, opening up and showing tensions in language use rather than continuing its domination, encouraging productive dissension rather than taking surface consensus as a point of departure (Alvesson and Deetz, 2000, p. 9).

Drawing from the fieldwork example, critical ethnography provides several ways to reexamine the symbolic violence of research and to expand our understandings of possible meanings embedded in the incident.

Herbert Blumer (1969, p. 2) reminds us that humans act toward things on the basis of the meanings that the things have for them in a communicative process of interpretation and fitting the meanings together. Unfortunately, most interaction contains multiple and often conflicting meanings that do not always fit neatly into paradigmatic interpretative frames. A critical conceptualization of prison culture as a communication process helps put the feces incident above in a new perspective so that the multiple meanings contained in the text of the incident do not become obscured in the public sphere of research where formatted meanings are limited by the conceptual currency of professional discourse. Borrowing from semioticians such as Roman Jakobson (1960), we can identify some of the varieties of meaning that might be embedded in the incident.

Social scientists generally would view the feces narrative as a referential meaning, one in which the researcher codes the "facts" within their surface context and then confers meaning drawn from a pre-given paradigm that selects or excludes what is important to know. In viewing the incident simply as "pathological behavior," nuances are lost and the fabrication process by which both the prisoner's and the researchers' meanings are produced is obscured. As a result, a unidimensional view of the meaning glosses over the complexity of cultural processes that originally created the meanings.

As the incident illustrates, the meaning(s) embedded in the flinging vary, depending on one's location in the social hierarchy. For prison staff, the meaning reflects aggressive and assaultive behavior of the prisoner; for students, victimization and embarrassment; and for the researcher, data. For the prisoner, however, the incident contains emotive meanings, such as "students are parading in here as if this was a zoo, and that pisses me off!" Or, it might reflect connotative meanings that express impulse, such as "Get away from my cell, now!" There might also be a phatic meaning that conveys prisoner culture rituals, such as, "Mr. Student, the prison norms require me to advise you that you are violating my space, and lacking any other means by which to communicate this to you, I opt to hurl shit at you!" Or, it could reflect a metalinguistic meaning that provides coded information, such as, "Although a prisoner, I do have some power, I am demonstrating it to you with this gift." Finally, the meaning might connote a poetic meaning in which symbols are presented for their own sake: "Why fling shit? Well, why not?"

Focusing on these possible meanings in isolation neither reveal the possible meanings as experienced by the prisoner nor integrate them into broader understandings about how cultures are experienced, managed, or resisted. But in combination, they help display the variegated nuances of a small slice of prison life and provide insights into the dual-edge quality of control and resistance.

Critical ethnography offers an antidote to the symbolic violence of conventional research in at least three ways. First, on the empirical level, it offers an oppositional discourse that shifts the prisoner's behavior from one of pathology to one more normal. Instead of viewing the incident in a discourse that reaffirms images of violence in prison and then develops justifications of and policies for greater control of prisoners, we can examine alternative meanings of the incident within the context of institutional controls and their debilitating consequences. The incident embodies a form of "primitive rebellion" (Milovanovic and Thomas, 1989) in which what conventionally might be interpreted as an irrational act of violence now becomes seen as a more normal and even natural response to an unnatural environment.

Second, by shifting the focus of analysis to the processes of prisoners' agency, we challenge the value-laden discourse of control and pathology. The focus instead is on an assessment of the variety of meanings of "deviant" behaviors and the cultural context that produces them. The shift allows us to view on the mix of factors from both within and outside the prison that are used as building blocks in the interactional processes of adapting to and resisting the pains of confinement.

Third, a critical approach provides suggestions for social action. Not only does it reframe how we approach and critique both our data and the processes by which we interpret it, but it also suggests that while isolating and imposing extreme deprivations may appear a solution to dealing with recalcitrant prisoners, such practices are only partially effective over the short term and may compound the problem over the long term. This helps balance both the security needs of staff and the more basic existential needs of prisoners as we pursue ways to reform prisons.

Alternative interpretations do not defend or justify violence or aggression of prisoners. Instead, they reflect recognition that things are not always what they seem. To reduce prison violence, we must include not only an alternative discourse in research, but also a broader framework for acting on the conditions that produce it.

Conclusion

There are, of course, problems with critical ethnography. After all, no single study or broad research perspective is flawless. The example above and the context used to frame it reflect an ideology based in social justice, the discourse is not grounded in an interpretive system intended to generate hypotheses or develop theory (although it is fully amenable to this), and issues of elitism and the standpoint problems of outsiders looking in are for the moment deferred.

But, science—and critique is part of the scientific project—is self-correcting. One task of those engaged in ethnographic critique lies in balancing the occasionally conflicting tasks of a priori conceptual analysis, interpretive narration, empirical rigor, and theory building, taking care not to reject such tasks as "positivistic" lest we substitute one intellectual dogma with another. This means that we must continually reassess our own project with the same rigor that we assess our foci of analysis, always bearing in mind that things are never what they seem, and that social justice is not simply a goal, but a vocation to which all scholars ought strive with credible critique.

References

Alvesson, M. and Deetz, S. (2000). *Doing critical management research*. Thousand Oaks, CA: Sage Publications, Inc.

Blumer, H. (1969). *Symbolic interactionism*. Englewood Cliffs, NJ: Prentice-Hall.

Bourdieu, P. (1991). *Language and symbolic power*. Cambridge, MA: Harvard University Press.

Bourdieu, P., and Passeron, J. C. (1977). *Reproduction in education, society and culture*. Beverly Hills, CA: Sage Publications, Inc.

Crotty, M. (1998). *The foundations of social research: Meaning and perspective in the research process*. Thousand Oaks, CA: Sage Publications, Inc.

Dewey, J. (1933). *How we think: A restatement of the relation of reflective thinking to the educative process*. Lexington, MA: DC Heath and Company.

Jakobson, R. (1960). Closing statement: Linguistics and poetics. In Thomas A. Sebeok (Ed.), *Style in Language* (pp. 350–377) Boston: Technology Press of MIT.

Lefebvre, H. (1971). *Everyday life in the modern world*. New York: Harper Torchbooks.

Milovanovic, D., and Thomas, J. (1989). Overcoming the absurd: Prisoner litigation as primitive rebellion. *Social Problems, 36* (February): 48–60.

Quant, R. (1967). *Critique: Its nature and function*. Pittsburgh: Duquesne University Press.

Schwalbe, M., Godwin, S., Holden, D., Schrock, D., Thompson, S., and Wolkomir, M. (2000). Generic processes in the reproduction of inequality: An interactionist analysis. *Social Forces, 79* (2): 419–452.

Smith, D. E. (1987). *The everyday world as problematic: A feminist sociology*. Boston: Northeast University Press.

Thomas, J. (1992). *Doing critical ethnography*. Newbury Park, CA: Sage Publications, Inc.

Thomas, J. and O'Maolchatha, A. (1988). Reassessing the critical metaphor: An optimistic revisionist view. *Justice Quarterly, 2* (June): 143–172.

Van Maanen, J. (1988). *Tales from the field*. Chicago: University of Chicago Press.

CHAPTER 4

What is Interpretive Ethnography?

An Eclectic's Tale

H. L. GOODALL JR.

The question that forms the title of this essay has been posed to me countless times over the years, usually by well-intentioned persons who expect to receive a singular, simple, and straightforward reply. It is a question that has never seriously been asked of me by other interpretive ethnographers, unless it was raised in a tone of complicit comic irony and performed as an intellectual exercise, as in the philosopher's query: *What is reality?*

Probably you are thinking: Why should an interpretive ethnographer *have* to ask it? After all, those of us who deploy this curious adjective and noun to describe what we "do" shouldn't have to ask each other what it means, right? But that is, I'm afraid, simply untrue. In fact, whenever we perform this adjective and noun professionally, we are actively engaged in asking not only *what* it means, but also *how* it is meaningful. We prefer to answer the question through a detailed examination of our work, and in a personal dialogue with readers/audiences about the processes that produced that work, rather than resort to a singular, nailed-down, debate-oriented argument by definition.

That is *not*, however, the answer I give to most people. I should say to most non-interpretive, non-ethnographic people. I tell them that interpretive ethnography is a way of studying and speaking about culture.

And await their next question.

If the next question is "how do you *do* that?" I have an interesting choice to make. In a rhetorical sense, it is clearly a matter of adapting my residual message (what does "it" come down to?) to my listener. In a literary sense, it is all about issues of representation—am I (to borrow Stuart Hall's terminology) mirroring a reality that actually exists or replacing it with a version that is aligned with my political and social goals? And, in an ethical sense, told forthrightly, my story forces me to confront my personal and professional shadows, which may or may not be appropriate for my listener or the social setting in which the question is raised. Being interpretive by choice and an ethnographer by calling, the truth is *never* simple and the outcome of expressing it is never easy.

So I have learned how to construct what I call a "layered account." A layered account is a many-storied story that continues to unfold, or not, depending on the responses I receive while telling it. For example:

> I begin my explanation with the statement that I usually spend a year or so living among those whom I am studying and writing about. While there—in situ, I might say, with the appropriate Latinate pronunciation delivered for learned effect—I take copious fieldnotes, I conduct in-depth interviews, I use all of my training to produce detailed observations of the local scene, climate, social and political relationships, kinship systems, and lifeways, and *I analyze culture by interpreting everyday routines, rituals, concerns, and conversations through my own lived experiences.*

At this point I know I have said enough if my listener nods appreciatively. Among authority figures—Deans, influential alums, and so forth—I have learned that this layer of my answer usually suffices, because it sounds rigorous and contains the magic word "conversations." Because I am in the communication field, saying that I analyze cultures by interpreting conversations—if my eclectic methods for doing so remain admittedly ambiguous—at least seems legit. The rest of what I have just said—academic-sounding talk about routines, rituals, and lived experiences—sounds appropriately difficult and perhaps even mysterious, which, in many ways, it is. Without having to risk anything conversationally themselves, and by being able to nod appreciatively and perhaps even utter the culturally sanctioned if equally ambiguous sentiment, "that's interesting," my listeners may not be more educated by my answer but they are usually satisfied.

But not always. If I get the impression that my listener wants more information, I then take a deep breath and continue to unravel the other narrative layers. "I make elaborate time charts and thematic graphs, more or less like William Faulkner did, of all the relationships and histories and turning point stories of the people involved. These days, whenever possible, I collect (and analyze) artifacts, take photographs (and deconstruct them), and make personal narrative videos to show interactive interviews and further document my time there." Then I pause. "Of course, the whole thing would be a sham if I didn't implicate myself in the framing and telling of the story and make a strong effort to give *something* back. They are, after all, sharing their lives with me. And I am the one interpreting the meanings of it."

For most people who ask me what interpretive ethnography is, this deeper layer, once told, tends to end the conversation. I don't know why. To the best of my knowledge, I've given some details about my work—not too many to appear boorish or egoist—and I've made a point of demonstrating my social conscience in a way that is neither threatening nor offensive. The most common response I receive is a quiet "Wow."

Maybe it's the way I say it.

What I have done is tell a version of the truth in the form of a story. The story *does* represent the truth—or I should say, regardless of how many layers unfold, they only ever reveal partial truths of my experiences. My account accomplishes this narrative objective by appropriating part of a common tale told for nearly a century by anthropologists and sociologists about fieldwork. John Van Maanen (1988) calls this genre of reporting "tales of the fieldwork" and teaches us that these stories belong to one of three literary subgenres: realist tales, confessional tales, or surrealist tales.

In the layered story I tell listeners about interpretive ethnography, I usually stop short of the Van Maanen-derived categories. That is too much explanation—one layer too far—for most people, unless they happen to share an interest in the history of ethnography. This abbreviated way of telling the story also usually gets me out of the conversation gracefully, but notice, please, that I haven't yet really answered the question, nor have I given a complete account of what *interpretive* ethnographers "do." For instance, I haven't gotten to the part about what you do when you "interpret" fieldnotes (the "studying" part of my initial response) nor said anything at all about the writing process (the "speaking" part of my response).

I'm not being evasive. Nor am I ashamed to talk about what I really do.

It's just that I've learned that explaining interpretive ethnography to people who don't practice it is like playing scholarly *Monopoly*. You can't go directly to "interpretive Boardwalk" without first accumulating and managing fundamental—and *disciplined*—narrative assets. It's the same balancing act in my classes. Students who enroll in my ethnography seminars are initially surprised to find a syllabus that devotes a good portion of the class to reading ethnographic "classics" and to learning the basics of fieldwork—observing, interviewing, note taking, and story writing. They maybe expect that guy with the rep I supposedly have for being "edgy" would begin with readings from the wilder prose of certain ethnographic rebels—say the surrealists—and move from there toward some radical outer limits of magical storytelling, which, if it exists, I guess we could call "Beyond Wow," or something.

But I don't play the game that way.

I just don't think it's a good idea.

Why not? Because interpretive ethnography is a *layered response to*, as well as a *critical extending of*, how we think about and do the work of being scholars.

Scholars are people licensed to find uncommon meanings in and about the
world and to act on them. I say "uncommon" not to privilege scholarly pro-
nouncements so much as to admit that we are granted cultural credentials that
attest to our having acquired knowledge, skills, and sensitivities—what Kenneth
Burke (1989) calls "equipment to think with" that are not readily available to
ordinary citizens. I say, "act on them," because scholars are also given the sacred
duty—and singular *moral* honor—of professing our uncommon meanings in and
to this world.

Viewed this way—which interpretivists often call "a framing device"—the
interpretive movement in the social sciences and in the humanities represents a
fundamental shift of perspective on *how* we do that. This, too, is a many-storied
story, itself containing many layers. For example, from a postmodern perspective,
one critical layer on the road to interpretive ethnography contains stories about
changes in the ways scholars are framed and the "work" that scholarship does in
the world. This layer represents a fundamental—paradigmatic—challenge to historically revered (usually scientific, mostly modernist) ways of knowing, being,
and doing (see Denzin, 1996, for an extensive discussion). From a Burkeian
dramatistic perspective, this challenge to the dominant paradigm is akin to force
of "the negative," which, for Burke, is captured in the powerful and defining
character of the "thou shalt nots" of the Ten Commandments.

For most of us eclectics who call ourselves "interpretivists," this evolving
radical shift in perspective means that we—in our lives and in our work—were
and are giving a moral response to modernist and scientific impulses. In this way,
interpretive ethnography *is* a way of studying and speaking in the world. Studying and speaking this way carries with it new scholarly identities and purposes.
The affirmation of our identity and purpose may be summed up—following
Burke, as I am wont to do—as three interpretive ethnography "thou shall nots":

1. Interpretive ethnographers shall not assume an objective, distanced,
   and politically removed relationship to those whom we study and
   write about. This interpretive commandment encourages us to make
   our work (including our relationships with those whom we study)
   both *intimate* and *vulnerable.*

2. Interpretive ethnographers shall not ignore the enormous influence
   of our personal history, gender, race, ethnicity, age, religion/spiritual
   beliefs, sexual orientation, and relative perceived beauty have on our
   lives, neither on the way we see and act in the world nor on the way
   others see and act toward us. This interpretive commandment
   encourages us to make our work *personal, interactive,* and *self-
   reflexive.*

3. Interpretive ethnographers shall not write in the omniscient third
   person, be limited by the format and style of a traditional scholarly

essay, nor should our prose and performances lack the qualities associated with good literature and/or art. This interpretive commandment encourages us to make our work more *evocative, narratively interesting, occasionally multi-voiced*, and intrinsically *dialogic*. It also establishes a new literary and professional standard for evaluation and critique of ethnographic writing and performance.

Interpretive ethnographers also try to extend the work of scholarship in the world by seeing ourselves as engaged citizens and framing our work as a form of meaningful social action. We strive to conduct ourselves—in our fieldwork, in our teaching, in our living, and in our writing and performing—with a sense of committed civic engagement. We are not simply "learning from" cultures, we are ethically responsible for giving something of value back to them. Viewed this way, "teachable moments" extend far beyond the classroom because our classroom is nothing less than the world.

If what I have just written strikes you as a bit high-minded, it is intended to be. The life of a scholar—traditional or interpretive—is a sacred calling and in answering it we have an enormous public responsibility. However, if what I have written also strikes you as a license for doctrinal preaching or ideological narrowness, then I must add a fourth interpretive commandment: *Thou shall not abuse scholarly privilege by using it as an ideological weapon.* Our work as scholars is inherently to promote diversity, democracy, dialogue, and the freedom of speech. To do that, we must continue to be *profoundly* open to differences of opinion and experiments in scholarly methods and forms of expression.

I hope you can see that being an interpretive ethnographer is more of an *attitude about studying and speaking* brought into the world than it is a strict methodology (see Goodall, 2000). It is also more about choices among ways of living a scholarly *lifestyle*, and using scholarly *energies* and *passions*, than it is a canonical allegiance to a set of sacred texts or practices.

This admission does *not* mean interpretive ethnography is undisciplined. Or irresponsible. Or that it is the by-product of mere circumstance and serendipity. Or that it is an excuse for being intellectually sloppy. Or that it serves as the last academic refuge of the procedurally weak.

It does mean that interpretive ethnography can't be learned from mastering a textbook or following a set of canned instructions. Much of what you learn to interpret—as well as how you choose to do the interpreting—depends on the kind of person you are, the life experiences you've had (including what you've read and discussed), as well as your ability and comfort level "hanging out" with people who are different from you. It also depends on what skills you have to build trust, get people to talk to you, and to use language. It is ultimately about *voice*—your own personal/scholarly voice, unique to you. Unlike the statistical tests that are used to validate quantitative studies, and which are supposed to come out the same regardless of who applies the test (which, I personally believe, is a bit of closeted fiction still adhered to by only the most unreflective social scientists), interpretive ethnographies are supposed to come out differently each time you do them because of who you are, how you see the world, and what language and communication skills you bring to the job.

— — — —

An attitude about speaking; a lifestyle choice; energy; passion. Fine words, these. Cool, even. But apart from acquiring an attitude, affecting a life-style, and pursuing the everyday interpretive life with passion and energy, how do we "do" interpretive ethnography?

When the adjective "interpretive" modifies the noun "ethnography" you get pulled into different ways of reading clues to a culture, and while you are doing that (and however you are doing that), some interesting personal questions connect you—your life, your goals, your purpose—to what begins to look and feel like a pattern. The clues about a meaningful pattern acts as an inducement to discover, and to create, connections among the complex intersections of selves, others, and cultural contexts. You will find that the boundaries among these deceptively ordinary terms "leak," are "permeable," "blur," and "merge." For this reason—and unlike more traditional social sciences—the clue you read about the pattern does not emerge as a clearly defined "problem" to be "solved," but rather as a *mystery* to be personally and culturally engaged (Goodall, 1989, 1991, 1996)

How do you "engage a mystery?"

This is where the importance of *your personal connection to the pattern* comes into play. This personal stake in understanding is a *resource* useful in evoking and creating reasons to, and motives for, interpreting meanings about others and contexts, as well as about yourself being meaningful there. The questions raised are about the hows and whys of persons and things, meanings and purposes, talk and action, silence and shadows, me and you, means and ends. As these questions are articulated and acted upon in fieldwork and especially through writing fieldnotes, they attain life as narrative offspring of the personal connection to a culture, they form storylines that organize and contribute meanings to the emerging tale of the fieldwork.

Our interpretive ethnographic work is *always* about the joining together of two otherwise disparate storylines—the story of the self who has the stake, asks the questions, and does the interpreting; and the stories of others who help us find or create meanings. In this way, interpretive ethnography springs from a personal urgency that is intimately connected to larger scholarly questions of meaning, purpose, understanding, and action.

The important phrase in the previous sentence is "intimately connected." To do interpretive ethnography is to connect your story to something larger than yourself. Because you are a scholar, that "something larger" is always partially drawn from our literature, our intellectual interests, our place in the academy and world. It is also drawn from whatever you understand to be your purpose, and your work, here on this blue planet. Your interpretive job is to find your personal connection to it and to story it to the world. This is our job, our professional license, our scholarly and civic responsibility.

— — — —

Allow me another analogy, this time between interpretive ethnography (as a way of speaking) and the development of interpersonal communication (as a way of relating). Interpretive ethnographic prose and performances construct relationships—close relationships—with our respective audiences. Relationships differ. They differ in their goals as well as in their communicative methods for attaining them. Relationships differ in modes of understanding, styles of interacting, and in the available artistry to satisfy deeply felt needs and desires. Some intimate relationships require a high level of self-disclosure whereas other, less intimate relationships, do not require as much disclosure—if any—at all. There is no one "right way" to communicate, or to disclose, that governs all relationships.

Within the interpretive ethnographic crowd there are those who provide rich autobiographical details—self-disclosures—to create a sense of intimate dialogue with readers/audiences, as well as to provide a personal context for interpreting meaning. However, among other interpretivists (and most traditionalists), the idea of including such material is practically, professionally, and politically problematic. For some scholars, these stories of the self occupy precious journal and monograph space that ought to be granted to others, particularly to those others who may have no public voice—oppressed and marginalized peoples. For still other scholars, it is simply inappropriate to their own scholarly or interpretive goals. My point is that interpretive authors develop *diverse ways of speaking* to readers, audiences, and the world. Just as there are no "ideal models" of personal relationships, there is no "one best way" to write or to perform interpretive ethnography.

Today, interpretive ethnography displays the most variety of literary forms—styles of speaking—currently available in the whole of the scholarly literature.

In addition to the categories put forth by John Van Maanen, we now have published interpretive ethnographies done in the genres of poetry, fiction, multimedia production, conversation, travelogue, memoir, dramatic performance, virtual report, and autobiography, as well as various creative works that blur even these diverse genres (for a representative sampling, see Bochner and Ellis, 1996, 2002).

What these genre experiments suggest is that the proper interpretive form for a given piece of work in the twenty-first century should emerge from its descriptive fieldwork, interpretive processes, and emotional content rather than from the limiting format of a nineteenth century traditional scholarly essay. What they also suggest is that ours is a creative activity that values artistic expression and careful attention to the craft of writing, speaking, and performing. Here again, interpretive ethnographers welcome and celebrate *artistic* diversity. Although we may not always agree with each other's practices, we are open to possibilities for expanding the boundaries of what we do and how we do it.

I hope you can now understand why the question that titled and framed this essay — What Is Interpretive Ethnography? — must remain without a singular, simple, or straightforward reply. Interpretive ethnography must continue to be defined by the worth of our individual, eclectic interpretive efforts, and the value of our diverse ethnographic products, rather than by strict adherence to a common definitional stance.

It's not the easy answer, but it is the right one. No one takes the interpretive turn because it is the "easy thing to do" in the academy. It's always easier to become mainstream, even if the work you do there is just as demanding. It's always easier to be able to clearly define who you are and what you do to people who quickly recognize what you are talking about. In most cases, it is easier *not* to have to implicate yourself, or your life history, in your writing, speaking, and performing.

So, no, people do not become interpretive ethnographers because it is an easy thing to do. In fact, among the "I became an ethnographer because . . ." storylines there are two that are quite common; neither one of them includes the idea that it is an easy thing to do. One account is that the choice to become an interpretive ethnographer is a false one — you don't so much "choose" interpretive ethnography as it chooses *you*. You may have been minding your own business when suddenly something happened — a reading, a lecture, a discussion, a moment at a conference, or a moment alone — and the impulse to become this kind of person — however you define it — became irresistible. You just *knew* this was who you were. From that point on you had to forget a lot of things that you once had thought important to learn. You had to learn a lot of new things that before probably seemed completely out of the question. But the question changed, and you changed. It wasn't easy, but it wasn't exactly a choice, either.

The other common tale has to do with a feeling of intellectual kinship and communion with the people who practice this form of speaking, this way of living the scholarly life. Interpretive ethnographers, as a breed of academic person — diverse and eclectic as we are — seem to be defined by a certain ineffable spirit, ways of being in the world and in the academy. I also believe this is true (but differently) to the experiences of scholars who do not choose to become interpretive ethnographers, which probably says a good thing about what it means to become "an academic" in general. Somehow, we recognize each other as belonging to the same experiential life form. We are joined together by the same impulses that divide us from others, and from other groups of academics. And we feel drawn to, or pulled in by, a clue to our identity and purpose that is somehow part and parcel of this interpretive practice.

Ours is an *interpretive community* of scholars. As you would expect to find in any community worthy of the label, we must continue to be characterized by ongoing dialogue, discussion, debate, and argument about what we do and how we do it, and even what we are doing it for. We may not ask each other what interpretive ethnography "is," but we will continue to talk about the studies we're involved in, discuss our own and other's work, and all that remains to be explored, uncovered, thought about, acted upon. When someone outside our area asks us that question, perhaps we will offer the kind of answer I've given in this story: it's a way of studying and speaking about culture.

Or perhaps not.

Either way, we will remain enlivened and unified in spirit through our quest to find meaningful the world, our place in it, and its splendid eclectic diversity.

References

Bochner, A., and Ellis, C. (eds.). (1996). *Composing ethnography.* Walnut Creek, CA: Alta Mira Press.

Burke, K. (1989). *Symbols and society.* Chicago: University of Chicago Press.

Bochner, A. P., and Ellis, C. (Eds.). (2002). *Ethnographically speaking: Autoethnography, literature, and aesthetics.* Walnut Creek, CA: Alta Mira Press.

Denzin, N. K. (1996). *Interpretive ethnography.* Walnut Creek, CA: Alta Mira Press.

Ellis, C., and Bochner, A. (Eds.). (1996). *Composing ethnography.* Walnut Creek, CA: Alta Mira Press.

Goodall, H. L. (1989). *Casing a promised land: The autobiography of an organizational detective as cultural ethnographer.* Carbondale, IL: Southern Illinois University Press.

———. (1991). *Living in the rock n roll mystery: Reading context, self, and others as clues.* Carbondale, IL: Southern Illinois University Press.

———. (1996). *Divine signs: Connecting spirit to community.* Carbondale, IL: Southern Illinois University Press.

———. (2000). *Writing the New Ethnography.* Lanham, MD: Alta Mira Press.

Van Maanen, J. (1988). *Tales from the Field.* Chicago: University of Chicago Press.

CHAPTER 5

Postmodernism, Ethnography, and Communication Studies

Comments and a Case

BRYAN C. TAYLOR

A perspective that acknowledges the imminence of death and the reality of mortality . . . positions me . . . in a particular way when . . . attempting to make sense of human experience. . . . It engenders a certain kind of mindfulness. It makes doing and writing and performing ethnography a particular path for waking up and preparing for death.

— Crawford, "Personal Ethnography"

Introduction

What is This Thing Called Postmodernism?

In the field of communication, ethnographers draw upon a number of theoretical traditions to ground their work. These range from "interpretive" theories of phenomenology, ethnomethodology, and symbolic interaction, to "critical" theories such as feminism and neo-Marxism (Lindlof and Taylor, 2002). This eclecticism creates a vibrant—but also potentially confusing—context for producing ethnography. Theoretical traditions typically involve complex narratives about human experience and social action. Accounts of these traditions sometimes gloss their internal diversity (e.g., disagreements over the implications of key claims for research methods) to emphasize their apparent distinctiveness. As a result, ethnographers attempting to grasp a tradition for the first time can be challenged by its seeming contradictions and messy entailments. Ideally, after they invest significant time and effort, this confusion resolves into sophisticated appreciation of a theory's potential (e.g., of the types of research questions that it alternately permits and prohibits).

While it is never easy, this process of "mastering" theory is especially challenging in the case of postmodernism. In this chapter, I attempt to explain why this is, address the implications of this condition for doing communication ethnography, and sketch a brief case that illustrates these claims. By the end of the chapter, you will hopefully be equipped to more reflectively engage postmodernism as a potential resource for your work.

We can begin by noting that, as a form of "critical" theory, postmodernism is generally concerned with studying the relationships between power, knowledge and discourse that are produced in the contexts of historical and cultural struggle between social groups. Beyond this summary, however, the definitional terrain quickly gets rough. This occurs for several reasons. One is that postmodernism is frequently invoked as an umbrella term to cover several different traditions that challenge various orthodoxies in social theory and research methods. These traditions include (but are not limited to) feminism, neo-Marxism, post-structuralism, and post-colonialism. Famous theorists associated with these traditions include Barthes, Baudrillard, Bhaba, Cixous, Deleuze, Derrida, Foucault, Jameson, Kristeva, Lacan, Lyotard, and Spivak. The problem here is that invocations of their work are often unreflective and inconsistent. Critics of postmodernism, for example, often wield (but do not rigorously define) the term to defend cherished traditions that they believe "it" threatens. Here, the term becomes a screen for the projection of anxiety. In other cases, speakers fail to explain the logic by which they have grouped diverse theories under the term. In this process, they blur important distinctions within and between those theories (e.g., by failing to distinguish their simultaneous affiliation with the *modernist* tradition of critical theory; Alvesson and Deetz, 1996).

Finally, postmodernism has developed a durable ambiguity because of the *enormous* work that it is called upon to perform by various speakers. That work involves adequately conceptualizing and engaging the daunting phenomena of *post-modernity*. This term is used to designate a number of dramatic, interrelated developments in twentieth-century political, economic, and social life that continue to resonate in the new millennium (Cooper and Burrell, 1988; Foster, 1983; Mumby, 1997; Strinati, 1995). These developments include:

- The disintegration of colonial systems historically ruled by imperial nation-states, and the subsequent dispersal of people, information, and products at accelerated rates across geopolitical boundaries (e.g., through immigration);
- The decline of industrial capitalism, and the rise of an information-age economy premised on the consolidation of "flexible" corporate control over markets (e.g., through the exploitation high-speed

information technologies), and the commodification of symbols and knowledge (e.g., as brands and intellectual property);

- The rise of global media systems whose scope and operations collapse barriers of space and time (e.g., to produce real-time coverage of international events). The commercial programming produced by these systems is pervasive and relentless. It saturates the contemporary life world and erodes historical consciousness. It implodes distinctions that have traditionally guided cultural members in navigating social reality, such as those between "high art" and "popular culture," "citizen" and "consumer," "reality" and "simulation," and "event" and "spectacle";

- A continuous dismantling and reassembly of artistic media, genres, and styles. This process produces texts characterized by *irony* (subversive mockery), *reflexivity* (self-consciousness), *bricolage* (creative combination of fragments), *intertextuality* (reference to other texts through quotation, homage and parody), *pastiche* (recycling of traditional forms to make the new-but-still-familiar) and *hyper-reality* (signifiers without signifieds). Here, surface, fluidity, and play constitute the dominant aesthetic. The artistic values of authorship, referentiality, depth, and tradition are all called into question;

- A general loss of ontological faith in "foundational" and "grand" narratives associated with modernity (e.g., of rationality and progress). This development is based on increasing recognition of the linguistic contingency of institutional authority (e.g., of religion, science, and politics). It renounces claims based on objectivity and universal warrants in favor of a skeptical "politics of the local." In this politics, discourses are viewed as perpetually contending for situational—but not enduring—legitimacy and authority. "Knowledge, instead of being an accurate representation of an external and objective order, is seen as the result of experiencing the world in terms of a particular cultural code or model. Thus, all knowledge is the result of a structuring discourse . . ." (Harms and Dickens, 1996, p. 212). This condition facilitates critical reflection on what "master narratives"—as intersections of power, knowledge and discourse—have wrought (e.g., reductionism). It restores to public consciousness marginalized cultural voices that relativize and challenge dominant narratives. In these performances, audiences learn alternative "tactics" for transforming relationships that are historically based on oppressive institutions such as racism and sexism. "The task," writes Judith Butler (1995, p. 39), "is to interrogate what the theoretical move that establishes foundations *authorizes*, and what precisely it excludes or forecloses" [emphasis in original].

- The "de-centering" of traditional forms of identity premised on totality, coherence, uniqueness, stability and essence (e.g., "the individual") in favor of those premised on partiality, plurality, fragmentation, paradox, and simultaneity (e.g., "the cyborg"). In this "death of the subject," identity is viewed not as the preexisting *referent* or *origin* of communication; it is instead the *effect* of discourses that arbitrarily construct and enforce preferred narratives of the self (including the discourses of "theory"; Lannamann, 1991). These discourses "suture" reflective human consciousness by providing temporarily stable linguistic contexts for meaningful orientation to Self, Other and World. Frequently, however, this suturing is a prerequisite for institutional goals of objectification, prediction and control (e.g., through diagnosis). The critical task becomes understanding—and ethically reflecting on—how discourses construct illusory (and precarious) experiences of coherence.

Implications of Postmodernism for Communication Ethnography

September 12: The evening is warm, stifling. Our fear is rising inside of us like bread dough. On-screen, a hand-held video camera tilts up the side of mortally wounded Tower One. Suddenly, piercing the billowing smoke, bodies plummet into—and then out of—the frame. They fall like rain, like carelessly tossed bags of trash. Each body carves the arc of a life *in extremis*. Months later, it feels like these bodies fell into me, and have been lodged there ever since.

While the above list is not exhaustive, it begins to establish some core themes of postmodern critical theory. That theory may be understood as a *response to* these conditions, and a *resource for* intervening in their ongoing production. What are the implications of postmodern theory for the conduct of communication ethnography? Optimistically, Manning (1995, p. 246) claims "postmodernism provides an opportunity for reinvigorating ethnographic research." But this opportunity is ambiguous at best. We can identify at least three challenges that communication ethnographers face as they orient to the resources of postmodernism.

The first involves adequately engaging a dense and agitated cultural *zeitgeist* characterized by crisis, schizophrenia, and nostalgia. These jagged forms of feeling emerge from the rapid transformation of social structures that make meaning itself a precarious accomplishment. Postmodern ethnographers vacillate between ecstasy and despair before a world of swirling signs: on the one hand, the rate and intensity of social action increase, and communication itself moves front and center as a social problem. At the same time, disorientation and emptiness haunt the ethnographic enterprise: more (of signs) is not necessarily better, or even enough. Rapid mutation can be either liberating or terrifying, depending on who is controlling the process, and how. Diverse voices may relativize authority and emancipate the oppressed; they are just as likely, however, to raise vexing problems of "undecidability" around equally compelling yet incompatible narratives (e.g., those associated with alien abduction, and "recovered memories" of sexual abuse). In this stormy epistemological weather, field-based research engaging the actual use and abuse of texts *in context* becomes even more important (Trujillo, 1993).

A second challenge involves designating the fields and sites of ethnographic research. This issue arises because elements of postmodernity have transformed traditional assumptions about the nature of fieldwork (Green, 1999). Specifically, the forces of globalization have undermined the isolation, stability, and uniqueness of "local" cultures that motivated generations of anthropologists to study and compare them. This development has forced researchers to acknowledge that research fields are increasingly multisited, partial, dispersed, and mediated. As opposed to singular, self-contained "locations," they are "spaces of flow" organized around "connections" between people, practices, events, and objects (Hine, 2000, p. 61). The surreal milieu of international airports is a case in point (Iyer, 1995). One implication of this development is that traditional criteria for valid ethnographies—such as physical "travel" to remote sites, and extended, immediate interaction with their members—are no longer universal or appropriate (Lyman and Wakeford, 1999). Instead, ethnographers adopt alternate strategies: they revisit the "foreign" middle-class life world of mass liberal societies produced by late capitalism (Marcus and Fischer, 1986); they move on-line (Jones, 1999); they punctuate interconnected sites to create a conceptually coherent scene of study; and they critically read media texts that saturate a scene as resources for sensemaking and social action among its inhabitants.

A third challenge posed by postmodern critique involves a general *crisis of representation* in the human sciences (Clifford and Marcus, 1986). This crisis stems from theoretical innovations that emphasize the centrality of discourse in shaping human understanding. A major theoretical influence here is that of *poststructuralism*, which rejects traditional claims that individuals "author" discourse as expressions of their unique essence, and that the material elements of spoken and written language ("signifiers") have stable referents in objective reality ("signifieds") (Chang, 1996; Hawes, 1998). Alternately, post-structuralism focuses on the way in which signs depend for their meaning on arbitrary, unstable (and often suppressed) relationships *with other signs* (e.g., racial identities such as "white" that necessarily invoke other racial signifiers as a basis for contrast). In this view, culture is a giant "rhizomatic" (root-like) field of interrelated sign systems; the meaning of any particular sign is stabilized only through ideological processes that constrain its "polysemic" potential for competing or subversive meanings (Hall, 1985). One implication of this argument for ethnographers is that their work products (e.g., field notes, monographs) may no longer be considered objective depictions of a stable Other. Instead, they are critically scrutinized for their ideological productivity (West, 1993).

Many qualitative researchers have chosen, subsequently, to abandon traditional forms of narration (e.g., "realism") to explore alternate writing formats that encourage reflection about the "politics and poetics" of their work (Ellis and Bochner, 2000; Richardson, 2000). In these formats, writers emphasize the embodied, collaborative, dialogic, and improvisational aspects of ethnography (Conquergood, 1991; Presnell, 1994; Van Maanen, 1995). They craft language that is impressionistic, slippery, evocative, and sensuous. They resist the temptations of neutrality, invulnerability, and abstraction (Tyler, 1987). Through the juxtaposition of fragments, they continually rupture their own authority, deferring closure and signaling the simultaneity of multiple, interconnected discourses.

> September 17: I am talking on the phone with a coauthor. Another male. Another version of coping. While I have (temporarily) abandoned work, he has embraced it. Each choice provides a different form of solace. Of shelter. We are discussing a manuscript whose pages we must cut. We are reviewing our options. "Remind me," he asks. "How is post-colonialism relevant for qualitative research?"

These strategies invite readers to collaborate in resolving "undecidable" issues of human experience. A recent example involves Bowman's (2000) poignant, multivocal, multimedia exploration of cultural myths surrounding the Great Depression-era "outlaw" John Dillinger, and their implications for both Midwestern culture and postmodern theories of performance. Like outlaws, Bowman concludes, postmodern ethnographers are "tricksters" devoted to confounding cultural order. They are also, however, vulnerable as targets of vengeful discipline (e.g., Shields, 2000).

A Case for Consideration: Notes on September 11th

The events surrounding September 11 create a "dangerous opportunity" for communication ethnographers wishing to engage postmodernism. Although these events are staggering, they compel our attention and challenge us to speak. Their aftermath ripples across mundane and extraordinary contexts: airliner cockpits, cell-phone conversations, presidential public address, grocery-store checkout lines, Afghanistan's mountain caves, and skyscraper offices with a view. In various ways, contemporary communication is haunted by these events, and ethnographers are poised to document how their meanings are constructed and used in highly consequential practices. In this process, however, ethnographers step into a volatile field of discourse in which cherished myths of personal safety and national identity have been—perhaps irrevocably—traumatized. It seems urgent that we say something, but what? How? And to whom? Since these events are still unfolding, and space does not permit full elaboration, I instead conclude by providing a collage of textual fragments that indicates how such ethnographies might develop. This collage will be successful if it evokes recognition of potential sites for postmodern ethnography of September 11th, and provokes discussion of how such work might be conducted.

> Morning in Manhattan. Excellent and fair. A mother brushes her daughter's hair. Millions to be made today, pal. The city's Greek chorus reads the op-ed page. A man looks at his stomach, sees a pile of ruin. I'm losing money here. Get to the office early. This could be the day. This is not the day. FedEx it. I'll fax it to you. Smoke condition at Forty-ninth Street. Woody Allen is washed up. They raised the rent on me. I'll put you through. Ewing is getting old, man. Please go see a doctor, Harry. Don't forget your lunch box. . . . A woman sits on the edge of the bed, remembering that yesterday's AIDS test was positive. We got serious racial problems in this city. It's not about the money. A beautiful apartment in this price range. I'm going to get liposuction.
>   —Harrison, 1996, *Manhattan Nocturne*

> The demigod of a U.S. military subject which euphorically enacted [in the Persian Gulf War] the fantasy that it can achieve its aims with ease fails to understand that its actions have produced effects that will far exceed its phantasmatic purview. . . . The[se] effects . . . have already inaugurated violence in places and in ways that it not only could not foresee but will be unable ultimately to contain . . .
>   .   —Butler, 1995, "Contingent Foundations"

> For the next fifty years, people who were not in the area when the attacks occurred will claim to have been there. In time, some of them will believe it. Others will claim to have lost friends or relatives, although they did not. This is . . . the counter-narrative, a shadow history of false memories and imagined loss.
>   —DeLillo, 2001, "In the Ruins of the Future

I believe the best the academician can do is to thickly describe, robustly interrogate, and directly challenge the authorized truths and official

actions of all parties who are positing a world view of absolute differences in need of final solutions.
                          —Der Derian, 2001, "Before, After, and In Between"

One can only hope that . . . as the ramifications sink in, as it becomes
clear how close the attack came to undermining the political, military
and financial authority of the United States, the . . . relativism of [post-
modernism] and the obsessive focus of [postcolonialism] will be
widely seen as ethically perverse. Rigidly applied, they require a form
of guilty passivity in the face of ruthless and unyielding opposition.
                                        —Rothstein, 2001, "Connections"

The story of Flight 93 is swiftly passing into the realm of American
mythology, a tale we will tell to our children and grandchildren just as
previous generations told tales of heroism during other wars. . . . Each
[speaker will] tr[y] in his or her own way to tell a story that can never
be known, but that should always be told, again and again and again.
                               —Burrough, 2001, *Manifest Courage*

Postmodernism maintains only that there can be no independent standard for determining which of many rival interpretations of an event is
the true one. The only thing postmodern thought argues against is the
hope of justifying our response to the attacks in universal terms that
would be persuasive to everyone . . . because our adversaries lay claim
to the same language.
                          —Fish, 2001, "Condemnation Without Absolutes"

The atrocities of September 11 have planted a question mark over the
very idea of modernity. Is it really the case that all societies are bound,
sooner or later, to converge on the same values and views of the world?
                          —Gray, 2001, "Where There Is No Common Power"

I often had a strange feeling in Afghanistan, a sort of temporal vertigo.
. . . History presents itself [there] in a disorderly montage, like one of
those heuristic displays in natural-history museums . . . rearranged at
random: pre-cold war, post-cold war, cold war, Buddhist antiquities,
Kalashnikovs. The timelessness of this jumbled history made me feel
like an old museum curator: time-transcendent, fascinated, and lonely.
                                        —Sifton, 2001, "Temporal Vertigo"

There is much I don't know about Osama bin Laden, but there is
something he doesn't know about me, and you, and the rest of us. He

doesn't know what a disparate culture we live in, how constantly at odds with itself it is. One paradox of our country is that the society that looks like such a monolith from without looks, from within, so fragmented.
—Todd, 2001, "The Way We Live Now"

In a day when hype and hyperbole have become a staple of cable news, when the word "reality" has become associated with stage-managed fame fests . . . words felt devalued and inadequate to capture the disasters. . . . Inevitably, many witnesses and television commentators . . . turned to film analogies to describe what they had seen.
—Kakutani, 2001, "Critic's Notebook"

In its desertion of every basis for comparison, the event asserts its singularity. There is something empty in the sky. The writer tries to give memory, tenderness and meaning to all that howling space.
—DeLillo, 2001, "In the Ruins of the Future"

References

Alvesson, M., and Deetz, S. (1996). Critical theory and postmodernism: Approaches to organizational studies. In S. R. Clegg, C. Hardy, and W. R. Nord (Eds.), *Handbook of organization studies* (pp. 191–216). Thousand Oaks, CA: Sage Publications, Inc.

Bowman, M. (2000). Killing Dillinger: A mystory. *Text and Performance Quarterly, 20:* 342–374.

Burrough, B. (2001, December). Manifest courage: The story of flight 93. *Vanity Fair:* 266–271, 328–332.

Butler, J. (1995). Contingent foundations: Feminism and the question of "postmodernism." In S. Benhabib, J. Butler, D. Cornell and N. Fraser (Eds.), *Feminist contentions: A philosophical exchange* (pp. 35–57). New York: Routledge and Kegan Paul.

Chang, B. G. (1996). *Deconstructing communication: Representation, subject, and economies of exchange.* Minneapolis: University of Minnesota Press.

Clifford, J., and Marcus, G. E. (Eds.). (1986). *Writing culture: The poetics and politics of ethnography.* Berkeley, CA: University of California Press.

Conquergood, D. (1991). Rethinking ethnography: Towards a critical cultural politics. *Communication Monographs, 58:* 179–194.

Cooper, R., and Burrell, G. (1988). Modernism, postmodernism and organizational studies. *Organization Studies, 9:* 91–112.

Crawford, L. (1996). Personal ethnography. *Communication Monographs, 63:* 158–170.

Der Derian, J. (2001). 9.11: Before, after, and in between. [Available on-line:] http://www.ssrc.org/sept11/essays/der_derian.htm

DeLillo, D. (2001, December). In the ruins of the future. *Harper's Magazine*: 33–40.

Ellis, C., and Bochner, A. (2000). Autoethnography, personal narrative, reflexivity: researcher as subject. In N. K. Denzin and Y. S. Lincoln (Eds.), *Handbook of qualitative research* (2nd ed.) (pp. 733–768). Thousand Oaks, CA.: Sage Publications, Inc.

Fish, S. (2001, October 15). Condemnation without absolutes. *The New York Times*. [Available on-line:] http://www.nyt.com

Foster, H. (Ed.). (1983). *The anti-aesthetic: Essays on postmodern culture*. Port Townsend, WA: Bay Press.

Gray, J. (2001, December). Where there is no common power. *Harper's Magazine*: 15–19.

Green, N. (1999). Disrupting the field: Virtual reality technologies and "multi-sided" ethnographic methods. *American Behavioral Scientist, 43*: 409–421.

Hall, S. (1985). Signification, representation, ideology: Althusser and the post-structuralist debates. *Critical Studies in Mass Communication, 2*: 91–114.

Harms, J. B., and Dickens, D. R. (1996). Postmodern media studies: Analysis or symptom? *Critical Studies in Mass Communication, 13*: 210–227.

Harrison, C. (1996). *Manhattan nocturne*. New York: Crown.

Hawes, L. C. (1998). Becoming other-wise: Conversational performance and the politics of experience. *Text and Performance Quarterly, 18*: 273–299.

Hine, C. (2000). *Virtual ethnography*. London: Sage Publications, Inc.

Iyer, P. (1995, August). Where worlds collide. *Harper's Magazine*: 50–57.

Jones, S. (1999). *Doing internet research*. Thousand Oaks, CA: Sage Publications, Inc.

Kakutani, M. (2001, September 13). Critic's notebook: Struggling to find words for a horror beyond words. *The New York Times*. [Available on-line:] http://www.nyt.com

Lannamann, J. W. (1991). Interpersonal communication research as ideological practice. *Communication Theory, 1*: 179–203.

Lindlof, T. K., and Taylor, B. C. (2002). *Qualitative communication research methods* (2nd ed.). Thousand Oaks, CA: Sage Publications, Inc.

Lyman, P., and Wakeford, N. (1999). Introduction: Going into the virtual field. *American Behavioral Scientist, 43*: 359–376.

Manning, P. (1995). The challenges of postmodernism. In J. Van Maanen (Ed.), *Representation in Ethnography* (pp. 245–272). Thousand Oaks, CA: Sage Publications, Inc.

Marcus, G. E., and Fischer, M. M. J. (1986). *Anthropology as cultural critique*. Chicago: University of Chicago Press.

Mumby, D. (1997). Modernism, postmodernism, and communication studies: A rereading of an ongoing debate. *Communication Theory, 7*: 1–28.

Presnell, M. (1994). Postmodern ethnography: From representing the other to co-producing a text. In K. Carter and M. Presnell (Eds.), *Interpretive Approaches to Interprersonal Communication* (pp. 11–43). Albany: State University of New York Press.

Richardson, L. (2000). Writing: A method of inquiry. In N. K. Denzin and Y. S. Lincoln (Eds.), *Handbook of qualitative research* (2nd ed.) (pp. 923–948). Thousand Oaks, CA: Sage Publications, Inc.

Rothstein, E. (2001, September 22). Connections: Attacks on U.S. challenge the perspectives of postmodern true believers. *The New York Times*. [Available on-line:] http://www.nyt.com

Shields, D. C. (2000). Symbolic convergence and special communication theories: Sensing and examining dis/enchantment with the theoretical robustness of critical autoethnography. *Communication Monographs, 67*: 392–421.

Sifton, J. (2001, September 30). Temporal vertigo. *The New York Times*. [Available on-line:] http://www.nyt.com

Strinati, D. (1995). *An Introduction to Theories of Popular Culture*. London: Routledge and Kegan Paul.

Todd, R. (2001, October 28). The way we live now: 10–28–01; Fragmented we stand. *The New York Times*. [Available on-line:] http://www.nyt.com

Trujillo, N. (1993). Interpreting November 22: A critical ethnography of an assassination site. *Quarterly Journal of Speech, 79*: 447–466.

Tyler, S. A. (1987). *The unspeakable : Discourse, dialogue, and rhetoric in the postmodern world*. Madison, WI : University of Wisconsin Press.

Van Maanen, J. (1995). An end to innocence: The ethnography of ethnography. In J. Van Maanen (Ed.), *Representation in ethnography* (pp. 1–35). Thousand Oaks, CA: Sage Publications, Inc.

West, J. (1993). Ethnography and ideology: The politics of cultural representation. *Western Journal of Communication, 57*: 209–220.

CHAPTER 6

An Ethics for Postcolonial Ethnography

MARIA CRISTINA GONZÁLEZ

When I sat down in 1991 to write the first draft of what would become my manuscript, *The Four Seasons of Ethnography,* (González, 2000) I did so quite freely and without self-consciousness. It was an act of expression that came out of my sincere desire to "see what would happen" if I opened to the possibility of envisioning ethnography with the eyes of my indigenous ancestors. Over the years, I shared photocopies and edited drafts with many students and colleagues, inviting the feedback that would help me to understand where I was not clear. I welcomed critique and feedback, and by hearing the multiple interpretations of my early drafts, I came to have a sense of how I was apt to be misunderstood. Each time I sat down to revise the manuscript prior to its eventual publication, it was a labor of love; I desired to sincerely express my ideas in a way that could be understood.

This desire to be understood forced me to explore the relationships of ontology to the epistemological assumptions behind our methodologies. The nature of what we believe is not only real but also the powerful determinant of all we see. Our relationship to what we know is equally influenced by the assumptions we hold about the nature of reality. These phrases are so familiar as to almost be cliché in our intellectual parlance. And it is precisely this colloquial nature of the vocabulary and phrases around the issues of ontology, epistemology, and methodology that concerns me. When our language becomes too familiar, as to stimulate agreement and eager head-nods before our minds have been actively engaged in a process of critical understanding, it is dead. And like the dead metaphors (Lakoff and Johnson, 1983) of our everyday idiomatic expression, the significance of what we are expressing when we discuss our ethnography can avoid any real depth of understanding. We begin to function at a level of assumed agreement, simply because we master the use of formulaic expression.

Such inorganic, dead discourse is the foundation of social engagement in conformity. Even resistance and protest can come to find the proper forms so that real critical examination need never occur, as long as people believe (because of the language they are using) that they are engaging in resistance and protest.

It is precisely this form of *dis*engaged discourse that led me to explore the creation-centered, organic, and spiritual ontology of my native ancestors as the place for a genesis of an embodied, living, breathing epistemology for ethnography. I was dying along with my thriving scholarship—the sacred *logos* was nowhere to be found, and although the structures of my social existence could be used to claim I was active as a scholar, my spirit knew that, in fact, I was in no way engaged from my core. Epistemology is about the relationship of the knower to the known. I wanted to have a passionate, enriching, and thriving relationship to that which I studied. And I wanted my approach to the use of research methods, my methodology, to be rooted in this passion—not in a received academic tradition that had as the most evident epistemology a relationship of professional dependence between knower and known.

As a woman of Mexican ancestry, I can trace the relationships between my ancestors to relationships of ethnographic origin. When the Spanish explorers first arrived on the shores of my indigenous cultural ancestors in Mexico, they brought with them religious scribes who kept meticulous records of all that was seen, all that transpired, all that was found. These early records, such as those of Fray Bernal Díaz del Castillo (1992), the companion friar to Hernán Cortés, provided the prototype for colonial writing of culture, or *ethnography*. Although meticulously and rigorously written, with rich description and cultural insights, what must be acknowledged in order for these early colonialist ethnographies to be fully appreciated, is that they were written in order to justify, legitimize, and perpetuate the colonization of those about whom the texts were written. Colonization implied cultural conquest; understanding the nature of those who were being colonized would facilitate the *conquista,* the conquest.

The determining realities of an ontology of such a colonialist stance are the relationships between colonizers and colonized, relationships where the multiple dimensions of basic human rights are seen as cast and molded by the colonizer to meet the needs for legitimized power and control as the particular society would see it. In the case of my ancestors, there was a blending of the political and religious colonizing forces of Spain, accompanied by the incredible epistemological policing of the Holy Inquisition of the Roman Catholic Church. Such an epistemological orientation contributes to the development of ideals that guide one's gaze of inquiry.

In *The Four Seasons of Ethnography*, I introduce four "guiding ideals" of the received view of ethnography. These guiding ideals are the cultural assumptions that shape the nature of reality within which one's research would be conducted. *Opportunism, independence of the researcher, entitlement, and the primacy of rationality* (González, 2000) reflect the colonialist ontology arising from the hotbed of medieval socioreligious politics. When we naively (and perhaps somewhat lazily) assume that the inherited voice of scientific literature is simply a product of the desire to engage in sound scientific method, we fail to look at the historical context within which the written form of science evolved. We also miss the opportunity to see the degree to which courage has played a major role in the production of knowledge that dares to stretch the boundaries imposed by those imbued with the authority to censor.

This was nowhere made clearer to me than in my reading of Sobel's (2000) biography of Galileo. In her book, she tells the story of Galileo's intellectual journey and his passion for studying the cosmos, leading to his eventual trial and sentencing by the Office of the Holy Inquisition. Embedded in the fascinating biography were excerpts and renderings of Galileo's scientific texts published prior, during, and after his ordeals with Rome. In an author's commentary within the biography, Sobel notes that prior to his fear of the inquisition, Galileo's texts were incredibly rich and creative narrative forms, typical of the scientific discourse of the time. They incorporated fiction, dramatic form, dialogue, and autobiographical narrative into the exploration and pursuit of theory. Once the threat of possible torture, death, and at best, destruction of one's research, became a real possibility, however, Sobel notes that Galileo's texts began to use a distanced voice, devoid of incriminating evidence or details that would tie him *personally* to his work. The possibility of punishment for one's personal involvement with one's research was the motivator for the neutral, distanced scientific voice—an epistemology of fear and suspicion.

At the same time, colonizing efforts in the Americas were shaping the epistemology of ethnographic texts by encouraging the reporting of topics likely to earn the explorers and *conquistadores* resources, titles, and endowments of land and property. The influence of the Christian ideology of conversion combined with this motivation to create an epistemology rooted in opportunism and entitlement. The primacy of rationality and independence of the writer were logical outgrowths from a social world in which the reality of torture and brutal death sentences for one's perspective was commonplace.

My struggle in writing *The Four Seasons* involved my awareness that I was writing my text for members of the academy, to an audience I assumed was deeply familiar with the received ontology (if not also unconsciously driven by it). I struggled to find a voice that would not reproduce the colonialist view. My text reflects this, in that the first half of the manuscript (González, 2000, 623–637), I consciously engage an audience I assume to be well grounded in colonialist assumptions. I further assume this audience might need some translation of concepts prior to reading the second half of the manuscript (González, 2000, 637–650), where I assume a more narrative style, engaging the language of ritual and ceremony modeled on my experience with elders and native teachers.

Since then, I have come to realize that while I described the ontology and alluded to the epistemology in depth, even highlighting methods that corresponded to each phase (season) of one's research (González, 2000, 639–640), I did not really explore the nature of the *methodology* that would emerge from this reality and relationship to one's knowledge. The *ethics* of a postcolonial ethnography were missing.

Colonialism, as I have framed it, along with religious-political imperialism, results in a form of silencing in scholarly writing. This silencing is insidious in that along with the obvious explicit censorship of texts and writings, it helps create the illusion of a free exchange of ideas. By culturally and politically coercing writers to manipulate interpretation for political and social survival, the nature of knowledge becomes a mirror of the boundaries set by the colonizing agents. From this perspective, authorship becomes industrial, with writers surrendering their *author*-ity to the colonialist voice. Along with the surrender of one's authoritative voice comes the elimination of evidence of context and incriminating intertextuality. To write scholarship easily becomes a feigning of community through adherence to enforced standards, rather than through an actual communal process of discovery and expression.

A colonialist ethnography, therefore, is one that is written primarily to serve the interests of agents who have taken upon themselves the privilege of owning the voices of others. Furthermore, systems of coercion and punishment seen as rational within the cultural realms they govern are established to set up a self-monitoring system of writers without standpoint. The views of culture presented cannot be understood without understanding the values of the agents who wield the authority to approve the text.

What then, would a post-colonial ethnography look like? And what would be the ethics of such an ethnographic method?

In *The Decolonial Imaginary: Writing Chicanas Into History,* Emma Pérez (1999) provides us with an example of what is *de*-colonial, as opposed to *post*-colonial. This distinction is very important, as I am not sure that it is immediately apparent. A *de*-colonial voice is one which attempts to undo the constructions of colonizing ontologies and epistemologies. The function of such a voice is to bring to awareness the functions and implications of the taken for granted realities in the colonialist discourse that surrounds us. Pérez, for instance, demonstrates the glaring absence of women from the writings about the history of Chicanos. She points out that for many years, even the idea of colonialism as the dominant force *today* was absent from the writing. This form of *de*-colonial voice is meta-ethnographic, in that it talks about the writing of culture, and therefore establishes an abstracted representation of the issues, very valuable in raising the awareness of colonization. I believe that this sort of writing can play a vital role in moving a colonized, hegemonically silenced author from a place of *received* agency (as in the "received knowledge" in *Women's Ways of Knowing* (Belenky, et al., 1986, 1997), to a place of recognizing that something has been "taken" from them. This,

I believe is parallel with Jacqueline Martínez' (2000) description of what she calls the "knowing unknown" a phenomenological stance within which one is aware there is a reality associated with one's existence other than that which was received. Still, there is no sense of what it might be, but there is the potential to discover.

It is from this cognizant place in the colonized mind that the post-colonial perspective is birthed. There is an awareness of colonization after having been woken from a hegemonic slumber, often accompanied with deep psychological and emotional malaise or anguish. This intense subjective suffering provides a just motivation to rebel against one's colonial history and to reject its contemporary influence. But just as with my Mexican ancestors who were clearly aware that they were being oppressed during those dreadful decades of conquest and inquisition, this awareness does not erase the reality of the colonization occurring. Accordingly, a *post*-colonial ethnography will have to do more than simply point out that colonization has taken place. There has to be some evidence that the domination of the creative mind has ceased. It is *post*-colonial—it is *after* the colonial. Simple rebellion, no matter how noble or righteous, often occurs in the very midst of the oppression. It is not until freedom from those agents of oppression has been attained that we can find if, in fact, their influence in shaping our realities has lost its control.

A post-colonial ethnography, therefore, is not merely an act of defiance, but one of great courage, in that unlike *pre*-colonial awareness, there is now a sense of coexisting within social systems that may or may not still be fully or partially in the creative grasp of the colonial fist. One's "buy-in" to the colonial systems of costs and rewards is tested. Does it determine what one says or doesn't? Do we feign free expression when we are aware that we made explicit choices not to express something because of the social implications? The ethics of a post-colonial ethnography must be able to provide a means for such obviously ambiguous readings to be made clearly.

Returning to the wisdom of my native teachers, I sought what would be the ethics for the telling of a people's story, their ethnography. The source of voice is spirit, equated with wind, *ehecatl*, in the native Nahuatl language of the Aztec Mexica peoples. To tell a story, one must use the wind, must harness this force without boundaries with culturally bound language, and allow its creative force to reach into the minds of others to create shared or competing realities. It is magic.

Most creation-centered peoples revere the wind. In the tribal Hebrew tradition, the word for spirit is *ruach*, also the word for wind. The native peoples of North America pray to the four winds, or the four directions. These four directions, (west, east, north, south) are augmented with the directions of earth and sky, symbolic of the transcendent father-protector energy and grounding mother-nurturing energy. Finally, there is a seventh direction, the place of the heart, or the inner wisdom, the place that in Jewish tradition is the home of the *Shekinah,* the indwelling presence of the Divine. The wisdom of the four directions blows continuously through us in the form of breath, the *prana*, or life-force of Hindu tradition. It is kept in place through a balanced sense of our spirit-matter (earth-sky) essence, and the appropriate use of this force, or *okra,* in the Akan tradition of Ghana, can manifest through sacred speech. All speech is sacred from a creation-centered perspective. Hence, all ethnography, or the telling of stories of cultural reality is sacred. And to call upon the wisdom of the four winds might not be such a bad idea. What follows are the four ethics, or wisdoms I offer as a means to a liberated ethnographic voice that shares stories within social constraints without ever feigning or surrendering their authenticity, or author-ity. The *okra,* the *ruach,* the *ehecatl* . . . is allowed to blow.

The Origins of an Ethics of Postcolonial Ethnography

A postcolonial discourse operates within the structures and social realities that were erected by colonialism, without being determined by them. This dynamic calls for the unequivocal knowing of one's voice, and the ability to communicate assuredly from this place. From a creation-centered perspective, what this requires is a constant use of the mother-father, earth-sky balancing dualism. In the Aztec Mexica Nahuatl language, this force is called "Ometeotl." It is not simply a concept of duality to be apprehended, comprehended and applied analytically. Rather, it is a *force,* to be embodied. This force of dynamic duality moves one to attain a positioning of existential equanimity, allowing standpoint to reflect, rather than deflect. As such, the colonialist context is defeated as determinant of one's voice and is transformed into an environment within which full agency can be exercised. Opening to this force is a form of spiritual surrender, and it is for this reason that I have referred to this sort of postcolonial ethnography as a *spiritual practice.* The practice of ethnography no longer exists primarily to serve the interests of colonialist agency. The methodology of such a postcolonial ethnography is therefore radically different, requiring the ethnographer to embody the postcolonial reality. It is from this embodied place of power that the ethics are born. The ethics are organic, stemming from the postcolonial position; they are not external, imposed, or legislative. One cannot create a postcolonial stance with ethics. Rather, the postcolonial stance produces the ethics.

Moving from purely verbal, logo-centric means of preparation for ethnography to multidimensional practices is essential for such a stance. Before one can act within the boundaries of the post-colonial ethics, it is vital that an ethnographer be firmly rooted in practices that ground her to the actuality of her material existence. Being comfortable in one's body, exploring the realms of sensuality fully, embracing the nature of living beings and the elements is essential to being a sound vessel for speech.

Along with this mother-spirit earth energy, a sound vessel for speech must also be willing to "let go" of her body, and to transcend the material reality, to acknowledge a reality in which there is nothing to hold on to, nothing to hold one back. Practices that allow this, such as meditation, ritual, chanting, dancing, or drumming, are all very powerful ways to connect to the father-spirit sky energy. When the earth and sky are both in balance, the seventh direction, or the heart, is perfectly open and situated to receive the wisdom of the four winds, and stories can be shared.

The ethics, which emerge from the person who opens to the embodiment of this dualistic force, are reflections of confidence and no longer reflect the hierarchically driven fears and apprehensions of the insecure colonial standpoint. Voice is the clear channeling of honest mindful experience. We begin to share stories without colonialist guile.

Four Ethics of a Postcolonial Ethnography

I purposefully have selected terms that are already imbued with colonialist meaning, to take advantage of the polysemic nature of language in order to transform the effective meanings of the language that surrounds us. This form of semiotic transformation can be as exhilarating as realizing one's shackles were never locked. The practice for such a transformative semiotic process is to allow the words to first reveal the taken for granted meaning we have for them, then to meditatively "let go" of this meaning, inviting the new interpretation to fill the spaces the accustomed meanings occupied. It is much more difficult to embody this practice than to conceptualize it, but my experience is that without such an embodiment of the transformation of meaning, there is no real transformation. A postcolonial stance reclaims the full body as participant in meaning. Not only the mind has been colonized. Without the subjugation of the body, the mind could never be held captive.

The first ethic: Accountability. From a colonialist perspective, when we think of the concept of accountability, we are concerned with the possible repercussions for not having followed "the rules" set forth by the imperial force. Let go of this meaning. Instead, begin to look at the word. Account-ability. The ability to account. To tell a story. The English language makes it more difficult to see the connection as easily, but when I see the word account, I think of the Spanish *contar,* which is the way we describe the telling of a story. A *contadora* is a storyteller. When we are *account*able, we are able to tell a story.

The ethic of accountability is not just the telling of the ethnographic tale. It is the telling of *our* story, of how we came to know the ethnographic tale. There is no natural boundary between a story and our learning of it. In order to know a story, it has to become part of us. What is the story of our story?

In practice, this ethic reflects itself in our ability to explain how we came to know what we know. What were the decisions and actions we made and took while engaging in our ethnographic research? While we discovered and opened to awareness and cultural knowledge, what were we challenged with? To what did we close ourselves? In telling this "story of our stories," we are fully accountable. We can, as Altheide and Johnson (1994) suggested, leave an "accountability trail." However, this trail is far longer than the frame of a simple "research study." Our accountability trail includes our whole life.

This accountability need not be fully shared in every telling of our ethnographic tales, but it is an *ability*. An ethical ethnographic tale holds implicit that the teller is able at any point to tell the story of the story. And that includes every decision, personal, professional, embarrassing or noble, self-serving or altruistic, that helped create the tale as it has come to be told. It's not so easy.

The second ethic: Context. The second ethic is closely linked to the first ethic, as all the ethics are interrelated in a dynamic sense of the united force that births them. The ethic of *context* is about the ability to describe the environment within which one's tale is told. It is an ethic of open-eyed mindfulness to one's surroundings. What were the political, social, environmental, physical, and emotional surroundings of one's story? What was happening in the lives of the people about whom the story is told? What features of the setting are vital to "getting" the story?

The first ethic of accountability leads one to describe context, and vice versa. What we will find is that the third ethic, *truthfulness,* is intricately woven into a tight braid with the first two ethics.

The third ethic: Truthfulness. In the practice of yoga, there are five yamas, or precepts, upon which an ethical practice of union (yoga) is based. One of these yamas is the precept of *satya,* or truthfulness. It is a truthfulness that is more than a simple consciously expressed truth. In a sense, the ethics of accountability and context rely upon such truthfulness. The third ethic of truthfulness, rather, exemplifies a sort of radical openness to *see* not only what is in one's social and environmental context, to see not only what one has actually done or said, but also to see that which is on the surface not visible. This seeming paradoxical form of seeing is the manifestation of true courage, an opening to the heart, a willingness to be absolutely existentially naked about one's purposes and issues in life. From such an exceedingly vulnerable position, the nectar of the tales that will pour out is sweet and pure. The colonized voice is polluted through the imposition of fearful, shameful, and dishonest filters. The postcolonial voice is a courageous voice, full of heart, fully aware of the colonial imperatives and rather than fighting against them, daring to speak nakedly *in spite* of them. Such a stable positioning of one's voice cannot be moved. It is a nonviolent stance.

The fourth ethic: Community. What we have so often called "audience," or "our colleagues," "the field," "our readers," is radically transformed through the fourth ethic of *community.* Community presumes not social and political unions of persons working together on issues or projects. Community here reflects what is created when naked stories are shared and one opens both in expression and receipt of those stories. The ethic of community implies that once we step forward with an ethnographic tale, we can no longer feign separation from those with whom we have shared that story. If there is misunderstanding or opposition, the ethic of community challenges us to further open ourselves that we might better be seen and understood. This is absolutely in contradiction to the notions of defensiveness inherent in colonialist, territorial, competitive approaches. We cannot respond without compassion to one who takes issue with our tales. However, compassion is not a weak surrendering of one's standpoint for the sake of another's comfort. Rather, compassion is the willingness to open one's self to see, hear, feel, taste and smell everything about another's experience—at the same time as we share our own experience without intentional or strategic, fearful distortion so that it might also be experienced by those open to community with us. Often the most compassionate sharing of one's tale will make others uncomfortable—not because we have chosen to be harsh, but because they are unaccustomed to our experience of reality.

The ethic of community cannot function without the ethic of truthfulness. In fact, all four of the ethics are intricately woven together and cannot be separated without harming the integrity of each. As we move through the four seasons of our ethnographic work, a rigorous and mindful practice of openness to the liberated cultural storyteller in each of us will lead us to an ethical postcolonial practice. We will find ourselves impelled by the sacred wind that can lead us to discover the organic ethics of postcolonial ethnography emerging. Attempting to practice our ethnography with these ethics can highlight where we are still captive to the colonial mind. I am excited by the potential of such a radical transformation of our practice. I am humbled by the depth of courage we are called to as a community of scholars drawn to understand how we come to make meaning in this frail existence. I welcome the wealth of cultural knowledge and wisdom we have yet to share with each other, free of the shackles of colonialist assumptions.

References

Altheide, D. L., and Johnson, J. M. (1994). Criteria for assessing interpretive validity in qualitative research. In *Handbook of qualitative research* (1st ed.), (pp. 485–499). Thousand Oaks, CA: Sage Publications, Inc.

Belenky, M. F., Clinchy, B. M., Goldberger, N. R., and Tarule, J. M. (1997). *Women's ways of knowing* (10th ed.). New York: Basic Books. (Original work published 1986)

Denzin, N. K., and Lincoln, Y. S. (1994). *Handbook of qualitative research.* Thousand Oaks, CA: Sage Publications, Inc.

Diaz del Castillo, B. (1992). *Historia Verdadera de la Conquista de la Nueva España* [Real history of the conquest of New Spain]. Mexico City, D.F.: Editores Mexicanos Unidos, S.A.

González, M. C. (2000). The four seasons of ethnography: A creation-centered ontology for ethnography. *International Journal of Intercultural Relations, 24:* 623–650.

Lakoff, G., and Johnson, M. (1983). *Metaphors we live by.* Chicago, IL: University of Chicago Press.

Martínez, J. M. (2000). *Phenomenology of chicana experience and identity.* New York: Rowman and Littlefield.

Pérez, E. (1999). *The decolonial maginary: Writing chicanas into history (Theories of representation and difference).* Bloomington, IN: Indiana University Press.

Sobel, D. (2000). *Galileo's daughter: A historical memoir of science.* New York: Penguin.

CHAPTER 7

The Beauty and Logic of Aesthetic Ethnography

ROBIN PATRIC CLAIR

Aesthetic, like the term *ethnography*, derives its root-meaning from ancient Greek. *Aisthetikos* means sensitive; *aisthanesthai* means to perceive. The Latin derivative of these terms, an infinitive — *audire*, means to listen.

The origin of philosophical conversations concerning aesthetics can be traced to antiquity. Greek philosophers proposed opinions on the topic which have engendered a continuing dialogue among scholars throughout the ages. Early on, Aristotle and Plato argued the merits of epic poetry. Plato suggested that artistic expressions were merely poor imitations of reality which should be set aside to allow reason and logic their privileged place in philosophical discussions. Aristotle, however, argued that "the aesthetic creation is more than an imitation. It speaks not only of what has passed, but also of what might be" (see Clair, 1998, p. 173). Aristotle turned the discussion of aesthetics toward an establishment of criteria that provided the grounds for declaring what constitutes art.

Before turning to varied discussions of aesthetics allow me to make one point regarding the meaning of *aesthetic ethnography* in relation to this ancient debate. It is important to note that aesthetics requires logical reasoning and logical reasoning relies on creativity. Although Aristotle and Plato dissected the two concepts — logic and art — they may very well exist in a simultaneous fashion. As noted earlier, aesthetics refers to perceiving, to listening, and to being sensitive. Logic, according to its Greek rudiments, refers to *logikos* — speaking, *logike* — techne, skill or art; *logos* — word; and *legein* — to speak, to calculate, to collect, and to gather. Logic is directly related to ethnography — collecting and gathering in technical and systematic fashion the cultural phenomenon so as to speak or write of culture. But aesthetics are equally linked to ethnography for we cannot

87

write or speak of culture if we have not perceived it in a sensitive fashion. Aesthetic ethnography necessarily and simultaneously contains the *aisthetikos* and *logikos*—the listening and speaking; the perception and the expression.

Over the ages, the two terms were relegated to their proverbial corners. And although this has caused what may be considered an artificial bifurcation, which has had some detrimental effects, it also allowed philosophers to wrestle with each term individually. Here I will focus primarily on the debates concerning aesthetics while weaving in their relationship to ethnography.

Reminiscent of Aristotle's notion that art holds possibilities for the future, Leo Tolstoy (1896/1960 as cited in Dickie, Sclafani, and Roblin, 1989) considered art an inherently ethical phenomenon. He judged art value by its potential to *infect* others with emotion that would stir them to action of the "highest moral good" (see Clair, 1998, p. 173). Activism on the part of anthropologists has waxed and waned over the years and taken several different forms (e.g., Allan Holmberg in conjunction with Cornell University developed schools, health care facilities, and initiated government policy changes in the name of ethnographic intervention in a poverty-stricken area of Peru; anthropological consultants have also been hired by the Peace Corps—for details on these and other examples see Cohen and Eames, 1982—but keep in mind that the question—whose moral good?—has come into sharp focus under the watchful eye of postmodern and postcolonial scholars). Nevertheless, Tolstoy's proposition on the power of the artistic creation as the means to enact change by infecting others can and has been applied to ethnography. Others, from the art world, however, focused less on macro-level ethics as portrayed by Tolstoy and more on the aesthetic experience as a moment of personal transcendence.

Bullough (1912), who drew from Kantian philosophy, argued that we must divest ourselves of emotion in order to reach an aesthetic experience. Bullough's divestiture of emotion or what he called "psychic distance" may be equated with Kant's transcendentalism. Bullough explains by using fog as an example. Fog may distress some people, leaving them with a vague sensation of uneasiness. However, if they transcend these initials perceptions of fog as a deterrent, then they can visualize fog on its own terms:

> The veil surrounding you with an opaqueness as of transparent milk, . . . observe the carrying power of the air, . . . note the curious creamy smoothness of the water . . . strange solitude . . . concentrated poignancy and delight. (p. 44)

The relationship of the aesthetic experience and phenomenology becomes quite apparent (see Clair, 1998). From Immanuel Kant, to Georg Hegel, to Martin Heidegger, to Maurice Merleau-Ponty, philosophers whose work is grounded in phenomenology have proposed that perception and interpretation of phenomenon explain how humans experience and engage the world. Transcendence was at the heart of understanding. This seemingly innocuous supposition has been challenged by feminists, who say that to lose sight of the cultural and political baggage that the phenomenon carries with it is to act in a less than ethical manner (see Hein and Korsmeyer, 1993). Transcendence may create an illusion of naturalness as if any phenomenon could exist without its cultural, aesthetic, political, physical, and spiritual associations (also see Clair and Kunkel, 1998). As Boas (1949) pointed out, "what we ascribe to human nature is no more than a reaction to the restraints put upon us by our civilisation" (p. 8).

Numerous philosophers contributed to definitions of the aesthetic experience and the artistic creation (e.g., aspects of form, substance, significance of composition, and effects on the audience) in hopes of determining their constitutive properties. But when Weitz (1977/1989) defined "art, art theory and the aesthetic experience as an open concept" (see Clair 1998, p. 174), aesthetic philosophers took notice. Weitz drew from Ludwig Wittengenstein's concepts to portray art and the aesthetic experience as well as art theory as a dynamic, fluctuating phenomena. Paraphrasing Weitz's concept, I wrote in 1998: "Art must challenge its own said boundaries because it is an inherently changeable, creative, open-textured activity" (p. 174). New debates surfaced in the wake of Weitz's claims.

Tilghman (1989), for example, agreed with Weitz and argued that art theory has little to do with art expression since art is an open activity. However, Dànto's (1989) work stands in contrast to these claims suggesting that artistic expression is both led by and defined by theory. Silvers (1989) suggested that theory may constrain and define art but theory itself is subject to change and therefore what counts as art or more specifically what counts as good art is subject to revision with each generation of new art theories. These thoughts led Dickie (1989) to suggest an institutional theory of art that argued that institutions (the art world) acted in a coproductive fashion with artists' creative expressions to continually codetermine the meaning of art. Each of these arguments could be applied to the concept of ethnography as well as to culture. For example, Sapir (1968) noted: "Culture implies creative participation . . . [yet] the individual is helpless without a cultural heritage" (p. 104). The concept of codetermination crosses disciplines. Thus, it is important to follow these debates as they developed.

Dickie's codeterministic concept may tell it like it is, yet it neglects to account for the political and elitist nature of the world. Hein (1993) pointed out that women's art still sits on the margins of the art world. In short, the codeterministic aspects reflect the prejudices of a patriarchal world (i.e., male-dominated institutions codetermined with primarily male artists what counts as art).

Applying these same arguments to ethnography would suggest that an academic world (and Euro-American one at that) attempted to define and theoretically regulate what counts as ethnography and often did so on the assumption that culture was a static entity. Generally speaking, defining the limits of what counts as ethnography was and continues to be done by elite ethnographers (perhaps an inescapable paradox since the acceptance of a marginalized theory would probably promote its founder to an elite level). However, one cannot possibly contain what counts as ethnography for very long under the premise that cultures are dynamic and that ethnographers are creative beings who express an interpretation of their world and the world of others. Nevertheless, as feminists have pointed out, it would be naive to think that power relations are absent in these academic ventures whether they are pursuant of art or ethnography. Thus, aesthetic ethnography must demonstrate a sensitivity to the power and politics of culture, to the dynamic and changing quality of culture and ethnography.

Karl Marx may not have been an ethnographer in the traditional sense, but he did expose the oppression and exploitation of working-class individuals as directly related to a loss of their aesthetic sense of well-being due to the onset of a capitalist culture. Marx argued that human beings "create according to the laws of beauty" (Marx, 1844, p. 140) and that the appropriation of one's work for another as in the assembly line manufacturing of goods results in a sense of alienation for the worker. The worker is separated from the praxis and the product, from the inspiration to the creation and even from a final appreciation. Marx let aesthetics fade into the background as he pursued economic critique, but Nietzsche put the issue in the forefront of his philosophical treatise.

Drawing from ancient Greek philosophies, Nietzsche argued that we live the illusion of being and "once we recognize the illusion, we inevitably see that we are not Being; instead we are Becoming. In other words, reality does not exist outside of the individual; rather realities are created" (see Clair, 1998, p. 177). Nietzsche argued that as we create realities we affirm ourselves as human beings. According to Nietzsche, it is the artistic endeavor that should be considered "the great possibilizer of life, the great seductress to life, the great stimulant of life . . . art is *worth more* than truth ([Nietzsche, 1901] Will to Power, 853, I and IV an unused draft for a preface for a new edition of *The Birth of Tragedy*—as cited in Hollingdale, 1973, p. 155). True to his own theories, Nietzsche created a world of his own and sadly that world was filled with misogynistic references (see Clair, 1998; Mahowald, 1983), which have at times been carried into the postmodern philosophies that he spawned.

Postmodern scholars of ethnography have drawn heavily from Nietzsche's treatise. They have added that the illusions of being may be represented as fragments of a created reality (e.g., Clifford and Marcus, 1986) and thus have encouraged ethnographers to move beyond their previous modernistic styles. But they must note that they, too, are creating a world. Reflexivity may assist ethnographers in seeing their own role in the creation of the culture. New insights may be gained by:

> Exploring the role of the scholar as artist, who both renders and creates an image which both reflects and creates a reality where the artist is part of both the creation and the audience (Clair, 1998, p. 194).

Relying primarily on Heidegger and Nietzsche's work, I (1998) provided an example by exploring how Conquergood (1994) discovered and created an image of South Chicago's street-gang members as caring individuals. He in turn provides an ethnographic report that creates a way for him and his academic audience to care for these marginalized youths who have themselves created a world in part based on an oppressive situation and in part based on their own ingenuity—the more danger they create; the more they create the need to care for one another and thus, their solidarity as a gang is reinforced (Clair, 1998). In short, "a reality conceived in care requires the development of a reality conceived in danger" (p. 195).

The creations expressed by ethnographers (i.e., the expression of the created cultural reality—the ethnographic expression) come in varied forms including narrative accounts, performance ethnography, videos, photographic essays, poetry, stories, and novels. Thus, ethnographies create a cultural phenomenon just as much as they represent one.

Focusing on style, John Van Maanen (1988) highlighted the rhetorical nature of ethnography by categorizing ethnographies as realist, confessional, or impressionistic tales. His choice of wording here suggests a connection to art which could provide stimulating metaphorical guidance. For example, to compare realist ethnography to the realist art movement may help to put the ethnographic practices and products in perspective. Artists as ethnographers and ethnographers as artists of the realist school attempt to render a life-like study of the reality that they believe exists as Truth. The impressionist-ethnographer attempts to see the reality as changing under the influence of altered light, as in Claude Monet's work, while maintaining an integrity of truth through substance or theme. Vincent Van Gogh criticized the impressionists, especially the pointillists, for their lack of emotion. The expressionists, like Van Gogh, bared their souls and shared the raw emotional response they experienced in relation to the world that exists in a reality that they perceive they must endure. Ethnographers, who grapple with personal and interpersonal struggles against a vibrant and exciting, or harsh and demanding culture, and who tell it in a dramatic or performative way are often providing expressionistic accounts. Each of these aesthetic ethnographies remains within a modernist framework.

However, abstract art movements such as Cubism and Surrealism wreck havoc with reality. Pablo Picasso's cubist work disjointed and fragmented reality. Salvatore Dali's melting watches and Georgio DeChirico's dream-like worlds asked us to accept an altered reality, a surreal vision of the world. From Dadaism to Minimalism, art movements challenged the grand narratives of what constitutes art and questioned the concepts of Truth, the rendering of Reality. Postmodern art movements are also reflected in alternative ethnographies many of which include a postmodern or postcolonial perspective. And each of these schools of thought promise exciting new approaches for the future of ethnography.

As Cohen and Eames (1982) suggest, "The future of any discipline is rooted in its past" (p. 393). Recognizing that debates on aesthetics drew their first breath in ancient Greece where ethnography was also born does not mean that European contributions of the past will guide our future. To the contrary, cultures that historically have been subjected to the ethnographic eye are currently engaging ethnography in novel ways and may provide new philosophical insights for the traditionally trained (see e.g., Uchendu, 1973).

"The Cherokee philosophy of aesthetics suggests that aesthetics is woven into every aspect of life and is inseparable from all creation" (Clair, 1998, p. 183). M. Awiakta (1993) attributes this to the Cherokee *habit of being* "where patterns and rhythms sustain the heartbeat of humanity" (Clair, 1998, p. 183). Specifically, Awiakta tells us that we move from "intellect to the intuitive and back again" (p. 177) in order to celebrate the "power of change and transitoriness balanced with the power of continuance. . . . This is the Great Law, the Poem ensouled in the universe. The people sing it, dance it, live it" (p. 178). This is culture.

Ethnographers have scrutinized, colonized, objectified, and reified the Other. Ethnographers have painted the Other's portrait and written the cultural story according to their own cultural assumptions. Thick descriptions (Geertz, 1973) and layered-accounts (Goodall, 2000) promise at least a modicum of truth, but the Other's own voice may give more verisimilitude than strategic maneuvers by academic outsiders. Sherman Alexie's (1995) novel, *Reservation Blues*; Leslie Marmon Silko's (1991) novel, *Almanac of the Dead*, Mary Ellen Crowdog's (1990) auto-ethnography, *Lakota Woman* all speak of culture in the most disarming way. And academic ethnographers may need to be *disarmed*. Vulnerability, the absence of defenses and pretenses, may be the only means to embrace the Other so that an aesthetic ethnographic rendering can emerge.

Not all aesthetic ethnographies need to be far from one's own cultural base. Tracy Kidder's (1993) short story, "The Last Place on Earth," is a magnificent portrayal of aging and death in a nursing home. Nadine Gordimer's (1975) short stories of life in South Africa, where she lives, have been described as "imaginative and compelling," as well as "piercingly accurate" descriptions of contemporary culture. Rich renderings of the unique ways of being in the world are based on more than sensory observations. Poignancy requires that we search out the visible and the invisible, listen to the words and the silences, smell the fear or the longing or the contentment, taste the night and touch the spirits of the people we wish to embrace.

Aesthetic ethnography asks ethnographers to set aside past dictates to categorize, compare, and analyze, while taking up, in a rigorous and creative manner, a vulnerable, sensitive, dynamic, and pulsating engagement with cultural ways of being in the world. This type of engagement may allow for poignant portrayals and mesmerizing images of cultural practices which in turn may be considered artistic expressions in and of themselves. After all, ethnography is art; art is a part of culture.

References

Alexie, S. (1995). *Reservation blues*. New York: Warner Books.

Aristotle (1989). The nature of Poetic imitation: from the *Poetics*. In G. Dickie, R. Sclafani, & R. Roblin (Eds.), *Aesthetics: A critical anthology* (pp. 32–47). New York: St. Martin's Press.

Awiakta, M. (1993). *Selu: Seeking the Corn Mother's wisdom*. Golden, CO: Fulcrum.

Boas, F. (1949). Foreword. In *Coming of age in Samoa* by Margaret Mead. New York: Mentor Book.

Bullough, E. (1912). 'Psychical distance' as a factor in art and an aesthetic principle. *British Journal of Psychology, 5*: 87–118.

Clair, R. P. (1998). *Organizing silence: A world of possibilities*. Albany, NY: State University of New York Press.

Clair, R. P., and Kunkel, A. W. (1998). "Unrealistic realities": Child abuse and the aesthetic resolution. *Communication Monographs, 65*: 24–46.

Clifford, J., and Marcus, G. E. (1986). *Writing culture: The poetics and politics of ethnography*. Berkeley, CA: University of California Press.

Cohen, E. N., and Eames, E. (1982). *Cultural anthropology*. Boston: Little, Brown and Company.

Conquerwood, D. (1994). Homeboys and Hoods: Gang communication and cultural space. In L. R. Frey (ed.), *Group communication: Studies of natural groups* (pp. 23–55). Hillsdale, NJ: Lawrence Erlbaum.

Crowdog, M. E. with Erdoes, R. (1990). *Lakota woman*. New York: Grove Weindenfeld.

Danto, A. (1989). The artistic enfranchisement of real objects: The art world. In G. Dickie, R. Sclafani, and R. Roblin (Eds.), *Aesthetics: A critical anthology* (pp. 171–182). New York: St. Martin's Press. (Original work published in 1964)

Dickie, G. (1989). The new institutional theory of art. In G. Dickie, R. Sclafani, and R. Roblin (Eds.), *Aesthetics: A critical anthology* (pp. 196–205). New York: St. Martin's Press.

Geertz, C. (1973). *The interpretation of cultures*. New York: Basic Books, Inc., Publishers.

Goodall, H. L., Jr. (2000). *Writing the new ethnography*. Walnut Creek, CA: Alta Mira Press.

Gordimer, N. (1975). *Nadine Gordimer: Selected stories*. New York: Penguin Books.

Hein, H. (1993). Refining feminist theory: Lessons from aesthetics. In H. Hein and C. Korsmeyer (Eds.), *Aesthetics in feminist perspective* (pp. 3–18). Bloomington and Indianapolis, IN: Indiana University Press.

Hein, H. and C. Korsmeyer (Eds.). (1993). *Aesthetics in feminist perspective*. Bloomington and Indianapolis, IN: Indiana University Press.

Hollingdale, R. J. (1973). *Nietzsche*. London and Boston: Routledge and Kegan Paul.

Kidder, T. (1993). The last place on earth. *Granta, 44*: 9–48.

Mahowald, M. B. (Ed.), 1983). *Philosophy of woman: An anthology of classic and current concepts* (2nd ed.) Indianapolis, IN: Hackett.

Marx, K. (1983). "Alienated Labor" from economico-philosophical manuscripts of 1844. In E. Kamenka (Ed. and Trans.), *The portable Karl Marx* (pp. 131–146) New York: Penguin Books. (Original work published 1844)

Nietzsche, F. (1973). The will to power 1870–1888 (W. Kaufman and R. J. Hollingdale, Trans.). New York and London: Vintage Books. (Original work published 1901)

Plato. (1989). The quarrel between philosophy and poetry: from the *Republic, Book X*. In G. Dickie, R. Sclafani, and R. Roblin (Eds.), *Aesthetics: A critical anthology* (pp. 20–31). New York: St. Martin's Press.

Sapir, E. (1968). Communication. In D. Mandelbaum (Ed.), *Selected writings of Edward Sapir in language, culture and personality* (pp. 104–109). Berkeley, CA: University of California Press.

Silko, L. M. (1991). *Almanac of the dead*. New York: Penguin Books.

Silvers, A. (1989). Once upon a time in the art world. In G. Dickie, R. Sclafani, and R. Roblin (Eds.), *Aesthetics: A critical anthology* (pp. 183–195). New York: St. Martin's Press.

Tilghman, B. R. (1989). Reflections on aesthetic theory. In G. Dickie, R. Sclafani, and R. Roblin (Eds.), *Aesthetics: A critical anthology* (pp. 160–170). New York: St. Martin's Press.

Tolstoy, L. (1989). Art as the communication of feeling: from *What Is Art?* In G. Dickie, R. Sclafani, and R. Roblin (Eds.), *Aesthetics: A critical anthology* (pp. 57–63). New York: St. Martin's Press. (Original work published 1896)

Uchendu, V. (1973). A Navaho community. In R. Naroll and R. Cohen (Eds.), *A handbook of method in cultural anthropology* (pp. 230–237). New York: Columbia University Press.

Van Maanen, J. (1988). *Tales of the field: On writing ethnography*. Chicago and London: The University of Chicago Press.

Weitz, M. (1989). Art as an open concept: from *The Opening Mind*. In G. Dickie, R. Sclafani, and R. Roblin (Eds.), *Aesthetics: A critical anthology* (pp. 152–159). New York: St. Martin's Press. (Original work published in 1977)

PART THREE

Dialogue and Interview as Expressions of Ethnography

CHAPTER 8

Ethnographic Interviewing as
Contextualized Conversation

CHRISTINA W. STAGE AND
MARIFRAN MATTSON

Ethnography is an exciting enterprise, the one systematic approach in the
social sciences that leads us into those separate realities that others have
learned and use to make sense out of their worlds. In our complex society
the need for understanding how other people see their experience has
never been greater. Ethnography is a tool with great promise.
—Spradley, *The Ethnographic Interview*

In-depth interviewing is one of the instruments of ethnography that aids
researchers in our attempts to describe and understand the unique experiences
of others. In this chapter, we question the assumptions that guide ethnographic
interview practice and challenge researchers to reconceptualize interviews as
contextualized conversations rather than traditional researcher-dominated interviews. We begin by comparing the tenets of interviewing and conversations. Contrary to traditional interviewing theory and practice, we then propose that
incorporating some conversational techniques may not only improve the interview process, but also would address some common questions and concerns
about qualitative research. Our companion chapter highlights exemplars of this
approach to ethnographic interviewing from our research.

Speech events have rules that guide participants in beginning and ending the
interaction, for example, taking turns, pausing, issues of proxemics, and even
asking questions. To learn about the speech event known as the interview,
Spradley (1979) suggests contrasting the elements of an interview with those of
a conversation. Spradley's book is often recommended as a starting point for
understanding ethnographic interviewing (Erlandson, Harris, Skipper, and Allen,
1993; Marshall and Rossman, 1995.)

Interviews

Ethnographic interviews are marked by three key elemental phases (Spradley, 1979, pp. 58–68). First, interviews begin with the *explicit purpose* of the interview being explained by the ethnographer to the research participant. The explicit purpose details why the interview is taking place, the goal of the interview, and the direction of the interview as envisioned by the interviewer. Second, the interviewer, through *ethnographic explanations*, offers particulars about how the goal of the interview might be achieved. In other words, after explicating the purpose of the interview, the researcher discusses how the interview might proceed using project explanations, recording explanations, native language explanations, interview explanations, and question explanations. While engaged in this phase of the interview, the researcher shares with the participant what aspects of that individual's experience the researcher would like to learn. In addition, the method of recording responses is discussed, the participant is encouraged to explain things in his/her own terms or language, and the form of the interview including the outline of questions is reviewed. For example, if the focus of an interview is questions that require the participant to recollect a certain set of events or if during the interview the researcher simply wants to clarify the meaning of some terms, that would be explained.

Third, after discussing the explicit purpose of the research project and providing ethnographic explanations, the researcher employs a variety of *ethnographic questions* to guide the interview. "Descriptive questions form the backbone of ethnographic interviewing," and they include grand-tour and mini-tour questions (Spradley, 1979, p. 90). Grand-tour questions ask participants to provide a verbal description of the significant features of the focus of the study. These questions usually emphasize space, time, events, people, or objects (Spradley, 1979, p. 87). Mini-tour questions are asked to learn about the details of things described in response to the grand-tour questions. For example, a grand-tour question for an organizational ethnography might be: "How do you decide who does what around here?" might be followed with a mini-tour question such as: "What are the guidelines for deciding who does what job?" Structural questions are used to clarify how individuals organize their knowledge and contrast questions help to differentiate between objects and events being described. For example, the question: "What are all the types of promotions available in your company?" provides insight on how participants organize their knowledge, whereas: "What's the difference between a promotion versus a transfer?" aids the researcher in distinguishing events.

Conversations

Conversations are contrasted to interviews in that the former is more informal and emergent while the latter is characterized by a variety of purposeful question types and a series of explanations (Spradley, 1979). Conversations are based on common understanding and are marked by a lack of explicit purpose, avoidance of repetition, balanced turn taking, use of abbreviation, occurrence of pauses, expressed interest, and curious ignorance by both parties.

What then can be learned by comparing interviews with conversations? Are there common pitfalls that researchers plunge into that could be avoided using a more conversational method? We, along with others (Oakley, 1981; Rawlins, 1998), contend that when complemented by the assets of conversations, ethnographic interviews can produce a more participant-respectful and insightful project that overcomes the common criticisms of ethnography. Consequently, research projects could benefit from consideration and incorporation of the following conversational techniques including problematizing the research context, redefining interviewer and interview participant roles, and contextualizing interviews.

Problematizing the Research Context

In the quote that opens this chapter the promise of ethnography is emphasized. Ethnography is a tool that will enable researchers to understand how others view their experience; however, many scholars have identified research practices that compromise the benefits of ethnography. Specifically, the need to understand rather than ignore any particular event or phenomena within the larger social milieu is addressed by scholars across multiple disciplines (e.g., Bantz, 1993; Marshall and Rossman, 1995; Oakley, 1981; Rawlins, 1998). Sociologist Michael Burawoy and his associates (1991), for instance, demonstrate and discuss the need to understand how external forces shape present social situations. They suggest that there is no need to follow conventional limits that suggest fieldwork be restricted to micro-level, ahistorical work or that macro-level, historically grounded work requires an exhaustive archival search. Thus, an interview need not focus exclusively on the direct experience of an interview respondent. If a respondent refers to historical texts recommended to the interviewer or local lore on the topic being explored there is a responsibility to consider such information and seek to understand the respondent's experience in relation to or in light of those referenced events.

Business and communication scholars also regularly remind readers of the need to appreciate that complex events and phenomena are embedded in social and cultural contexts (Boyacigillar and Adler, 1991; Stohl, 2001). Additionally, the work of feminist scholars highlights this issue. For example, standpoint theory not only seeks to understand lived experience within the context of larger social concerns, but it also demands attention be paid to the experiences of those who are marginalized and/or are absent in our work (Harding, 1987). And Oakley (1981) emphasizes the need to critically consider the interviewer/respondent relationship within the traditions/confines of the research practice.

Redefining Interviewer and Interview Participant Roles

In addition to a responsibility to understand events as they are framed by a larger social context, there is a need to address issues surrounding the notion of knowledge creation including who is afforded the opportunity to create knowledge in the process of research. Tanno and Jandt (1994) argue for the need to extend the research process to include participant groups as research peers. Further, they suggest that researchers engage in a dialogue with research participants, thereby redefining the participant role as one of coproducer of knowledge. Blurring the lines between researcher and participant roles provides those who will be defined an opportunity to participate in their portrayal. Fine (1994) advocates that researchers "work the hyphens." By this she means, "that researchers probe how we are in relation with the contexts we study and with our informants . . . invite researchers to see how these 'relations between' get us 'better' data, limit what we feel free to say, expand our minds and constrict our mouths." (p. 72). These authors and others (e.g., Clifford and Marcus, 1986; González, 1996; Rawlins, 1998; Tanno, 1997) implore researchers to realize the power of their position as researcher, accept the responsibility that comes with portraying others, and learn to share the power of representation in ethnographic work.

Why, you might be wondering, should ethnographic researchers have an obligation to address these concerns? Lincoln and Guba (1985) outline the distinct characteristics of naturalistic or ethnographic research and two of these characteristics speak directly to this question.

> Characteristic 1: Natural Setting. . . . realities are wholes that cannot be understood in isolation from their contexts, nor can they be fragmented for separate study of the parts. Characteristic 2: Human Instrument. The researcher elects to use him- or herself as well as other humans as the primary data-gathering instruments . . . because of the understanding that all instruments interact with respondents and objects but that only the human instrument is capable of grasping and evaluating the meaning of that differential interaction (p. 39).

Therefore, if as ethnographic researchers employing any method, including interviewing, we want to realize the promise of which Spradley (1979) speaks, we need to consistently and mindfully engage these concerns. Failure to address these concerns would result in what Watzlawick (1984) terms "a trap." We must be careful not to assume that merely doing research in a natural setting with humans as both the instruments and data results in ethnographic research. To believe that merely going through the motions of ethnography and interviewing in a particular way will yield the rich promise is to be ensnared in a research trap. To avoid such traps, researchers need to heed these cautions and not separate the goals and methods of the research project from the context in which the study is embedded. Also, ethnographers must carefully construct their relationships with participants.

Techniques for Contextualizing Interviews

How might contextualization be accomplished? We conclude this chapter by suggesting several techniques to assist researchers in exploring the context that frames their study including ways to constructively blur the traditional interview roles within the researcher-participant relationship. The following chapter provides a demonstration of these techniques by providing a variety of examples from our current research projects.

Pause to reflect and prepare. In conversations, unlike traditional interviews, there are often pauses. For those in conversation, pauses serve as natural breaks allowing time to reflect or time to wait before changing the topic of conversation (Spradley, 1979). Researchers often move to avoid or fill pauses. They usually operate under strict deadlines and do not plan for pauses, or simply do not feel comfortable being quiet through a pause. We suggest that researchers consciously pause to reflect on the context in which the focus of their study resides.

To encourage this reflective process, González (1996) presents a framework for ethnographic research as a metaphorical four season process. Spring is a time for preparation and reflection before the hot summer of data collection. Fall is characterized by data analysis with the bounty of the fall harvest dependent upon the preparations of the spring and the hard work of the summer. Writing occurs in the winter when the cold reminds the ethnographer to be careful and thoughtful in what is presented. Across the seasons of ethnography, González (1996) emphasizes preparation and reflection and in doing so, expands our notion of what counts as facets of the research process. Rawlins (1998), too, suggests that researchers practice reflexive awareness to gain an understanding of, "one's indebtedness to others in the ongoing construction of selfhood; one's limited abilities to achieve absolute knowledge of others or self; and one's temporal and spatial finitude despite the enlarging capabilities of symbolic systems" (p. 362).

Pay attention to context. Strauss (1978) emphasizes that preparation for research must involve contexualization. He studies negotiation and contends that to fully understand this practice the various contexts of negotiation must be considered. That is, the researcher must strive to understand both the larger transcending circumstances surrounding an event and the properties of the immediate setting that directly impact the event. Based on Strauss' notion of negotiation contexts, we suggest that researchers develop contextual questions. Contextual questions, developed in conjunction with research questions, guide the analysis of the research context and begin prior to and continue during and after interviewing. In other words, contextual questions are developed to focus researchers' attention on the circumstances that influence and shape the emphasis of their study. Thus, the research process is marked by and integrated with pauses during which the researcher reflects on the larger context that surrounds the study.

Paying attention to context shares aspects of building theoretical sensitivity (Strauss and Corbin, 1990). Following our adaptation, researchers would work to build contextual sensitivity throughout the duration of the research project. Contextual sensitivity comes from literature, professional and personal experiences, and analytical processes (Strauss and Corbin, 1990). Using contextual questions as a guide, relevant historical and current, mediated and print literature should be selected and pondered. Professional and personal experiences are reflected upon. Reflection on these experiences identifies involvement with similar events that might be useful, and it helps researchers to more fully understand what they bring to the project and how that knowledge impacts the research process (see also Lincoln and Guba's 1985 discussion of *tacit knowledge*,). Contextual sensitivity continues to be built through analytical processes as the researcher enters the field and interacts with participants and data (Strauss and Corbin, 1985). Thus, the process of paying attention to context is a constant interplay, guided by contextual questions, between the researcher, participants and the stimulus of sources within and surrounding the context.

Balance turn taking through reciprocal participation. In addition to incorporating pausing and contextualizing, the art of conversation offers another opportunity to avoid the traps of traditional ethnographic interviewing. Balanced turn taking and reciprocal participation rather than one person dominating the talk and the process marks most conversations. In order to include interviewees in the research process, Tanno and Jandt (1994) suggest working with research participants when asking questions, interpreting data, validating conclusions, and presenting knowledge. Interview protocols need to be developed and structured in a manner that recognizes the usual flow of conversation given the focus of the study. Seeking the input of one or more participants to review the protocol is most useful. While talking with participants during the planning and implementation of the research, the researcher must really listen to and remember participant words and concerns. There may be an unrealized angle to the study that participants recognize and are trying to tell the researcher, however, the researcher has to listen to be able to grasp it. Also, ask participants for resources or information on how to learn more about the issues identified in contextual questions. In general, Rawlins (1998) advocates an ethnographic stance that uses conversational norms that require speaking as equals. Indeed, he considers speaking as equals, "as a means-to-a-beginning and a beginning-in-itself" (p. 362).

Balance is an issue not only while gathering data but also during data analysis. Once the process of data analysis begins, check interpretations of the data with participants. Lincoln and Guba (1985) suggest *member checking* as a way to test interpretations with stakeholders. If there are differences in interpretation be sure to adequately represent these complexities in the written report. And when writing, researchers need to consider forms of presentation or venues that will make the information accessible to more than those who subscribe to academic journals.

Finally, the conversation is ongoing. Goffman (1959) pictures culture as an ongoing conversation in which we're not aware of the beginning and we're not likely to be cognizant of its end. With this in mind, interviews should not be bound by artificial beginnings and endings. Two examples that demonstrate this quality come from the work of Conquergood (1994) and Clair (1994). Conquergood's extensive ethnography of the South Chicago street gangs with intense in-depth conversational style interviews are not *ended* when Conquergood leaves the urban neighborhood. To the contrary, he gives the gang members his office phone number in order to stay *in touch*. Similarly, Clair's in-depth interview with one man concerning the sexual harassment that he reports encountering at work does not stop after one interview. Clair revisits the story that the man wrote about his work-related problem and interviews him several times during the course of the research project and even shares concerns from the blind reviewers at the journal of publication with him. In short, the interviews should not be forced to fit within the time constraints or number of interview constraints.

Ethnography, and ethnographic interviewing in particular, is a research method with tools of great promise. For researchers to realize that promise in their work, we suggest that interviews be approached as contextualized conversations. Contextualized conversations have the goal of answering research questions, however, they require researchers to pause and reflect on context and include research participants in a reciprocal process. Use of these techniques not only answers often-voiced critiques of qualitative work; it positions researchers to more fully realize the promise of ethnography.

References

Boyacigillar, N. A., and Adler, N. J. (1991). The parochial dinosaur: Organizational science in a global context. *Academy of Management Review, 16*: 262–290.

Bantz, C. R. (1993). *Understanding organizations: Interpreting organizational communication cultures*. Columbia, SC: University of South Carolina Press.

Burawoy, M., Burton, A., Ferguson, A. A., Fox, K. J., Gamson, J., Gartell, N., Hurst, L., Kurzman, C., Salzinger, L., Schiffman, J., and Ui, S. (1991).

Ethnography unbound: Power and resistance in the modern metropolis. Berkeley, CA : University of California Press.

Clair, R. P. (1994). Resistance and oppression as a self-contained opposite: An organizational communication analysis of one man's story of sexual harassment. *Western Journal of Communication, 58:* 235–262.

Clifford, J., and Marcus, G. E. (Eds.). (1986). *Writing culture: The poetics and politics of ethnography.* Berkeley, CA: University of California.

Conquergood, D. (1994). Homeboys and hoods: Gang communication and cultural space. In L. R. Frey (Ed.), *Group communication in context: Studies of natural groups* (pp. 23–55). Hillsdale, NJ: Erlbaum.

Erlandson, D. A., Harris, E. L., Skipper, B. L., and Allen, D. A. (1993). *Doing naturalistic inquiry: A guide to methods.* Newbury Park, CA: Sage Publications, Inc.

Fine, M. (1994). Working the hyphens: Reinventing self and other in qualitative research. In N. K. Denzin and Y. S. Lincoln (Eds.), *Handbook of qualitative research* (pp.70–82). Thousand Oaks, CA: Sage Publications, Inc.

Goffman, E. (1959). *The presentation of self in everyday life.* Garden City, NY: Doubleday.

González, M. C. (1996, March). *The four seasons of ethnography.* Paper presented at the ethnicity and methodology conference, Arizona State University, Tempe, AZ.

Harding, S. (Ed.). (1987). *Feminism and methodology.* Bloomington, IN: Indiana University.

Lincoln, Y. S., and Guba, E. G. (1985). *Naturalistic inquiry.* Newbury Park, CA: Sage Publications, Inc.

Marshall, C., and Rossman, G. B. (1995). *Designing qualitative research* (2nd ed.). Thousand Oaks, CA: Sage Publications, Inc.

Oakley, A. (1981). "Interviewing women: A contradiction in terms." In H. Roberts (Ed.), *Doing feminist research* (pp. 30–61). London: Routledge and Kegan Paul.

Rawlins, W. K. (1998). "From ethnographic occupations to ethnographic stances." In J. S. Trent (Ed.), *Communication: Views from the helm for the 21st century* (pp. 359–362). Boston: Allyn and Bacon.

Spradley, J. P. (1979). *The ethnographic interview.* Orlando, FL: Harcourt Brace Jovanovich.

Stohl, C. (2001). Globalizing organizational communication: Convergences and divergences. In F. M. Jablin and L. L. Putman (Eds.), *The new handbook of organizational communication.* Thousand Oaks, CA: Sage Publications, Inc.

Strauss, A. (1978). *Negotiations: Varieties, contexts, and social order.* San Francisco: Jossey-Bass.

Strauss, A., and Corbin, J. (1990). *Basics of qualitative research: Grounded theory procedures and techniques*. Newbury Park, CA: Sage Publications, Inc.

Tanno, D. V. (1997). "Names, narratives, and the evolution of ethnic identity." In A. Gonzalez, M. Houston, and V. Chen (Eds.), *Our voices: Essays in culture, ethnicity and communication* (2nd ed.). Los Angeles, CA: Roxbury.

Tanno, D. V., and Jandt, F. (1994). Redefining the "other" in multicultural research. *Howard Journal of Communication, 5*: 36–45.

Watzlawick, P. (1984). *The invented reality: How do we know what we believe we know? Contributions to constructivism*. New York: W. W. Norton.

CHAPTER 9

Contextualized Conversation

Interviewing Exemplars

MARIFRAN MATTSON AND
CHRISTINA W. STAGE

In the preceding chapter, we argued that in an effort to achieve the unique promise of ethnography for communicating the experiences of others (see Spradley, 1979), the traditional method of ethnographic interviewing needs to incorporate the assets of interpersonal conversations. Further, we suggested that a reconceptualization of interviewing practice must include redefining interviewer and interviewee roles as coparticipants in the creation of knowledge while continually emphasizing the contextualization of the interview conversation. As part of this endeavor, we proposed three techniques for contextualizing interviews including pausing to reflect and prepare, paying attention to context, and balancing turning taking through reciprocal participation. In this chapter, we demonstrate our reconcepualization of ethnographic interviewing as contextualized conversation by highlighting, from our research, examples of the techniques we propose.

As Bandura (1977) and others (Hutchinson and Neuliep, 1993; Anderson and Millan, 1995) have established, modeling is essential to the developmental learning process. One way to model behavior is by providing exemplars, or case examples (see Yin, 1994), to illustrate best practices and promote parallel knowledge and action. The following examples, organized by the technique they refer to, aptly illustrate how contextualizing interviews creates conversations that expand the depth of ethnographic discovery. Also, the variety of research topics and projects (i.e., intercultural, health, and organizational communication) from which these examples were drawn speaks to the potential breadth of this perspective for ethnographic interviewing.

Pause to Reflect and Prepare

Contextualizing an interview as part of the larger research project takes time and requires conscious pause. The time spent preparing oneself for the research project has been characterized by González (1996) as the spring of ethnography. This time of preparation serves several purposes. First, researchers become aware of their position with respect to the research project. Building awareness of one's position to something uncovers personal experiences, tacit knowledge, and other issues that could aid, or interfere with the project. Second, this time of preparation and reflection helps researchers become aware of their voices, which in turn contributes to the presentation of qualitative work. If researchers are not aware of their voices, it becomes very difficult to separate the voices of researchers from the perspectives of the research participants. The following examples demonstrate different ways to prepare for ethnographic interviewing.

Training and Observation

After being asked to join an interdisciplinary research team that focused on aviation safety, Mattson (2001; Mattson, Petrin, and Young, 2001) realized that to prepare for conducting ethnographic interviews she and the communication students working on the project needed to immerse themselves in the environment of the aviation maintenance technicians they proposed to study. Their preparation unfolded in two phases. The first phase was training. By taking university courses with students studying to become aviation maintenance technicians, they learned the necessary jargon to interact in this environment along with many of the licensing programs, which were part of mandatory federal regulations designed for the aviation industry. They also participated in plant trips and job-shadowed maintenance technicians. All of these training experiences helped to strengthen their practical knowledge (Giddens, 1993), which enabled them to interact more effectively with the maintenance technicians once they began the second phase of their preparation which consisted of participant observation.

In the second phase, the researchers engaged in participant observation of two airplane maintenance teams for six weeks. The maintenance teams allowed them full access to observe and participate in daily work activities. Their participation in discussions during meetings was accepted and encouraged; maintenance technicians were always willing to talk and answer questions, and they were permitted to investigate any job as long as they followed the standard safety precautions they had learned during their training. Sometimes they were allowed to participate in menial tasks such as sweeping the airplane hangar or stuffing literature into seat pockets. However, they were not allowed to perform work on the airplanes because they were not licensed maintenance technicians. During their daily observations, which spanned about six hours, they jotted brief notes to later remind them of what they had observed. Immediately after the observation period, they went to a computer in the airplane hangar facility, and using their jotted notes, typed extended fieldnotes (Lofland and Lofland, 1995).

Their acceptance as part of the maintenance teams was evident when, during a regularly scheduled planning meeting of the maintenance team leaders, one of the researchers was asked to "work the job board" (i.e., review and assign jobs), a task normally rotated among the lead maintenance technicians. This provided evidence that the teams considered the researchers to have sufficient training and practical knowledge to know how to interact in the aviation maintenance environment. Later when they conducted ethnographic interviews, the maintenance technicians were very willing to participate because they considered the researchers credible and genuinely interested in their work.

Thinking/Planning and Journaling

Stage (1996, 1999) examined the degree to which Thai employees in American subsidiary organizations, doing business in Thailand, participate in the creation of the organizational communication cultures within the subsidiary organizations. She describes the preparation for this research as follows. The spring for this project centered around two activities: (*a*) thinking about and planning for the project, and (*b*) journaling about the project. The thinking and planning involved three stages. First, discussions with members of the university community enabled the researcher to determine the appropriateness and feasibility of the project. Second, advanced Thai language training at Arizona State University and in Thailand helped the researcher gain the necessary credentials to explore funding opportunities and lay the groundwork for conducting research in Thailand. Third, the search for funding for this project began two years prior to the actual proposal of the project.

In addition, journaling was a valuable tool for preparation of the human research instrument (Lincoln and Guba, 1995) both emotionally and theoretically (González, 1996). In terms of emotional preparation, journaling can assist researchers in evaluating their position prior to entering the field. Though one cannot and should not attempt to avoid culture shock, journaling about previous experiences, how these situations were handled, and what can be learned from these experiences provides the researcher with a base on which to build.

Further, through journaling the various roles of the researcher become sorted out which aids in the development of contextual sensitivity. In this particular project, Stage (1996) played many roles—all integral to the collection and analysis of data. For example, the researcher was an instructor of MBA students, a graduate student, and a woman from the United States living abroad. Building contextual sensitivity through past experiences and the issues that were encountered and contexts in which the research occurred was continually important. Contextual sensitivity was built through journaling about the researcher's experiences as a Peace Corps volunteer in Thailand from 1987–1989, a summer spent studying at Chaing Mai University in 1994, and developing a reading list that addressed the Thai business environment, Thai culture, and the United States-Thai relationship. As Burawoy and his associates (1991) explain, focusing on the macro-determinants of everyday life helps researchers to understand the external forces that shape everyday activity.

Though these techniques are not the only avenues available to researchers for pausing to reflect and prepare, they do provide poignant examples. Most importantly these examples demonstrate how an individual researcher or a research team can prepare, how techniques can be used separately or in combination, and that any context—domestic or international—needs to be reflected upon and prepared for. The previous examples also illustrate that the techniques surrounding ethnographic interviewing are not mutually exclusive endeavors. That is, as the researcher is pausing and preparing for the project, the context of study is likely to be considered. However, for the purposes of illustration and in the interest of emphasizing the need to contextualize the interview process, we treat paying attention to context as a distinct issue.

Pay Attention to Context

Although the need to contextualize our research is not a novel idea, we contend that it is often overlooked. To aid ethnographers in understanding both the larger transcending circumstances surrounding their study and the properties of the immediate setting that directly impact their work, we suggest consciously developing contextual questions alongside research questions.

Contextual Questions

Contextual questions focus the researcher's attention on what might be shaping the project. For example, in Stage's (1996, 1998) study of Thai managers working in American-owned subsidiaries in Thailand contextual questions were posed to provide an understanding of the environment in which the organizations were operating and employees were working. The goal was to gain a level of understanding about the economic, historical, and political dimensions of the United States-Thai relationship, in addition to cultural aspects that would influence the workplace.

The first question addressed the relationship between the countries where the parent and subsidiary were located. The second question examined the specific relationship between the parent organization and the subsidiary location.

The third question looked at the relationship between employee culture and the resulting organizational environment, while the fourth question asked how this situation as a whole could best be understood.

Contextual question 1. How do sociohistorical circumstances shape the communicative negotiations of employees in American-Thai parent-subsidiary organizations doing business in Thailand?

Contextual question 2. How does the relationship between American-Thai parent-subsidiary organizations doing business in Thailand shape the communicative negotiations of organizational employees?

Contextual question 3. How does employee culture shape communicative negotiations of employees in American-Thai parent-subsidiary organizations doing business in Thailand?

Contextual question 4. How is(are) the organizational communication culture(s) best understood and how does this shape the communicative negotiations of employees in American-Thai parent-subsidiary organizations doing business in Thailand?

Paying attention to context by developing and addressing contextual questions helped Stage (1996, 1998) learn about the nature of the Thai-United States relationship and how that history in turn shaped attitudes among Thai employees about working in companies that originate in the United States versus Japan or Europe. By examining how Thai employees described the workplace, the contradictory forces that shaped the nature of their jobs was highlighted. Finally, consideration of how Thai employees perceive themselves as members of the organization revealed that Thai employees regard themselves as a group separate from the organization as a whole. And though many Thai employees have learned how to have voice in the organization, they are sometimes subjected to ethnocentric acts and sentiments by other non-Thai employees that reinforce Thai employees' feelings that they are not part of the organization.

Balance Turn Taking Through Reciprocal Participation

Balanced turn taking and reciprocal participation rather than one person dominating the talk is one of the hallmarks of conversation and an important component of ethnographic interviews. Balancing the input of researchers and participants can take many forms including using informants, working with participants to develop the research protocol, letting the participants choose the language of the interview, listening to participants, and member checking.

Informants

For a researcher to engage in a reciprocal process, someone to exchange ideas with is as essential to the researcher as listening during actual interviews. Thus, partnering with informants is an integral part of ethnographic fieldwork (Bernard, 1994; Lincoln and Guba, 1985). According to Bernard (1994), there are two types of informants. *Key informants* play a central role during the inquiry. They help the researcher by providing in-depth information; they may aid in the analysis of data, provide introductions to important people, and entrée into desired research settings. General *informants* provide the researcher with essential information and insight but on a less regular and less personal basis.

During Stage's (1996) study of Thai managers, her key informant was introduced to her by a mutual acquaintance. The acquaintance recognized similarities between his friend and the researcher. The acquaintance's friend worked in human resources, specifically in American subsidiaries doing business in Thailand and many years earlier, his graduate education was made possible by a grant from the Fulbright Foundation. Interestingly, Stage wanted to study the experience of Thais working in American subsidiaries doing business in Thailand and the Fulbright Foundation was funding her research effort. This key informant helped develop the interview protocol and advised the researcher to conduct one-on-one interviews rather than focus groups to be sensitive to certain aspects of Thai culture. He also provided letters of introduction that were critical in gaining organizational entrée in Bangkok.

General informants also were helpful in providing information about everyday life in both Thai and international companies in Bangkok. Stage's (1996) general informants were Thai students in the Business Communication course she taught at a Thai university. The class was based on an American textbook that in many situations did not have examples relevant to the students' workplace experiences. Therefore, Stage taught the concepts and ideas behind business communication and the students taught her related issues and important considerations specific to the Thai workplace.

Working With Participants To Develop Research Protocol

Reciprocal participation of researchers and participants can also occur by working with participants in the ongoing development of the research protocol or the interview process. For example, in Stage's (1996) study of Thai managers she learned that although beginning an interview with biographical or demographic information is discouraged in the United States, it is the appropriate method for laying the foundation for a conversation in Thailand—especially a conversation with someone you have never met. During the asking of the first interview question, interviewees also questioned her. This exchange established or clarified the social hierarchy between people. In Thailand it is important to know if you are talking with someone who is more or less important than yourself. Your importance in the hierarchy is determined by a combination of age, education level, what country your degree is from, the title you hold based on your work, the reputation of your family, and so forth.

An initial exchange like this also builds common ground between people that facilitates conversation. Stage (1996) connected with many of the interviewees, as they had either attended the university in Bangkok where she was teaching or had friends that had graduated from there. With interviewees who were approximately the same age, she was at an equal or more important place in the social hierarchy because she was pursuing doctoral studies and was funded by the Fulbright Foundation (a well-known program in Thailand). With interviewees who were older, she was less important in the social hierarchy but because of her position as a student they were very interested in assisting with the project.

Also, as excerpts from her fieldnotes illustrate, Stage realized through the reactions of her participants that she designed and was conducting her interviews in a culturally sensitive way.

> At the end of several interviews where no Thai was spoken, when interviewees were asked if they had any further questions, they asked if I knew Thai language? When I responded yes, they said they could tell I spoke Thai by the way I conducted myself. When I asked them for more details, they would respond—you are very polite. Self-reflection on my behavior during the interviews made me realize that I was very soft-spoken, smiled a lot, maintained a stooped body posture to show respect, and my note taking directed my full attention away from the interviewees allowing them time to think without feeling pressured to respond immediately. The placing of my first interview question and taking notes versus tape recording were all suggestions given to me by my key informant. To be honest, the "polite" actions were a result of previous experience in Thailand; they were not consciously planned.

Choosing the Language

Being culturally and contextually sensitive also extends to issues of language use during an interview. Many of Stage's (1996) interviews with Thai managers highlight this. She relates that all the interviewees spoke excellent English, a requirement for employment in American-owned organizations. Stage speaks Thai and found that when discussing aspects of Thai culture that impact organizational life using Thai helped to clearly define and understand culturally unique terms and seemed to establish rapport between her and the interviewees. For example, if an interviewee was explaining the need to sometimes show deference to a Thai superior they would ask her if she knew *"kreng-jai"* the Thai term that refers to this concept. The interviewees were sometimes surprised and always pleased that she knew Thai. Some would then quiz her in Thai about where she learned Thai (i.e., in the Peace Corps) and if she could eat hot Thai food (i.e., loves it!). They would then switch back to English and complete the interview.

In addition to sometimes using Thai words when discussing cultural terms (or the ability to eat hot food), each interviewee had their own way of referring to the Americans with whom they worked. Depending on the language choice of the interviewee the terms American, *farong*, or "ex-pat" were used interchangeably. *Farong* is the Thai word for foreigner and "ex-pat" refers to ex-patriots or people from any country living and/or working overseas. Being prepared to allow interview participants to choose the language they felt comfortable with when discussing various aspects of their culture enriched the depth, breadth, and contribution of this intercultural study.

Brann and Mattson (2001) also encouraged interview participants to choose their own language to define breaches of patients' confidentiality in a hospital setting. Although the medical and popular literature provided some direction on how confidentiality breaches have been defined in the past, none of the existing definitions considered patients' perspectives. Realizing this, the researchers interviewed patients to understand how they define and describe breaches of patients' confidentiality. Each unique definition commonly articulated that breaching confidentiality involved unauthorized persons (i.e., friends, family, coworkers, employers, insurance companies), including anyone who did not have the patient's overt or implied permission, obtaining this knowledge. The definition developed from these interviews not only extended the literature, but more importantly provided patients a voice on the issue (for another example study see Clair, 1993).

Really Listening

Another aspect of establishing reciprocal participation during interviews involves uncovering the complexities of your study by really listening to participants even if their responses seem irrelevant to the focus of your study. Although it is important to maintain the focus of your research, the apparent tangents participants discuss may have import for future research and should be considered carefully before being dismissed as irrelevant. For example, one level of analysis in Stage's (1996, 1999) study of Thai managers focused on Thai employees' perceptions of how the parent organization viewed itself and how these views might in turn impact the ability of employees in the American-owned subsidiary organization to do business in the subsidiary location in Thailand. By really listening to the ideas expressed by interviewees (and not rejecting them as irrelevant), she soon realized that a company's image of itself was only part of the puzzle. A company's ethical stance was also an important component deserving attention.

The purpose of the original study that generated these intriguing interview data was not to determine whose ethics apply in the international business arena; however, the study highlighted the discrepancy in ethical standards and the awkward and stressful position this created for Thai employees in the subsidiary location. For example, one employee explained, "We really have an ethics and safety focus. The ethics are good but also hurt us. We have trouble getting permits from the government and dealing with them because of the ethical standards we have to maintain." Follow-up work on such comments made by Thai employees during ethnographic interviews has resulted in a series of studies that are attempting to determine constructive, proactive ways of addressing ethical discrepancies in global organizations (e.g., Mattson and Stage, 2001). Additionally, the ability of Thai employees to use both Thai and English in the subsidiary workplace was further explored (Stage, 1998).

In Mattson's (1999) study of HIV test counseling, her preparation included visiting several clinics to have an HIV test while observing the process. Although the focus of her study was the counseling session prior to the blood draw for the HIV test, her initial observations and informal discussions with clinic workers and patients alerted her to some breaches of patients' confidentiality. For example, when patients came to the clinic for their prescheduled, anonymous HIV test, receptionists and other staff often drew attention to patients and the reason for the visit by talking too loud about their visit either to them or about them. One receptionist called out to a patient, "Okay, the counselor is ready to see you for your HIV test" while pointing at the patient who was sitting in a general waiting room filled with patients and visitors. In a few cases, patients became so upset they left the clinic without having the HIV test. Based on her experience, then, Mattson was asked to consult with a number of clinics on how to keep the HIV test counseling process confidential for patients.

Member Checking

Reciprocal participation in ethnographic interviewing also takes place through member checking. Member checking refers to channeling one's research interpretations back to the research participants or knowledgeable individuals (Lincoln and Guba, 1985). Although member checking has traditionally referred to conveying the finished product, we, like Lincoln and Guba (1985), prefer that a provisional report be taken back to participants for their feedback including, corrections, amendments, and extensions prior to finalizing the draft.

For example, given the circumstances of Stage's (1996) study of Thai managers working in American-owned subsidiary organizations, it could have been years before there was an opportunity to return to Thailand with a draft of the final product for the participants to review, but she felt it was important that the initial interpretations of the data be checked. An invitation to guest lecture in an MBA program in southern Thailand provided the opportunity. Correspondence with the program revealed they had heard about the research and given the nature of their MBA program were interested in hearing about the work. Their program took place in the evening, meaning most of the students worked during the day. Fortunately, most students worked for several United States parent-subsidiary organizations in southern Thailand. Additionally, many of the program's faculty consulted for American companies and were also interested in and willing to comment on the project.

Stage's (1996) fieldnotes from the project offer a pointed illustration of a member-checking scenario.

> Thank goodness they could relate to what they heard in tonight's presentation! I was very nervous—all this work and what if they thought I was full of hot air? Both the students and the professors gave me good feedback and several things to think about.

Specifically, in an attempt to understand the extent to which Thai employees negotiate their organizational communication cultures, Stage (1996, 1999) reported a great deal of freedom to pursue immediate job tasks within the office. However, when employees conducted business with outside clients, companies varied greatly in recognizing the norms of their local Thai customers and several examples of Thai employees being embarrassed by their company's policies were provided. The response from the group to this report contained much laughter and immediate sharing of "silly" requirements of American companies and how to work your way around those requirements.

Mattson (2001) also employed member-checking in a structuration theory analysis of the best (e.g., changing an engine) and worst (e.g., cleaning the lavatories, changing the grease soaked krueger actuators) jobs assigned to aviation maintenance teams. After interviewing (and observing) lead maintenance technicians and team members about the criteria used to determine the rules, resources, and sanctions that guided their decisions about which team would be assigned which job, she wrote a thick description (Geertz, 1973) of the process. Later she returned to the leads and team members to ask if she had accurately characterized the nature of the jobs and the decision making involved in job assignment. After revising the document based on their feedback, her observations were confirmed by team members.

There are many ways to foster reciprocal participation when conducting research. Though the idea of reciprocal participation might cause some to fear losing focus in their research effort the examples provided here demonstrate that reciprocal efforts lead to a more complex understanding of a given phenomena and often illuminate subtleties and complexities that would not be captured otherwise. Additionally, reciprocal participation with informants, in the development of research protocols, when choosing language, by listening, and member-checking provides research participants a role in the creation of knowledge and a voice in the presentation of findings. Clearly the examples in this chapter do not exhaust the possibilities or the extent to which reciprocal participation is possible, our goal was to demonstrate the potential of such efforts.

Through interviews that are shaped as contextualized conversations, we have come to realize the promise of ethnography alluded to by Spradley (1979). While the challenge of that promise injects our research with excitement, it also compels us to recognize that in attempting to understand the phenomenon of human experience we must respect the people whose stories we convey by mindfully pausing to reflect and prepare, paying attention to context, and encouraging reciprocal participation.

References

Anderson, R. B., and Millan, P. Y. (1995). Effects of similar and diversified modeling on African American women's efficacy expectations and intentions to perform breast self-examination. *Health Communication, 7*: 327–343.

Bandura, A. (1977). *Social learning theory*. Englewood Cliffs, NJ: Prentice Hall.

Bernard, H. R. (1994). *Research methods in anthropology: Qualitative and quantitative approaches* (2nd ed.). Thousand Oaks, CA: Sage Publications, Inc.

Brann, M., and Mattson, M. (2001). *Toward a typology of confidentiality breaches in health care communication: An ethic of care analysis of provider practices and patient perceptions*. Manuscript submitted for publication.

Burawoy, M., Barton, A., Ferguson, A. A., Fox, K. J., Gameson, J., Gartell, N., Hurst, L., Kurzman, C., Salzinger, L., Schiffman, J., and Ui, S. (1991). *Ethnography unbound: Power and resistance in the modern metropolis*. Berkeley, CA: University of California Press.

Clair, R. P. (1993). The use of framing devices to sequester organizational narratives: Hegemony and harassment. *Communication Monographs, 60*: 113–136.

Geertz, C. (1973). *The interpretation of cultures*. New York: Basic Books, Inc., Publishers.

Giddens, A. (1993). *New rules of sociological method* (2nd ed.). Stanford, CA: Stanford University Press.

Gonzáles, M. C. (1996, March). *The four seasons of ethnography.* Paper presented at the ethnicity and methodology conference, Arizona State University, Tempe, AZ.

Hutchinson, K. L., and Neuliep, J. W. (1993). The influence of parent and peer modeling on the development of communication apprehension in elementary school children. *Communication Quarterly, 41*: 16–25.

Lincoln, Y. S., and Guba, E. G. (1985). *Naturalistic inquiry.* Newbury Park, CA: Sage Publications, Inc.

Lofland, J., and Lofland, L. H. (1995). *Analyzing social settings* (3rd ed.). Belmont, CA: Wadsworth.

Mattson, M. (1999). Toward a reconceptualization of communication cues to action in the Health Belief Model: HIV test counseling. *Communication Monographs, 66*: 240–265.

———. (2000). Empowerment through agency-promoting discourse: An explicit application of Harm Reduction Theory to reframe HIV test counseling. *Journal of Health Communication, 5*: 333–347.

———. (2001). *Dualities in rhetorically structuring team work: Extending the conceptualization of communication in Structuration Theory.* Manuscript submitted for publication.

Mattson, M., Petrin, D.A., and Young, J. P. (2001). Integrating safety in the aviation system: Interdepartmental training for pilots and maintenance technicians. *Journal of Air Transportation World Wide, 6*: 37–64.

Mattson, M., and Stage, C. W. (2001). Toward an understanding of intercultural ethical dilemmas as opportunities for engagement in new millennium global organizations. *Management Communication Quarterly, 15*: 103–109.

Spradley, J. P. (1979). *The ethnographic interview.* Orlando, FL: Harcourt Brace Jovanovich.

Stage, C. W. (1996). *An examination of organizational communication cultures in American subsidiaries doing business in Thailand.* Unpublished doctoral dissertation, Arizona State University, Tempe, AZ.

———. (1998). *Talk like a "Farong." Communication patterns of Thai employees in American organizations doing business in Thailand.* Paper presented at the Western States Communication Association convention, Denver, CO.

———. (1999). Negotiating organizational communication cultures in American subsidiaries doing business in Thailand. *Management Communication Quarterly, 13*: 245–280.

Yin, R. K. (1994). *Case study research: Design and methods.* Thousand Oaks, CA: Sage Publications, Inc.

CHAPTER 10

Hearing Voices/Learning Questions

WILLIAM K. RAWLINS

"Communication with the other can be transcendent only as a dangerous life, a fine risk to be run."
—Emmanuel Levinas, *Otherwise than Being or Beyond Essence*

If one listens with concern, one might hear in many contemporary expressions of ethnography a growing variety of expressions of regard for others, which in turn embodies a call, a call to place ourselves in question, if not in suspension. This call is addressing us, whoever and wherever we "selves" are—we, who have principal access to the means of amplification and thereby silencing. In this crucial, recurring, postmodern predicament, there are also those who seem to be encouraging, yearning for and turning to what may be termed ethnographic stances toward being and learning with others (Ellis and Bochner, 2000; Rawlins, 1998).

Among the multiple ways of characterizing or assuming such a stance, I highlight what I consider some key convictions here. Confessing the prevalence of hierarchy in human social formations and gross disparities in the circulation of resources and power, embracing such a stance involves striving to converse with others on equal footing. Such a project of learning about the human condition works to renounce an exalted self as the center from which all things are known and measured. In contrast, other persons are addressed as coparticipating subjects of discourse instead of objects or targets of knowledge acquisition (Kauffmann, 1990). Pursuing one-sided objectivity, detached and disembodied from our contingent subjectivities, is considered a mutually demeaning and distorting activity. We realize that as we objectify others we objectify self (Laing, 1971). In this emerging context, objectivity loses its mystique, its grip, its penchant to stare and

---

I would like to thank Devika Chawla, Lainey Jenks, Sandy Rawlins, and Natalie Sydorenko for reading and commenting on this chapter.

snare. In its place cosubjectivities arise and thrive; "We are seeking conversation, not classification" (Rawlins, 1998, p. 361).

Ethnographic living and learning is avowedly relational in cast (Bateson, 1972; Rose, 1990). Understanding others is partially a projection of our own self-conceptions, even as these self-understandings are largely derived from others' responses to us. Acting out of our unique spatiotemporal vantage points, we address and are addressed by a vivifying and challenging world of others (Bakhtin, 1981; Holquist, 1990). Our limited comprehension of our own as well as others' existences constitutes a profound reason for *humility* as we face this world. Meanwhile, whatever understandings we have achieved about our being-in-the-world, we have accomplished with others. This indebtedness to others for our own humanity constitutes a profound reason for *goodwill* toward others (Bateson, 1993).

This ethnographic stance appreciates the differences making up our lives and the ongoing exigencies of defining relationships. Differences are regarded as enlivening, as always arising in and through relationships, and as constituting the basis for self- as well as other-recognition (Bateson 1972; 1979). Differences, which make us all who we are, are respected and sustained. They are not transcended or merged through a self-ordained empathy. Describing this outlook in another essay, I wrote: "Instead, self seeks the other's point of view and images of self's being, without necessarily relinquishing self's point of view or converting other's point of view into self's" (Rawlins, 1998, p. 361).

But in the reaching out and reaching in of ethnographic discourses, we confront paradox; namely, is it inherently an act of self-privileging to seek to learn more about others? Is it intrinsically a patronizing conceit? Are we not imposing the responsibility of educating self onto the other through our seeking purposefully to learn about her/him? Worse yet, don't our questions embody a thirst for knowledge about others occasioned by the desert of sameness composing our own horizons? But what if we don't ask, don't care, don't try? Where does that leave us? How else are openings intentionally created for mutual learning? For relinquishing and sharing the floor?

I believe there are honorable reasons to seek, to learn, and to understand more about other persons' (and reflexively our own) practices, experiences, and ways of life. Though opportunities for doing so are admittedly unequally distributed, I do not consider it *inherently* colonizing nor self-aggrandizing to strive for greater awareness concerning "the canon of human experience," to attempt to appreciate from their own standpoints others' being-in-the-world, their life conditions (Bateson, 1993, p. 118).

We are finite beings. But in seeking to understand more fully other persons and ways of life, we can strive to embrace this ethnographic stance as we embody our questions to various degrees and durations of encounter, immersion, or living together with others. For multiple reasons, we may have only limited opportunities to speak with others and only restricted amounts of time to be in their presence and in their domains. However, we also may dwell with them for indefinite periods of time; they may already constitute a significant part of our worlds and we theirs (Jenks, 2001). But there is always much to learn, more than we can imagine. Any one of us conceivably may have questions to ask the person beside us, across the walkway, in the next room, county, or continent. They may have questions for us as well. How can we talk?

Surely, we (must) have questions. That is one reason why we seek out conversation with others. But true learning usually generates more questions than it answers. More questions about these others; more questions about ourselves; more questions concerning self's and other's asked and unasked questions. Why did or didn't you or I ask *that* question? The one that needed most to be raised? How do we know whether or not we and other persons are hearing the same question asked over and over again, when we think we are asking different questions? One way is to devote ourselves to trying to grasp what the other is saying to us and what it seems to mean to her or him. Hearing the other is the priority. We need to listen diligently for clues concerning how our questions are being heard and regarded. We need to risk discovering that our projects are misguided. In short, we need to experience our conversations with others as opportunities to learn the questions we should be asking, as well as to hear and respond to the questions the other has for us.

Hearing Voices

As Bakhtin (1981) teaches us about all speaking sites, numerous discourses and voices intersect in the ethnographic conversation. In listening to one's own voice(s), a person walks fine lines among duly hearing, being distracted by, and catching oneself mouthing certain vernaculars. One hopefully remains alert to speaking in one's inherited or inscribed tongues of privilege and objectification, of "authoritative discourse" (Bakhtin, 1981, p. 344). As one turns toward others, it is important to attend to the discourses threatening to make one's own speech deafening, even as one focuses on hearing the voice(s) of the person(s) with whom you are speaking right now, at this moment.

It is a hallmark of postmodern times to encourage the expression of multiple voices, diverse stories, and to interrogate the legitimacy of master narratives (Lyotard, 1984; Frank, 1995, 1997). As Arras observes: "Another way to depict the implications of postmodernism for ethics is to describe it as an 'ethics of voice'" (1997, p. 80). But in order for speaking to attest to any self's possibilities and convictions, one's voice must be heard. Listening and hearing honors the gift of self that is speaking; it renders voice meaningful. In Frank's (1995) words: "Listening is hard, but it is also a fundamental moral act; to realize the best potential in postmodern times requires an ethics of listening" (p. 25).

Hearing others is not a passive enactment of being-in-conversation. Hearing *voices*, it says something about you that is critical. It identifies you as someone who has postponed speaking, someone who is reserving and respecting the space of talk for (an)other. It announces you as someone potentially open to the other's voice, at least in this moment when he/she is speaking. Listening in this way is a committed, active passivity. It is an opening in practice, conscientious listening. Gurevitch (1990, p. 188) amplifies this resolutely ethical quality of listening to others:

> Listening may indeed be linked to curiosity and interest in what the speaker will say. But the ethical aspect of listening refers particularly to granting the other with the power to establish self-presence as a source of meaning and authority. . . . The task of the listener is an active part, to open toward the other, to evacuate, (even if for brief and rapid exchanges) space and attend to the presence of the Other I.

Even so, this speaking constituted by your listening matters only if you actually do hear, only if you allow the other person's voice and stories to reach you, to change you. For if you really hear what the other is saying, you cannot remain the same. You are not the same. Something of value has been shared with you. Hearing the other's words, stories, concerns, and particulars tells you this.

Remember as well that to perform a hearing is to grant an opportunity for someone's case to be heard; in a judicial sense, it is a time and place for testimony, for justice to be served. As he celebrates the virtues of storytelling in particular, hear Arthur Frank's eloquence in this regard:

> Storytelling is *for* an other just as much as it is for oneself. In the reciprocity that is storytelling, the teller offers herself as guide to the other's self-formation. The other's receipt of that guidance not only recognizes but *values* the teller. The moral genius of storytelling is that each, teller and listener, enters the space of the story *for* the other. Telling stories in postmodern times, and perhaps in all times, attempts to change one's own life by affecting the lives of others. Thus all stories have an element of *testimony* . . . (1995, pp. 17–18, original emphasis)

The politics of experience loom large in these evanescent moments when a voice is offered for your ears to receive, to make welcome. For you to take on its own terms, the terms of the other. Perhaps your face and ears are burning now; perhaps your mouth is dry. Perhaps your cheeks are wet with tears. You're aware of your own posture, your heart and your stomach. Others' truths can be hard to swallow, especially when they implicate you and yours. You very well may need to *do* something differently now. You asked for it. Arras (1997) concurs, "But once one actually sits down to listen to the other's story, one opens oneself not simply to the possibilities for acquiring sympathy and tolerance, but also to the possibility of radical self-transformation" (p. 74).

We're not exactly talking about dialogue here, although hearing other voices and stories can assuredly lead to or serve dialogue. We're not really talking about airing your convictions here; we are talking about a hearing. Hearing comes first. Hearing comes before speaking. In this context your hearing speaks louder than your saying. It announces and makes possible who you are and who you are trying to become. Dedicated listening enacts a suspended or altered context of power. It is a form of surrender, a vulnerability and susceptibility to others (Levinas, 1991), a readiness—an "uncommitted potentiality for change" (Bateson, 1972, p. 396). Are we ready to listen, ready to hear others? Ask yourself; then listen.

Learning-Hearing-Questioning-Learning

Gregory Bateson viewed human communicators from birth as participating in an uninterrupted sequence of contexts of negotiating and learning premises for communication with others (Rawlins, 1987). Doing so speaks our humanity. We have our reasons for talking with other people just as they have their reasons for talking with us. The similarities and/or differences in our respective reasons for talking together may themselves constitute further reasons for talking. But even though asymmetries in our circumstances may persist, I do not believe that we pursue understanding with and about others necessarily in bad faith. As students of the human condition, ethnographers perform potentially honest, morally instructive, and life-affirming work. I am talking here about ethnography's core concern as continually aspiring to a mutually edifying stance toward conversation with others.

Being present to the other is a path to becoming other than ourselves. Can we come to experience speaking with others more and more as placing our knowledge and our projects, our selves in question? Learning the most meaningful questions to ask arises from listening, learning, and responding to the questions being posed to self. To question others is to place ourselves in the ethical position of striving to hear their voices, their responses. To question ourselves is to place ourselves in the ethical position of striving to hear how others are hearing our voices, our questions, and asking their own. What transpires is not merely information exchange, but an opportunity to grow older together (Schutz, 1970) and to change in a space surrendered to, entered into, and created with the other. We face each other as another self, embracing this moment in time and space as a gift of presence.

There are transformative values in being able to speak, to lift one's voice, but a listener is necessary to receive the speaker's testimony. "The challenge," as Frank reminds us, "is to *hear*" (1995, p. 101, original emphasis). Becoming a different person, and a susceptible ethnographer, begins with hearing, recognizing, and addressing different questions.

References

Arras, J. D. (1997). Nice story, but so what ?: Narrative and justification in ethics. In H. L. Nelson (Ed.), *Stories and their limits: Narrative approaches to ethics* (pp. 65–88). New York: Routledge and Kegan Paul.

Bakhtin, M. M. (1981). *The dialogic imagination: Four essays*. Austin, TX: University of Texas Press.

Bateson, G. (1972). *Steps to an ecology of mind*. New York: Ballantine Books.

— — —. (1979). *Mind and nature: A necessary unity*. New York: E. P. Dutton.

Bateson, M. C. (1993). Joint performance across cultures: Improvisation in a Persian garden. *Text and Performance Quarterly*, *13*: 113–121.

Ellis, C., and Bochner, A. P. (2000). Autoethnography, personal narrative, reflexivity. In N. K. Denzin and Y. S. Lincoln (Eds.), *Handbook of qualitative research* (2nd ed.) (pp. 733–768). Thousand Oaks, CA: Sage Publications, Inc.

Frank, A. W. (1995). *The wounded storyteller: Body, illness, and ethics*. Chicago: The University of Chicago Press.

— — —. (1997). Enacting illness stories: When, what, and why. In H. L. Nelson (Ed.), *Stories and their limits: Narrative approaches to ethics* (pp. 31–49). New York: Routledge and Kegan Paul.

Gurevitch, Z. D. (1990). The dialogic connection and the ethics of dialogue. *British Journal of Sociology*, *41*: 181–196.

Holquist, M. (1990). *Dialogism: Bakhtin and his world*. London: Routledge and Kegan Paul.

Jenks, E. B. (2001). Searching for autoethnographic credibility: Reflections from a mom with a notepad. In A. P. Bochner and C. Ellis (Eds.), *Ethnographically speaking: Autoethnography, literature, and aesthetics* (pp. 172–188). Walnut Creek, CA: Alta Mira Press.

Kauffmann, R. L. (1990). The other in question: Dialogical experiments in Montaigne, Kafka, and Cortazar. In T. Maranhao (Ed.), *The interpretation of dialogue* (pp. 157–194). Chicago: The University of Chicago Press.

Laing, R. D. (1971). *Self and others*. Middlesex: Penguin.

Levinas, E. (1991). *Otherwise than being or beyond essence*. Dordrecht: Kluwer Academic Publishers.

Lyotard, J. (1984). *The postmodern condition: A report on knowledge*. Minneapolis, MN: University of Minnesota Press.

Rawlins, William K. (1987). Gregory Bateson and the composition of human communication. *Research on Language and Social Interaction, 20*: 53–77.

— — —. (1998). From ethnographic occupations to ethnographic stances. In J. S. Trent (Ed.), *Communication: Views from the helm for the 21st century* (pp. 359–362). Boston: Allyn and Bacon.

Rose, D. (1990). *Living the ethnographic life*. Newbury Park, CA: Sage Publications, Inc.

Schutz, A. (1970). Interactional relationships. In H. R. Wagner (Ed.), *Alfred Schutz on phenomenology and social relations* (pp. 163–199). Chicago: University of Chicago Press.

CHAPTER 11

Sighted, Blind, and In Between

Similarity and Difference in Ethnographic Inquiry

ELAINE BASS JENKS

I'm a fully sighted individual. Seems odd to say that, doesn't it? I mean, of all the characteristics about myself that I could share, such as age, gender, race, sexuality, marital/parental status, education, occupation, or geographic location, I chose visual acuity. Of course, I haven't always thought of myself as a fully sighted individual. In fact, I never thought of my vision as part of my self-concept until I started studying communication and visual impairment.

I'm a fully sighted self who studies blind and visually impaired others. I study people who are different from me. It is the issue of studying a "different" other that intrigues me. For Rawlins (1998) reminds us that "all differences arise from and are only possible in relationships" (p. 361). And since all relationships exist through communication, as an ethnographic researcher, I seek to learn from, with, and about others through conversation (Rawlins, 1998).

Further, because I want to share what I learn about communication and visual impairment with the sighted world, I find myself in the position of engaging in a second level of conversation. Specifically, I am a (sighted) person who studies people who are different (*because* they are different/blind). Yet, the goal of my research is to convince others (the non-different/sighted) that they (the different/blind) are not that different/blind ("blind" here in the nonvisual acuity sense) after all.

Thus, in this essay, I explore the tension between difference and similarity of self and other in ethnographic inquiry. First, I discuss how the concept of difference plays out in conversations between the sighted and the blind. Then, I examine how my experience as an ethnographer of communication and visual

127

impairment is shaped by my "in between" positions. These positions include being the parent of an eleven-year-old boy who has been visually impaired since birth, living simultaneously in the worlds of the sighted and the blind, and being a researcher who is a participant in the topic being studied.

Difference

Gregory Bateson (1979) writes: "Information consists of differences that make a difference" (p. 110). It follows, then, that differences that don't make a difference are not information. For example, it wasn't really information for me to write at the start of this essay that I'm a fully sighted individual because the world is predominantly sighted. However, writing that my eleven-year-old son has low vision is "information" because being visually impaired in a sighted world is a significant difference.

Yet Rawlins (1998) reminds us that we should ask the question, "Who *determines* (italics added) the 'differences which make a difference'" (p. 361)? In relation to blindness, it's obvious that the sighted world has determined that a lack of visual acuity is an important difference. I believe the reasons blindness is treated as a significant difference are because sighted people do not have a lot of contact with visually impaired individuals, because sighted people do not exactly understand visual impairment, because sighted people are scared of blindness, and because sighted people set the rules of interaction.

First, according to the American Foundation for the Blind (2001), ten million people in the United States are blind or visually impaired. Of this number, one-half are individuals over the age of sixty-five. Thus, for the average American, knowing a child, adolescent, or young adult who is blind or visually impaired is relatively unusual. I'll mention here that not all disabilities are considered differences that make a difference. For example, three to five million people in the United States suffer from anosmia which is a lack of sense of smell/taste (The Anosmia Foundation, 2001), yet people without olfactory disorders tend not to separate the world into those who can smell/taste and those who cannot. Of course, anosmia is an invisible disability, but so are most visual impairments. Thus, disability status alone does not determine difference.

Second, blindness is a disability that is virtually impossible for sighted people to understand. Most sighted people believe that if they close their eyes (and try to function), they have approximated blindness. This behavior is a misconception in two ways. Closing one's eyes doesn't approximate blindness because most blind people don't live in total darkness. Ten million Americans are blind or visually impaired, but only 130,000 of these individuals (1.3%) have no light perception (American Foundation for the Blind, 2001). Further, sighted individuals can't approximate blindness, because they know what 20/20 vision looks like. Blind and visually impaired individuals either never had full vision or don't retain the image. As G. Kleege (1999) writes: "It has been more than a quarter of a century since I could make eye contact, and I have no memory of what it feels like" (p. 126). Thus, visual acuity that differs from one's own is a difference that can't be completely understood by either the sighted or the blind.

Third, the sighted are scared of blindness. This fear permeates literature dating back to Oedipus and Tiresias, and is shown in the misconceptions the sighted hold about the blind. These myths include the belief that those who do not see or who do not see well have lost mental abilities along with their sight, that the visually impaired have better senses of hearing, taste, touch, and smell than the sighted, and that the blind have special powers allowing them to see into other's souls (Hine, 1993; Wagner, 1986). The Canadian National Institute for the Blind (2001) states that the sighted also fear "the loss of what we feel may be normal contact with others, the threat to our ability to be mobile, and the potential loss of our independence" (p. 3). Thus, from the perspective of the sighted, the "different-ness" of blindness is a difference to be feared.

Fourth, sighted people set the rules of interaction. That is, the blind are expected to adapt to the conventions of the sighted with few or no accommodations being made by the sighted for the visually impaired. The best example of this phenomenon is the issue of eye contact. Most basic communication textbooks discuss the importance of individuals maintaining eye contact with one another (e.g., Adler and Rodman, 1997), and some of these books even discuss differences in eye contact behavior between individuals from different cultures (e.g., Trenholm and Jensen, 2000). But I've yet to see a communication textbook that tells individuals about people who can't make eye contact (because they can't see others' eyes). Interestingly, this topic has been discussed in the visual impairment literature (e.g., Fichten, Judd, Tagalakis, Amsel, and Robillard, 1991; Raver and Drash, 1988; Raver-Lampman, 1990). Blind and visually impaired individuals are routinely told to turn their faces toward sighted individuals when talking together. The reason for this is to make the sighted person feel more comfortable (and possibly more accepting). No one, blind or sighted, needs to look at the other's eyes in order to hear what is being said. Yet, because listening is associated with looking in the sighted world, people who can't look are asked to simulate eye contact.

Clearly, sighted individuals determine which differences make a difference (Rawlins, 1998). While not all disabilities are considered significant differences, blindness is. Further, neither sighted nor blind individuals can fully understand this difference, because it is impossible to experience the world through the other's visual acuity. Additionally, visual impairment is a difference both misunderstood and feared by the sighted. And finally, sighted people expect (and blind people are taught) to adjust eye "contact" to the rules of the predominantly sighted world.

In Between

I am an ethnographic researcher of communication and visual impairment. I'm also the parent of a child who has been visually impaired since birth. I would not have become an ethnographer of this topic if my oldest son were fully sighted. I would not have a special interest in the topic; I would not have read about the topic; I would not have spent six weeks conducting ethnographic research at a day camp for visually impaired children; I would not be writing about the topic; and I would not view my work as a "quest" (Frank, 1995, p. 115) to enhance communication between blind, sighted, and visually impaired others if my oldest son had been born with ordinary visual acuity.

But he wasn't. And here I am. A person who finds herself "in between" others. In between the worlds of parents with children who have special needs and those who don't. In between the worlds of the sighted and the blind. In between the worlds of the researcher and the researched.

Special Needs

I find myself both identifying with and separating myself from other parents who have children with special needs. First, Linton (1998) points out the irony of the word "special" when referring to people with disabilities (p. 15). She mentions that whole professions are built around the word "special," but that the word does not mean "exceptional" or "extraordinary" (*American Heritage Dictionary*, 1982, p. 1172) when referring to children or education. I learned early on that "special" can have two meanings when I told my younger, fully sighted son that his older brother needed to be closer to me to see a picture book because he had "special" eyes. My younger son replied, "I want special eyes, too," meaning, of course, that he wanted to be closer to me. Sitting between my sons during book reading, while eliminating the word "special" from any description of my older son's visual acuity, solved both problems at once.

Almost all the social scientific research on parents of visually impaired children outlines the same pattern of coping with a child's low visual acuity (Ammerman, Van Hasselt, Hersen, and Moore, 1989; Correa, Silberman, and Trusty, 1986; Haring, Lovett, and Saren, 1991; Herring, 1996; Leinhaas, 1992; Masino and Hodapp, 1996; Nixon, 1988; Reinhardt, 1996). Specifically, parents acknowledge negative emotions, but only as initial sensations. After these early negative emotions, the literature assures parents that they will feel better if they learn to cope. The most common form of coping is getting information, particularly from other parents of visually impaired children.

The most specific work on coping is by Tuttle (1986) who offers a seven phase model of adjusting to visual impairment in the family. The stages are physical or social trauma, shock and denial, mourning and withdrawal, succumbing and depression, reassessment and reaffirmation, coping and mobilization, and self-acceptance and self-esteem. One can almost see the upward trajectory of this model. Tuttle (1986) does say that he believes coping is an adjusting process that continues throughout life, but he states that if these new skills are mastered, future setbacks will only be temporary.

This pattern of things-were-bad-but-now-they're-better found in the social scientific research is echoed in an oft-reprinted essay by Emily Perl Kingsley (1987) that parallels having a new baby to planning a vacation. Kingsley writes that raising a child with a disability is like ending up in Holland when the trip was planned for Italy. Her point is that Holland isn't bad, it's just different than Italy, "slower paced, less flashy," and that everyone else you know is "busy coming and going from Italy" (p. 9). Kingsley suggests that parents of children with disabilities stop mourning the trip to Italy and learn to enjoy Holland.

The model of coping offered in the printed literature does not mirror my experience of raising a visually impaired child, but I'm not sure I'm supposed to say this aloud. After all, I'm trying to demonstrate that blind and visually impaired others are not that different from those with sight. Yet, I also know that I have conversations with the teachers of my oldest son about adaptations needed in the classroom (like sitting near the front of the room and having printed materials enlarged) that I never have with the teachers of his younger brother. I know that I've had to think differently about issues as varied as toilet-training (we made the water blue to solve the contrast problem of a white toilet on a white floor) and sports activities (he prefers indoor soccer because he can hear where the ball is).

I believe that coping should be thought of as ongoing, ever-changing, and relational. More of a spiral than an upward journey. Even if I believe I've completely accepted my son's visual impairment (meaning I acknowledge that he needs adaptations to accomplish some tasks without wishing he had better sight), I still have to continuously negotiate coping about my son's visual acuity with others. These others include family members (who seem very uncomfortable with words like "impairment" and "disability"), friends (who ask about my older son in a concerned tone of voice never used when asking about his younger brother), educators (who vary in their willingness to listen to yet another concerned [read that: interfering] mom), medical personnel (who rarely consider the social aspects of visual impairment), and sometimes, even strangers (who range from the people who stare to the people who comment, and who are found everywhere—from grocery stores and swimming pools to movie theaters and playgrounds).

Thus, there are plenty of differences between raising a visually impaired child and raising one who is fully sighted. But there are lots of similarities, too. My oldest son still fights with his little brother, ignores my repeated requests to make his bed, prefers television watching to homework accomplishing, and sometimes just wets his toothbrush instead of really cleaning his teeth. I believe the reason I don't totally think of myself as the parent of a different other is that my son has low vision, but is not blind. Or to use Kingsley's (1987) metaphor, if fully sighted is Italy and blind is Holland, then my family lives somewhere in Central Europe.

Visual Impairment

When my son was first born, I couldn't imagine thinking of him as visually impaired. I didn't think of him as partially sighted. I didn't think of him as anything other than a boy whose eyes were crooked and shook a little. I didn't know words like strabismus and nystagmus until years later. Even when I found out that he had an underlying retinal cone dysfunction, I still didn't think of him as visually impaired. Moreover, I never would have associated him with people who are blind.

In fact, I can still remember the first time a person used the word "blind" in relation to my son. He was three years old and had just been diagnosed with a cone dysfunction. I was told to have him evaluated by educators of the visually impaired in order to find out what services he would need when he became old enough for school. Two teachers had been observing my son playing for about an hour when one of the women looked at me and said, "It'd be easier if he were blind."

"Excuse me," I said, thinking that I hadn't heard her correctly.

"It'd be easier if he were blind," she said again.

"It would?" I replied.

"Yes," she explained, "It'd be easier to tell other people. People understand blind. Blind means not seeing. Only your son has vision. But he doesn't have normal vision. He has what we call low vision. People don't know what that means. People know what blind means."

Of course, that teacher was right. I have spent the last eight years explaining that my son can see even if he can't see across a room. Further, because I can't approximate my son's visual acuity, I don't really know what my son can and cannot see. I've been told that if I look out of a car windshield when it is raining hard before I turn the wipers on, I will have simulated his vision. Only I know what that windshield looks like when the wipers are working. Plus, I'm not trying to read, ride a bike, or play kickball through that rainy windshield, so I can't ever really understand this difference between my oldest child and me.

Further, I find that my son can't really understand this difference either. He routinely overestimates my visual acuity. He'll hold up a book from across the room and ask me to read a particular word to him. It's as if my visual ability is to him what X-ray vision would be to me. Further, I find that my experience with my older son's visual impairment has led me to underestimate the visual acuity of his fully sighted younger brother. When my younger son was about two and a half, he pointed out the kitchen window and said, "Squirrel in tree." I looked out the window, saw a squirrel in a tree, was surprised he could see what I saw, and realized that I'd never pointed out an airplane, a star, or a cloud to him because, well, I'm not sure why. Because I underestimated his visual ability? Because I didn't want his older brother to know what he was "missing?" Or because I was unsure how to adapt to the fact that one of my sons was visually impaired and the other was fully sighted?

Regardless of the reasons, my oldest son's low vision has placed him between the world of the fully sighted and the world of the blind. He can see, but he can't see well. This makes him sighted enough for some situations (he doesn't use Braille or a white cane and he plays kickball at recess), but blind enough for other situations (he uses a closed-circuit television to enlarge the print in his textbooks and he plays pitcher in kickball, because he can't field the ball). Before I had my son, I never realized there was a whole world in between sighted and blind.

A world that's hard to explain to others. A world where people can "pass" as sighted and/or self-identify as blind (Uttermoheln, 1997, p. 309). A world where visual acuity can fluctuate based on illness or fatigue. A world where one visual impairment might be completely different from another—where some people see through blurred vision, some through tunnel vision, some through peripheral vision, and some in black and white (American Foundation for the Blind, 1999; Sacks, 1996; 1998). A world that's not fully sighted, but not quite blind.

Researching Sight

Each summer, my son spends six weeks at a day camp for blind and visually impaired children and teens. I conducted an ethnographic study at the camp during the summer of 1999 (Jenks, 2001). Because I'd been reading about the topic of communication and visual impairment, and because I'd been raising a visually impaired son for 8-1/2 years at the time, I assumed I'd react differently than the typical sighted person to what I witnessed at the camp.

That is, I assumed I was one of the enlightened sighted. I assumed I was a person who would not have, much less enact, the misconceptions the sighted hold about the blind. I assumed I would look at the children and teens I met as people first. I assumed I was a sighted self who was somehow separate from, and different than, other fully sighted individuals. After all, I knew about the world between the sighted and the blind, didn't I?

It turns out that my choices were far more stereotypical than enlightened. For example, the first time I interviewed a fourteen year old, totally blind camper, I couldn't believe she couldn't see anything. Of course, that sounds absurd to admit, because I was interviewing her *because* she was blind.

Here's part of our exchange:

Me: Do you know what your visual acuity is?
Camper: I don't have any.
Me: Not at all?
Camper: No.
Me: Do you have perception of . . .
Camper: A little, I can see the sun.
Me: Okay. So even in a room, as far as knowing if the light is on or off . . .
Camper: I can't tell.
Me: Can't tell. And how about like shadows or ...
Camper: I can't tell.
Me: Not at all. Okay. Okay.

Notice that my question is answered in her first reply, but I kept asking her follow-up questions because inside I was thinking all sorts of sighted-self thoughts. Thoughts I didn't think I should be having. Thoughts like how it seemed impossible that this person couldn't see anything at all because she looked like an average teenager except for the folded-up white cane hooked to the belt of her shorts.

My stereotypical sighted-self behavior wasn't isolated to that one interview. For instance, I was continually surprised that the campers could do things like swim and hit baseballs and make crafts and play bingo. Of course, these activities were accomplished through accommodations such as using baseballs that beep and large print or Braille bingo cards. But being amazed by visually impaired people's accomplishments is a very typical sighted reaction.

During my interviews with the adult camp counselors and the teen volunteers (all sighted individuals), I asked them to describe for me how they felt when they knew they would be coming to a camp for people who are blind or visually impaired. I found that no matter how recent that experience was (some volunteers were in their first year at the camp), or how distant (some counselors had been at the camp for 10–15 years), everyone seemed to remember exactly how they felt:

15-year-old volunteer: When I first came here I was kind of scared, because I didn't know what to expect and I didn't know how to act around the kids.

16-year-old volunteer: I was a little intimidated. I was afraid that I wouldn't know what to do and that, like, I'd have to be cautious about what I say and stuff like that.

27-year-old counselor: I was very excited. And then I got very scared. I guess more frightened. I didn't know what to expect.

48-year-old counselor: I was very, very nervous. Like the first day. I can remember being very nervous.

While each sighted person initially felt uncomfortable, every person I interviewed described a different reaction now:

15-year-old volunteer: I thought it would be different, but it's really just like a regular camp and the kids are normal, they're like normal kids and they play around and they love to play baseball and soccer and just like little kids stuff.

16-year-old volunteer: But I'm like totally different now. More like at ease and it's just like going to camp with normal kids that don't have visual problems.

27-year-old counselor: But after the first week or so I was here, it didn't take long, and you know, just realize that these kids are kids who happen to have a visual impairment.

48-year-old counselor: It probably just took one day and that's it. [And then you weren't nervous?] No. No. They're kids. You know, they're kids who have a vision problem.

The sighted volunteers and counselors articulate the view that the blind and visually impaired campers aren't that different after all, even though each sighted person I interviewed expressed some apprehension about communicating with the campers before they met them. As one thirty-year-old counselor said,

I thought everybody was going to be like totally blind. I didn't even think about levels of visual impairment at all. Not even close. . . . I mean, right when I walked up and I see everybody moving around I'm like, you know, "Where are all the blind kids?" And . . . it's wasn't a big deal. I think I really picked up on it right away and I said, "Well, these kids are just kids," you know? I mean, it wasn't that big a deal.

This comment summarizes some of the differences between the sighted and the blind and visually impaired. First, sighted people usually think blind means no visual acuity at all. Second, sighted people hold misconceptions about non-sighted people including the assumption that visually impaired people are impaired in other ways—hence, this counselor's initial surprise when he saw campers "moving around." And third, if sighted people have contact with visually impaired people, they start to realize that the differences are not a "big deal" after all.

Ethnographic inquiry is fraught with tensions between similarity and difference of the self and other. While the goal of our conversations is to learn from, with, and about others, every researcher also ends up learning about the self (Rawlins, 1998). This essay is a reminder that even if the Other is part of our family, there can be differences that make a difference. We, as ethnographers, need to recognize these differences, to acknowledge how we are positioning ourselves in relation to others, and to remind ourselves we may not know for sure about what or whom we are seeking to learn.

References

Adler, R.B., and Rodman, G. (1997). *Understanding human communication*, (6th ed.). Forth Worth, TX: Harcourt Brace College Publishers.

American Foundation for the Blind. (1999). What is low vision? Retrieved from http://www.afb.org/info_document_view.asp?documentid=213

———. (2001). Statistics and sources for professionals. Retrieved from http://www.afb.org/info_document_view.asp?documentid=1367

American Heritage Dictionary (1982). 2nd College Ed. Boston: Houghton Mifflin Company.

Ammerman, R. T., Van Hasselt, V. B., Hersen, M., Moore, L. E. (1989). Assessment of social skills in visually impaired adolescents and their parents. *Behavioral Assessment, 11*: 327–351.

Anosmia Foundation. (2001). Introduction. Retrieved from http://www.anosmiafoundation.org/intro.shtml

Bateson, G. (1979). *Mind and nature: A necessary unity*. Toronto: Bantam Books.

Canadian National Institute for the Blind. (2001). Myths and misconceptions about blindness. *Living with vision loss: A handbook for caregivers*. Retrieved from http://www.cnib.ca/pamphlets_publications/lwvl/chapter1.htm

Correa, V. L., Silberman, R. K., and Trusty, S. (1986). Siblings of disabled children: A literature review. *Education of the Visually Handicapped, 18*: 5–12.

Fichten, C. S., Judd, D., Tagalakis, V., Amsel, R., and Robillard, K. (1991). Communication cues used by people with and without visual impairments in daily conversations and dating. *Journal of Visual Impairment and Blindness, 85(9):* 371–378.

Frank, A. W. (1995). *The wounded storyteller: Body, illness, and ethics*. Chicago: The University of Chicago Press.

Haring, K. A., Lovett, D. L., and Saren, D. (1991). Parents perceptions of their adult offspring with disabilities. *Teaching Exceptional Children*: 1–10.

Herring, J. (1996). Adjusting to your child's visual impairment. In M. C. Holbrook (Ed.) *Children with visual impairments* (pp. 49–72). Bethesda, MD: Woodbine House, Inc.

Hine, R. V. (1993). *Second sight*. Berkeley, CA: University of California Press.

Jenks, E. B. (2001). Searching for autoethnographic credibility: Reflections from a mom with a note pad. In A. Bochner and C. Ellis (Eds.), *Ethnographically speaking: Autoethnography, literature, and aesthetics* (pp. 172–188). Walnut Creek, CA: Alta Mira Press.

Kinglsey, E. P. (1987). Welcome to Holland. Retrieved from http://www. downsyn.com/holland.html

Kleege, G. (1999). *Sight unseen*. New Haven: Yale University Press.

Leinhaas, M. M. (1992). Low vision, blindness, and the complicated family. *Journal of Vision Rehabilitation, 6*: 5–13.

Linton, S. (1998) *Claiming disability: Knowledge and identity*. New York: New York University Press.

Masino, L. L. and Hodapp, R. M. (1996). Parental educational expectations for adolescents with disabilities. *Exceptional Children, 6*: 515–524.

Nixon, H. L. (1988). Reassessing support groups for parents of visually impaired children. *Journal of Visual Impairment and Blindness, 82*: 271–278.

Rawlins, W. K. (1998). From ethnographic occupations to ethnographic stances. In J.S. Trent (Ed.), *Communication: Views from the helm for the 21st century* (pp. 359–362). Boston: Allyn and Bacon.

Raver, S. A., and Drash, P. W. (1988). Increasing social skills training for visually impaired children. *Education of the Visually Handicapped, 19(4)*: 147–155.

Raver-Lampman, S. A. (1990). Effect of gaze direction on evaluation of visually impaired children by informed respondents. *Journal of Visual Impairment and Blindness, 84(2)*: 67–70.

Reinhardt, J. P. (1996). The importance of friendship and family support in adaptation to chronic vision impairment. *Journal of Gerontology, 51*: 268–278.

Sacks, O. (1996). *An Anthropologist on Mars*. New York: Vintage Books.

— — —. (1998). *The Island of the Colorblind*. New York: Vintage Books.

Trenholm, S., and Jensen, A. (2000). *Interpersonal Communication* (4th ed.) Belmont, CA: Wadsworth Publishing Company.

Tuttle, D. W. (1986). Family members responding to a visual impairment. *Education of the Visually Handicapped, 18*: 107–116.

Uttermoheln, T. L. (1997). On "Passing" through Adolescence. *Journal of Visual Impairment and Blindness, 91(3)*: 309–314.

Wagner, S. (1986). *How do you kiss a blind girl?* Springfield, IL: Charles C. Thomas, Publisher.

PART FOUR

Personal Narrative as an
Expression of Ethnography

CHAPTER 12

Ethnography as the
Excavation of Personal Narrative

ROBERT L. KRIZEK

My father passed away about ten years ago and I have my fondest memories of my father in this ball park. He used to take me out here frequently and I have some real strong memories of my father here . . . (Fan, male, final game at Old Comiskey, 9/30/90)

I never asked for his name; labels didn't seem necessary that day. He did tell me his age, forty-three, a year older than me, and introduced me to his son. Before our brief conversation ended he confided in me, struggling to conserve what remained of his fragile composure, "I'm here to reconnect one more time with those memories while I still can."

Beyond the demographic similarities of gender and age, I share other, more personally meaningful characteristics with this fan whose life crossed mine at the closing of Old Comiskey. I, too, have my fondest memories of my father, George Krizek, in Old Comiskey Park. Whether real or imaginary, I have very vivid recollections of my father at my very first Sox game. I was six years old that summer of 1954, and the White Sox played the new York Yankees. I remember the smell of hot dogs and the cool dampness of the Park's inner caverns. I remember having a Sox cap atop my head, a bag of peanuts in one hand, and my father's assuring grip in the other as we traveled to our assigned seats. We, my father and I, sat in section 213, seats 21 and 22, in the upper deck far down the rightfield line—not very good seats. As I attended games at Comiskey throughout my adult years, I would often take the time to sit in those seats and enjoy the strong feelings of warmth and contentment that would come over me. I would sit there and reminisce about a relationship I never quite understood.

—Krizek, "Goodbye Old Friend," 1992b

In the following essay, I share some of my answers to three questions that challenged me for the first time as I wrote about the closing of Old Comiskey Park back in graduate school (see Krizek, 1992a, 1992b). They were born out of a need to feel a sense of congruence between what I was doing as an ethnographer-in-training and what I was learning in my communication seminars, between a method that spanned disciplines and my discipline. I continue to ask them even today in regard to my current research endeavors. "What exactly is it that makes this a communication study?" "What makes this communication study an ethnography?" And, "If I am the research instrument, how much autobiographical detail/personal information should I include when writing my ethnographic understandings?" My answers, to a greater or lesser extent, all involve issues of personal narratives. I make no claims as to the "correctness" of my answers, only that they make sense to me. Hopefully, however, my answers will provide some insight for other ethnographers, especially those in communication, to help guide their ethnographic practices and to help them answer their questions.

The "Big" Question

For me, the biggest of all the questions I confronted as a graduate student and still confront today, both as a social researcher and a mentor of graduate students in communication, is: "What exactly is it that makes this a communication study?" It is a question that strikes at the heart of disciplinary identity, perhaps at disciplinary contribution. Before offering an answer, one answer to that question, however, let me first provide you with a brief glimpse of what it is that attracts my research attention. At its core what I study is meaning, the meaning individuals have for the events, places, and practices that inhabit their lives. For me it's about understanding lived human experience, person by person.

Richardson (1990) tells us that if we wish to be faithful to the lived experiences of people then we should value the narrative. In my research, I embrace Richardson's agenda for understanding the lived experiences of people and follow her advice. The inherent "value" I accord the narrative is reflected in my decision to focus on personal narratives, "the stories people tell about their lives" (Rosenwald and Ochenberg, 1992, p. 1) as the grist of my understandings. Rosenwald and Ochenberg (1992) continue by telling us that, "Personal stories are not merely a way of telling someone (or oneself) about one's life; they are a means by which identities are fashioned" (p. 1). I frame my research as the excavation of personal narratives. It is a process of "digging," of uncovering, of actively pursuing the stories people tell about their lives, their experiences, and their identities. It is a process by which I elicit, witness, collect, and ultimately represent the personal narratives performed by those I encounter while I'm attempting to understand whatever place, event, or practice I'm attempting to understand.

Perhaps the most effective way for me to help you make sense of the previous sentence is to quickly outline one of my research interests—non-routine public events. I frame non-routine public events as social occasions not given over to mechanistic routine, and, much like Turner's (1981) social dramas, they involve performance and enactment. In addition, I define them in large part as the media events identified by Dayan and Katz (1992) as "epic contests of politics and sports, charismatic missions, and the rites of passage of the greats" (p. 1). I expand upon their categories, however, by including the seemingly endless "once-in-a-lifetime" ceremonies commemorating past notable incidents or marking the important milestones of significant institutions. For me the label of non-routine public events encompasses a wide variety of occasions such as a papal mass, the passing of the Olympic torch, the closing of a venerable old sport stadium, the funeral of an ex-president, or the fiftieth anniversary of the Normandy landing. There is an almost inexhaustible list of non-routine public events in today's postmodern world.

Although these events may span a vast range of occasions, my interest in them centers on something they share. The vast majority of us experienced all five of the events mentioned above and most non-routine public events through the alternative of live (or videotaped) coverage fed to us by a few elite media institutions. For all five of these events it was, therefore, the newscasters and reporters who became the authors of our experiences in regard to them. They became the filters of our experience and knowledge. Ordinary people, individuals not in these professions, therefore, have lost their status as "superior knowers" (Gergen, 1991) in regard to these events.

Zelizer (1993) claims of journalists that they "are skilled tellers of events who reconstruct and often displace the activities behind the news" (p. 189). I would add to Zelizer's assertion that journalists also "reconstruct and displace" the meanings behind the events. By contrast, I offer the excavation of personal narratives, with a specific focus on meanings and identities as revealed in the personal narratives of the event-goers. These are the individuals who, for some reason, selected the "other" alternative. They chose or, perhaps, were compelled by accidents of their biographies to attend the event. Through the excavation of their personal narratives, I am able to "see" the event more clearly as they place it within the context of their lives.

Carr (1986) asserts that the act of telling stories has no terminal value in and of itself. The story for Carr is always embedded in some larger temporal context and field. In regard to personal narratives, that larger context involves the temporal stretch of the narrator's life story. A non-routine public event, therefore, has a temporal structure and meaning beyond clock time, beyond the moment, beyond the news. It, the event, resides and can be understood within the context of the event-goers' life stories. In the excavation of their stories I am not, however, looking for THE essence of the event. Rather I am searching to place the event and re-present it within the lived experiences and identities of the event-goers. By doing so I offer an alternative to the disembodying and often normalizing readings of these events promoted by newscasters, reporters, and other "reconstructors" of the human experience.

"So what exactly is it that makes this a communication study?" My answer—what I do is excavate and re-present personal narratives. And while communication certainly does not "own" the exclusive rights to the use or examination of personal narrative, what we (at least some of us in our discipline) do understand in regard to personal narrative's liminal status connecting life as lived, life as experienced, and life as told can inform our research practices in very distinct ways. In short, I offer one possibility, among many, for researchers grounded in the theoretical sensitivities of the communication discipline and who wish to study lived human experience, person by person—their personal narratives.

Before I move onto my second question, one more issue remains in conjunction with the excavation of personal narratives. Although my research example focuses on non-routine public events, if examined closely many of these events mark beginnings and endings of sorts. Carr (1986) tells us that beginnings and endings naturally cast us into a story mode as we look backward or forward from a particular significant point. As such, I contend that the excavation of personal narratives would be a valuable research exercise in any situation or occasion that marks a significant beginning or ending—birth or death, openings or closings, the start of a new relationship or the demise of an old one. The applications for the excavation of personal narratives may be as extensive as the number of non-routine public events available for our research gaze. I will, however, continue to use my research regarding non-routine public events to demonstrate my points and support my arguments throughout the remainder of this essay.

Question Two—and a Potentially Controversial Answer

My answer to the second question, "What makes this communication study an ethnography?" might be controversial for some. The issue of what constitutes ethnography has been discussed at great length over the past several decades. I joined the conversation when I read Clifford and Marcus (1986), Geertz (1973), and Putnam and Pacanowsky (1983) back in the late 1980s early in my graduate school career. From them I learned that ethnography involves both "doing" and writing. In responding to this second question I focus primarily on the "doing" of ethnography. In answering the final question, I focus more on the writing of ethnography.

For me, whatever else ethnography is, its "doing" requires the researcher to go "there" to understand "them." It's what I learned from Agar (1980), and Lofland and Lofland (1984), and Spradley (1979, 1980). In fact, I unknowingly might even be borrowing the phrase "go there to understand them" from one of them. Please realize, however, that while I believe an ethnographer must go "there" to understand "them," I recognize that part of going "there" might include, in many research undertakings, staying "here," and part of understanding "them" might include a reflexive examination of "me." Under no circumstances, however, at least for me, does ethnography, including the ethnographic excavation of personal narratives, involve simply staying "here" and understanding or studying "me." As such, and here might be some controversy, I find the label autoethnography problematic if, for the social researcher, it means only staying "here" and studying or understanding "me."

I do not, however, find the knowledge gained from self-reflection, introspection, autobiography, or autobiology (Payne, 1996) problematic or of questionable worth. In fact, I believe just the opposite. All knowledge is valuable if it helps the social researcher as a reader or writer gain insight into the human condition. And yet, each different form of knowledge calls for a different set of criteria for judging it and, likewise, each different form of knowledge allows for different types of claims to be made. So while all forms of knowledge are valuable, for me ethnographic knowledge is gained ultimately by going "there," which allows for claims to be made about "them" (remembering "here" may be part of "there" and "me" may be part of "them"). One final note on knowledge and claims. The knowledge gained from staying "here" and understanding "me" can be holographic by nature (see Talbot, 1991) in that in each part we recognize the whole. Knowledge gained from going "there" and understanding "them" (or "we"), however, used to support or supplement the "here" and "me" knowledge, or vice versa, can be much more powerful than knowledge gleaned from the holographic image of "me" when making claims about the social collective.

For now this is enough said regarding claims and knowledge related to going "there" versus staying "here." In my next section, I will address the benefits of understandings gained from the intersection of ethnography, autobiographical detail, and personal narrative. For now I'll leave the discussion of autoethnography and new ethnographies to others (see Bochner and Ellis, 2001; Goodall, 2000), and turn my attention to my rationale for wanting to excavate personal narratives by "doing" ethnography.

Simply put, in my attempt to understand non-routine public events within the temporal span of individuals' lives, my communication study assumes an ethnographic stance because I go "there" to understand "them." For example, in my research on the meaning of non-routine public events such as the closing of Old Comiskey Park, I engage the event-goer in the flow of the event, on their terms, when all their senses are actively engaged in experiencing the event. I walk and talk with them as they make their way to and from the event, as they wait in lines, or as they sit or stand next to me. During this flow the event-goers are hearing the music or other sounds, seeing the visual symbols, tasting the food, smelling the incense, and touching the sacred people and objects (Turner, 1981).

They are physically, emotionally, some perhaps spiritually, as well as cognitively immersed in experiencing the event.

The researcher, then, temporarily joins that experience and through informal yet guided conversation invites the event-goers to reflect on their attendance. A question, "So why is it important for you to be here today," or a comment, "I'm surprised so many people came out to hassle the crowds" are contributions the researcher might interject into the conversation that create that moment of reflection. In the spontaneous interactions of ethnographic encounters, the storyteller is no longer free to monitor his or her speech as he or she normally would in a formal interview (Langellier, 1989). In creating this moment of reflection within the ongoing experience of the event, as the researcher I not only engage the rational, strategic being, but also the nonrational, nonstrategic experiencing body. For a researcher seeking an embodied understanding this move is critical.

In addition to this experiential reason, there are practical considerations for electing an ethnographic approach to understanding non-routine public events as well. Beyond the fact that the one place all the event-goers will be is the event, there is a second practical consideration, one beyond the nature of these events, this one stemming from the nature of personal narrative itself. Stern and Henderson (1993) claim that personal narratives exhibit the trait of site specificity. One gets selected for telling here, while another there. And only rarely are these performances of personal narratives planned, rather they emerge from the mixture of the specific components of the event of narration: the context, the situationally salient identity of the teller (often unwittingly uncovered during the excavation of the narrative), and the current psychological stance of the individual stemming from the interplay of the context and identity (Robinson, 1981). The responsibility of deciding which story to tell, when, and to whom rests in the teller influenced by the context and the "I" of this end point. Each telling of a personal narrative, therefore, has meaning for a specific site and interactional partner, in other words, for a particular event of narration (Polkinghorne, 1988). To collect personal narratives before or after the event (or any other phenomenon) would be to engage a different "I" at a different end point. To collect personal narratives other than ethnographically, going "there" to understand "them," would simply diminish the possibility of witnessing a truly embodied performance.

There is another person, however, who shares in the partnership of the ethnographic encounter with the event-goer, the social researcher. My reasons for selecting an ethnographic approach for the excavation of personal narratives have relevance for this "other" person as well. In regard to the practical, by locating him or herself amidst the ongoing construction of experience, the researcher is able to witness those moments when various individuals, driven by joy or grief, pride or disdain, display their emotions. The researcher observes laughter, tears, an anxious walk, or a silent moment alone. She witnesses those moments that enhance a storyteller's trustworthiness. In other words, in an ethnographic encounter the researcher has contextual clues to help determine whether or not the narrative has situationally relevant coherence and fidelity (see Fisher, 1984, 1987, 1991). Upon noticing these behaviors, watching them first from a respectful distance, she can ascertain if and when it would be appropriate to approach and comment on what she sees. If the moment appears too painful or private, the researcher moves on. It is important to realize that without the use of ethnographic techniques these moments may pass never having been articulated. An occasion for the researcher to access meaning and identity passes, but more importantly, perhaps, an opportunity for the event-goer to tell (and "hear") his story passes as well. Perhaps even an occasion for him to confront an aspect of his identity in the articulation of a personal narrative slips by. Or perhaps, by extension, even an opportunity for the social researcher to engage some aspect of her own identity in the words of others is lost as well.

So "Why is it ethnographic?"

I go "there" to understand "them," and, in "doing" so, I create opportunities for better understanding the lived experience of others as well as for better understanding me.

The Final Question

"How much autobiographical detail/personal information should I include when writing my ethnographic understandings?"

I conclude my contribution to this volume by discussing how the ethnographic excavation of personal narratives will, at times, intersect with the primary identities and personal narratives of the ethnographer. In excavating (the eliciting, witnessing, collecting, and re-presenting) the personal narratives of those in attendance at non-routine public events, there exists the potential for the researcher to recognize some aspect of her primary identities or a storyline from her life story in the personal narratives performed by others. These stories possess a type of narrative fidelity for the researcher. They correspond to some aspect of her identities that, upon hearing, "rings true" for her. In these instances the researcher makes a connection with those she encounters at the level of identity, the most basic level of human understanding (MacIntyre, 1981). This connection then elicits a performance (this could be for an internal audience only) of a personal narrative by the researcher and a possible confrontation when a prereflective identity occurs, this time for the researcher. This performance may contribute new insight and meaning for the event, place, or practice under study.

In the scenario just described, the personal narratives of others precipitate a confrontation with identity on the part of the researcher. The researcher now joins the event-goer, each an investigator of prereflective identities, each a narrator seeking meaning by accessing her of his life story through a personal narrative.

None of this, however, requires an ethnographic encounter or even face-to-face interaction. At one time or another, in reading an interesting short story, while watching an episode of ER, or skimming the third page of the sports section, we all have recognized ourselves in another person's story. Their words elicit a recognition of our story and we connect the past to the present, the "here" with the "not here" of our lives. We assign value to our past behaviors or evaluate some course of action we may have taken, or worse yet, didn't take. Maybe we just catch upon a memory trace that reminds us who we are, and somehow in all of this we gain insight to an identity or meaning. Although an ethnographic encounter is not a necessary condition for these moments of reflection and insight to transpire, it does, nevertheless, because it is an embodied way of knowing which provides a potentially strong catalyst in stimulating access to meanings and identities.

But the question remains, "How much autobiographical detail/personal information should I include when writing my ethnographic understandings?" Based on my ethnographic experiences, I would assume that every ethnographic involvement elicits some insight into some aspect of our identity or past, it does for me, but not all provide a connection to one or another of the ethnographer's primary identities or "star groups" (Turner, 1981). According to Turner, a star group classifies as one "to which we owe our deepest loyalty and whose fate is for us of the greatest personal concern" (p. 145). This group could be a family, a dyadic relationship, an international religious group, an occupation, or a social affiliation. An individual identifies most deeply with a star group and finds fulfillment of her or his major social and personal desires by identifying with such a group. It is in our star groups that we most look for love, recognition, prestige, self-fulfillment and other tangible and intangible benefits and rewards.

Our primary identities, however, consist of more than just our memberships in star groups. Our primary identities include our most significant social and professional roles as well the most compelling and meaningful experiences of our lives. The ethnographer should, I would hope, be a person who devotes time to understanding him or herself. If we are the research instrument then we should have some grasp of who we are and what's important to us. González (2000) recommends the use of guided journaling for ethnographers in pursuit of self-understanding. The guiding ideals for her approach state that journaling should "demonstrate an enlightened need for particular types of insight, an awareness of specific aspects of the human instrument which must be examined and honed in order to improve the quality of field research" (González and Krizek, 1994, p. 16). We should, therefore, know something about our membership in star groups, our most significant social roles, and our own life story so that we can recognize intersections when we encounter that "something" in the personal narratives of others.

While I believe Goodall's (2000) position on revealing our ethnographic personality in order to build credibility when writing our ethnographic representations, there is a difference between enlightening our readers in regard to our "ethnographic stance" and connecting our personal narratives to the personal narratives of those we encounter. I believe at times there is too much of the former and not enough of the latter. I find this somewhat ironic. After years of ethnographers only identifying themselves as white males (if that), it seems that some have made the ethnographic conversion as an avenue to a personal catharsis—as a way to tell others about what they eat or drink, about their neuroses, about their past. At times we simply tell our readers about who we are without connecting to broader cultural discourses or issues. Certainly we need to recognize our connections and write about them, but mainly as these connections further illuminate the reader's understanding of the cultural event, place, or practice.

As an ethnographer interested in excavating personal narratives in order to understand aspects of lived human experience, I move between the roles of editor and author in my ethnographic representations. The extended quote opening this essay provides an example of both. The important issue to remember here is that the event (or place or practice) and/or the event-goers assume the role of a facilitator, a relational partner of sorts in the constitution and reconstitution of identity. From the smell of the incense to the emotion of a patriotic song, from the tears of a woman weeping over her dead husband as she pays her respects at a funeral of a president to the words of an event-goer remembering his father, all aspects of the social phenomena we study possess the power to spark a story within us about us. We need to recognize and write about the times when our identities and personal narratives intersect with those we encounter. For me this isn't an option, it is an ethnographic requirement.

Preskill and Torres (1999) tell us that questions are the gateway to knowledge. I suggest that ethnographers, whatever their theoretical disciplines, should ask themselves important questions about their ethnographic scholarship and their disciplinary contributions. For those of us raised in communication, I have responded to some of these questions by focusing on issues of personal narrative, labeling my approach the excavation of personal narratives. There certainly are more answers than the ones I've provided. For me the important thing, however, is not whether or not my answers to the three specific questions I pose in this essay are "correct," but rather that I've taken the time to ask these questions and that I have answers that make sense for me. There was, however, a fourth question—"Who am I"—implied in this essay that ethnographers need to consider if they are to be skilled at their craft and move beyond inscribing their ethnographic stance (Goodall, 2000) to contributing meaningful personal narratives. If we are the research instrument and if it is our responsibility to decide when and how to inscribe ourselves in our ethnographic re-presentations, then we must take the time and do the work to know ourselves (excavate our own personal narratives) as sons and daughters, lovers and neighbors, men and women before we tell our readers what we know about others.

References

Agar, M. H. (1980). *The professional stranger: An informal introduction to ethnography.* Orlando, FL: Academic Press, Inc.

Bochner, A. P., and Ellis, C. (2001). *Ethnographically speaking: Autoethnography, literature, and aesthetics.* Walnut Creek, CA: Alta Mira Press.

Carr, D. (1986). *Time, narrative, and history.* Bloomington, IN: Indiana University Press.

Clifford, J., and Marcus, G. E. (Eds.). (1986). *Writing culture: The poetics and politics of ethnography.* Berkeley, CA: University of California Press.

Dayan, D., and Katz, E. (1992). *Media events: The live broadcasting of history.* Cambridge, MA: Harvard University Press.

Fisher, W. R. (1984). Narration as a human communication paradigm: The case of public moral argument. *Communication Monographs, 51*: 1–22.

———. (1987). *Human communication as narration: Toward a philosophy of reason, value, and action.* Columbia, SC: University of South Carolina Press.

———. (1992). Narration, reason, and community. In R. H. Brown (Ed.), *Writing the social text: Poetics and politics in social science discourse* (pp. 199–217). New York: Aldine de Gruyter.

Geertz, C. (1973). *The interpretation of cultures.* New York: Basic Books, Inc., Publishers.

Gergen, K. J. (1991). *The saturated self: Dilemmas of identity in contemporary life.* New York: Basic Books, Inc., Publishers.

González, M. C. (2000). The "four seasons" of ethnography: A creation-centered ontology for ethnography. *International Journal of Intercultural Ethnography, 24*: 623–650.

González, M. C., and Krizek, R. L. (1994). *Indigenous ethnography.* Paper presented at the Western Speech Convention, San Jose, CA.

Goodall, H. L. (2000). *Writing the new ethnography.* Walnut Creek, CA: Alta Mira Press.

Krizek, B. (1992a). Remembrances and expectations: The investment of identity in the changing of Comiskey. *Elysian Fields Quarterly, (11)*2: 30–50.

———. (1992b). Goodbye old Friend: A son's farewell to Comiskey Park. *Omega Journal of Death and Dying, 25*: 87–93.

Langellier, K. M. (1989). Personal narratives: Perspectives on theory and research. *Text and Performance Quarterly, 9*: 243–276.

Lofland, J., and Lofland, L. H. (1984). *Analyzing social settings: A guide to qualitative observation and analysis* (2nd ed.). Belmont, CA: Wadsworth Publishing Company.

MacIntyre, A. (1981). *After virtue.* Notre Dame, IN: University of Notre Dame Press.

Payne, D. (1996). Autobiology. In C. Ellis and A. P. Bochner (Eds.), *Composing ethnography: Alternative forms of qualitative writing* (pp. 49–75). Walnut Creek, CA: Alta Mira Press.

Polkinghorne, D. E. (1988). *Narrative knowing and the human sciences*. Albany, NY: State University of New York Press.

Preskill, H., and Torres, R. T. (1999). *Evaluative inquiry for learning in organizations*. Thousand Oaks, CA: Sage Publications, Inc.

Putnam, L. L., and Pacanowsky, M. E. (Eds.). (1983). *Communication and organizations*. Beverly Hills, CA: Sage Publications, Inc.

Richardson, L. (1990). Narrative and sociology. *Journal of Contemporary Ethnography, 19*: 116–135.

Robinson, J. A. (1981). Personal narratives reconsidered. *Journal of American Folklore, 24*: 58–85.

Rosenwald, G. C., and Ochberg, R. L. (1992). *Storied lives: The cultural politics of self-understanding*. New Haven, CT: Yale University Press.

Spradley, J. P. (1979). *The ethnographic interview*. Orlando, FL: Harcourt Brace Jovanovich College Publishers.

— — —. (1980). *Participant observation*. Orlando, FL: Harcourt Brace Jovanovich College Publishers.

Stern, C. S., and Henderson, B. (1993). *Performance: Texts and contexts*. New York: Longman.

Talbot, M. (1991). *The holographic universe*. New York: HarperCollins Publishers, Inc.

Turner, V. (1981). Social dramas and stories about them. In W. J. T. Mitchell (Ed.), *On narrative* (pp. 137–164). Chicago: The University of Chicago Press.

Zelizer, B. (1993). American journalists and the death of Lee Harvey Oswald: Narratives of self-legitimation. In D. K. Mumby (Ed.), *Narrative and social control: Critical perspectives* (pp. 189–206). Newbury Park, CA: Sage Publications, Inc.

CHAPTER 13

Telling the Story of Birth

PAAIGE K. TURNER

Telling the story of birth:

Of all the things I recall about my daughter's birth, the one thing that seems the most out of place is hearing, "Susan will pick you up for the dance soon," as my daughter's head was crowning. It was the second time that Dana's (the midwife) daughter had called in ten minutes. As I lay on the bed trying to push out a nine pound, twenty-one inch little girl I thought, "Why is she taking this call?" I had done everything I could to get the birth I wanted . . . natural, beautiful, well-planned and still focus was being shifted away from me.

The moment of birth, the emergence from one world to another, is perhaps one of the most personal moments a mother or child will ever experience. Our private experiences, however, are often defined and negotiated in very public ways such that the boundaries between the personal or private and the public become reciprocally fluid, negotiated, and political (Clark and Lange, 1979; Deetz, 1992; Fraser, 1989; Parkin, 1990). In this essay, I explore how desires, including my own, are inhibited and enabled by American cultural beliefs and practices that locate the experience of birth within the public domain. Specifically, the belief that individual freedom and control are gained by participating in forms of bureaucracy that simultaneously offer freedom while taking control.

In America, the telling of birth stories are ritualized performances that reflect and construct our beliefs about the relation of science and nature, our private and public bodies, and control and freedom, (Davis-Floyd, 1992; Pollock, 1999; Turner, 2002). According to Pollock (1999), the birth story is cultural, personal, and metamorphic. The telling is simultaneously a performance of birth, body, and macro-micro politics where the center shifts and moves. They are continually constituting and reconstituting public and private yet they are always both. Birth stories are the origins of our beliefs about birth and the counter rituals that re/ritualizes. They are told in, around, and against other narratives; the personal narratives of those giving, attending, regulating, and even studying birth. For me, the stories are heard against past stories that are made present as images reverberate, reinforce, and challenge the narrative to which I am currently listening. Or, sometimes, the narrative I am listening to reconstructs my understanding of the past—my past.

It is in the interplay of the stories told by certified nurse-midwives (practicing with a license), lay midwives (practicing without a license), and my own experiences as a client and researcher that I have come to see that all of us rejected bureaucratic control while at the same time seeking bureaucratic protection. Bureaucracy's goal to eliminate ambiguity and provide certainty offered to us the opportunity to have the freedom we sought in the form of an absolute. In doing so, however, we became caught in a web of discursive closure (Deetz, 1992). We accepted and did not challenge the system that defined what would be an appropriate time, place, or mode of discourse (Ferguson, 1984; Fraser, 1989). As such we defined freedom as "freedom from the decisions of others rather than the freedom to participate in collective decisions" (Deetz, 1992, p. 155).

For the birth of my first child I chose a freestanding birth center run by certified nurse-midwives over a hospital birth or a birth with a lay (paid, unlicensed midwife). I neither wanted my labor to be "on the clock," nor wanted the hospital or it's schedule to tell me who would hold my hand. I wanted to be free from the bio-medical community's control where my body would be viewed as a machine waiting to breakdown (Bortin, Alzugaray, Dowd, and Kalman, 1994). I wanted to know that as my ability to control my body ebbed away, the person that *I* had picked would take it up and carry it forward for me.

I chose the certified midwife because if needed she could walk into the hospital with me and, even though I would be under a doctor's direct care, she could still supervise my labor. She was licensed (e.g., sanctioned) to walk across the threshold of the hospital and provide them with medical information that could be vital to my health and baby. After the birth of my child, I talked with lay (e.g., unsanctioned) midwives and their stories reinforced that I had made the "right" decision. While none of them ever left or failed to provide needed information, they all told stories concerning the precarious situation they were in when they entered a hospital.

One such story was told by Margaret (a lay midwife) about a situation that almost caused her to leave midwifery. During one transport where the baby required major resuscitation, she went in and gave the people the straight scoop. "They . . . were grateful for the information I gave them, you know, they indicated that my efforts had saved the baby's life." Later the doctor grilled the parents as to whether the midwife had been licensed or not. According to Margaret, the doctor told the parents,

> If she wasn't licensed, if she was licensed that's fine. She handled this appropriately. But if she wasn't licensed, she practiced medicine without a license and needs to be reported, because she's practicing illegally. And the dad looked at the guy and said, "Well, what did you want her to do?" And he said, "She should not have practiced medicine. She should have called an ambulance. You know? Wrapped the baby up and called the ambulance. And the dad just looked at him totally dumbfounded, like, you know, I wouldn't have my daughter, you know, if she had done that.

Margaret did eventually come under investigation for this incident, but the parents supported her and told the investigator that the father had "caught" the baby and that Margaret was just "a friend" attending the birth. This was the second time Margaret had come under investigation and it scared her. She considered quitting, but instead chose to work towards a licensing law for direct-entry or lay midwives. The retelling of this story positions the father, not Margaret, as the hero. It further positions the doctor as the enemy rather than the licensing system. Both certified-nurse midwives and lay midwives told me stories where individual doctors and nurses created problems for them but never did they call into question the larger system (Turner, 1998).

While we talked about the benefits and limitations of licensing, neither one of us stepped outside the discussion of licensing to comment on the fact that the legal system had created a threat that only it could eliminate. Indeed, in the state that Margaret operated, a person assisting a birth without a license could be charged with either a misdemeanor or a felony, depending on if they were a nurse or a lay midwife. Nurses, who were licensed by the nursing board, were typically charged with a misdemeanor. Lay midwives, however, were typically charged with felonies under the Medical Practice Act, which prohibited the practicing of midwifery without a license. These laws, presumably, deferred because of the varying degrees of risk associated with the differing individuals. However, the differing penalties also discursively positioned identical behaviors on the part of nurses and lay midwives as more or less deviant, depending upon the degree to which the individual participated in the larger, biomedical community.

What I didn't realize was that because of those laws and my desire to choose who would be with me throughout my labor—regardless of the location—my ability to have the birth attendant I wanted was being defined. Thus, while the licensing laws may have served as a structure to ensure "quality care," they also performed a specific ideological function (Fraser, 1989). That is, the licensing laws interpreted my needs for support and a safe labor according to officially sanctioned interpretations that defined licensing as the only appropriate means for establishing competence—and I opted for the license.

"Susan will pick you up for the dance soon." I worked so hard to have the birth I wanted, to ensure my freedom to choose and retain control. Yet, as my daughter's head crowned, the focus had shifted from me. As a "client," I should have received her full attention. After all I (and my insurance company) was paying for it; I had talked with her about what I wanted, and I was in labor. Yet, I never said anything, even during the "exit interview" when I was asked if there was anything I would have changed about my experience. Ferguson (1984) argues, "it is important to remember the complexity of bureaucratic domination, its ability to both *suppress* and *produce* its victims" (p. 90). As a client, I felt suppressed by the formal procedures that were in place to provide feedback about my experience. As a part of the post-birth appointment, the midwife, who had assisted the birth, asked us if there was anything we felt uncomfortable with during our birth. I said "no." I remember feeling that I had missed my opportunity to say that I found it inappropriate for the midwife to receive personal phone calls during labor, but the formal space for comment was gone and I didn't know how or to whom to bring it up. It was as if the formal space negated other options for me to express my needs. "Do it here, now, or forever hold your peace because you got your chance." It was not till much later, in a different context, that I got another "formal" chance.

During a casual conversation with the other birth attendants, they mentioned some problems they had with Dana. "It seemed kind of strange that she took a phone call during my labor," was my response. Their whole bodies gave off a sigh of relief. Julie (a birth assistant) said that they had not wanted to say anything because I had said that my birth was perfect, but that they were very upset with Dana. She had done some other things that they thought were unacceptable (e.g., leaving the premises during labor), and they had filed a complaint with the licensing board. They asked me if I remembered if she brought the phone on the bed. I said she had and asked why that was important. Julie told me that Dana had "broken the sterile field" and asked me if I would be willing to talk with the licensing board. I said sure.

Later, I realized that something was bothering me. In all of my the stories, I listened to I never heard a midwife talk about the need for a sterile field. In fact, they talked about women who gave birth on couches, in tubs, or even on the toilet—hardly a sterile environment. Ferguson (1984) states: "to embrace the administrative roles would be to lose those dimensions of oneself that do not coincide with one's organizational roles" (p. 91). It was clear to me that they were concerned about the quality of care that my original midwife provided. Yet, rather than address it as an issue of midwifery (e.g., she was not with woman) they addressed it in terms that would be deemed appropriate by the licensing review board because that was the only discourse that would be heard. In doing so, however, they defined themselves and midwifery according to the vocabulary offered by the licensing board. And while that vocabulary was not consistent with their beliefs, it did offer them a form of protection. All they had to do was accept the licensing board's control to define what would count as a valid argument.

While I would like to say that I saw this and chose not to participate, I didn't. I had sought to reject the bureaucratic control a hospital would impose upon my body, yet I was happy to use some of those same channels to reprimand the midwife. While I was upset that she did not attend my labor in the manner that I wanted, my confirmation that she broke the sterile field was the only thing I offered. I didn't talk about how I interpreted my own need to "be with woman." My fear of being alone during labor, my desire to be—for once—the absolute center of attention, my longing to be able to focus my mind and body on my own self and not have to puzzle out someone else's behavior, my hope that I could be so caught up in a moment that everything else falls away, to give birth. Instead, the midwives and I accepted that we had to arrange our needs and concerns in a manner that would be recognized. In doing so, however, we participated in what Fraser (1989) calls the internalization of need interpretations (p. 169). Our needs were interpreted as the need to ensure compliance with current licensing requirements. This interpretation, however, can and did work to all of our disadvantage. It closed off discussions about why we could only appeal to the sterile field and not to "being with woman." We never talked about why there were two criminal penalties rather than one. We never discussed why a father could "catch" a child without a license, but not a midwife. Instead, we told a story that allowed us to place the ritual of birth within the public domain, and subsequently, gained and lost both control and freedom.

References

Bortin, S., Alzugaray, M., Dowd, J., and Kalman, J. (1994). A feminist perspective on the study of home birth: Application of a midwifery care framework. *Journal of Nurse-Midwifery*, *39*(3): 142–149.

Clark, L. M. G., and Lange, L. (1979). *The sexism of social and political theory.* Toronto: University of Toronto Press.

Davis-Floyd, R. (1992). *Birth as an American Rite of Passage.* Berkeley, CA: University of California Press.

Deetz, S. A. (1992). *Democracy in an age of corporate colonization.* Albany: State University of New York Press.

Ferguson, K. E. (1984). *The feminist case against bureaucracy.* Philadelphia: Temple University Press.

Fraser, N. (1989). *Unruly practices: Power, discourse and gender in contemporary social theory.* Minneapolis, MN: University of Minnesota Press.

Parkin, W. (1990). Private experiences in the public domain: Sexuality and residential care organizations. In J. Hearn, D. L. Sheppard, P. Tancred-Sheriff, and G. Burrell (Eds.), *The sexuality of organizations* (pp. 110–124). London: Sage.

Pollock, D. (1999). *Telling bodies: performing birth*. New York: Columbia University Press.

Turner, P. K. (1998). *Labor as Work: The Discursive Construction of* Midwifery. Unpublished Doctoral Dissertation. Purdue University, West Lafayette, IN.

— — —. (2002). Is childbirth with midwives natural?: The gaze of the feminine and the pull of the masculine. *Qualitative Inquiry, 8*: 652–669.

CHAPTER 14

Watching the Watchers

Making Sense of Emotional Constructions Behind Bars

SARAH J. TRACY[1]

For nearly one year, I engaged in participant observation with correctional officers at a county jail and state women's prison. My quest? To better understand and tell a story about the emotional dilemmas faced by those who keep, watch, care for, and guard society's deviants. Criminal justice research paints a picture of correctional officers as hardened, cynical, stressed out, ritualistic and alienated (Poole and Regoli, 1981; Walters, 1986)—problems that have been linked to high levels of turnover, job dissatisfaction, psychological distress, and a life expectancy of fifty-nine years old (Cheek, 1984). Survey studies have pointed to a number of variables related to officers' stress and burnout, including danger, strained relations with administration and coemployees, lack of influence, negative social image, and lack of social support (Huckabee, 1992). However, the past burnout and stress research with correctional officers has rarely gone beyond measuring certain variables and comparing them to officer's self-reported burnout levels (Tracy, 2001). While past research provides information on the *amount* of stress and burnout among officers, it does little to examine *why* certain variables play a role in the emotional well-being of officers and *how* emotional challenges are constructed through day-to-day work experiences.

This shortcoming is not unique to the criminal justice literature. As noted by Fineman (1996), concepts of emotion have generally been subsumed by

This chapter is based upon data gathered for my dissertation, expertly advised by Stanley Deetz at the University of Colorado. This project was partially supported by the College of Public Programs, Arizona State University.

seemingly more "rational" categories, such as employee morale, attitude, affect, or job satisfaction. This issue is more than one of semantics; these conceptualizations encourage an understanding of emotion as a "state" that can and should be counted or measured, leading to research questions that ask "how much" rather than "what kind" (Hochschild, 1983). Solely counting and measuring emotion in organizations, however, is somewhat akin to asking someone at the end of a gourmet meal, "how much taste did it have?" Such a question ignores the subtleties of spices and textures, the spiffiness of presentation, and the harmony of flavors working together. Likewise, a sole focus on "how much emotion" glosses the nuances and contextualized nature of interactions and communicative processes—fundamental ingredients of the organizational emotional experience that can best be understood through observing "real-time" emotion.

To better flesh out the interaction picture, I thus turned to ethnographic methods. As Fineman (1993) declared, "the method makes the feelings" (p. 221). As such, I utilized "a 'tracer' form of ethnography where the investigator follows people and their moments over time, in situ" (Fineman, 1993, p. 222). Over the course of eleven months—May 1999 through March 2000—I traced the work life of correctional officers, interacting with 109 research participants who were employed at a county mixed-gender jail, Nouveau Jail (NJ) and a state women's prison, Women's Minimum (WM). The primary source of data was fieldnotes from 80 hours of shadowing correctional officers in their day-to-day work and 33 hours of serving as a participant or participant-observer during training sessions. Additionally, I examined a number of training documents and conducted 22 in-depth recorded interviews with correctional employees: 10 with NJ officers, nine with WM officers, and three with organizational supervisors, including the WM Warden, NJ Captain and NJ Sheriff.[1]

This chapter provides a mini case study that illustrates several puzzling emotional constructions among officers and how these constructions make sense in light of the norms and contradictions that mark the correctional officer profession. My hope is that the overview demonstrates how participant-observation was a critical method for being able to understand how and why correctional officers evidence certain emotional constructions.

Emotion Behind Bars

Upon entering the correctional scene, I knew that I was interested in better understanding the burnout and emotion dilemmas faced by this largely misunderstood and ignored group of workers. Specifically, I wanted to better understand how officers engaged in "emotion labor," a term coined by Hochschild (1983) and considered to be work that includes "knowing about, and assessing as well as managing emotions, other people's as well as one's own" (Hochschild, 1993, p. x). Furthermore, using social constructionist notions of emotion (e.g., Harré, 1986), and post-structuralist viewpoints of identity formation (Foucault, 1977, 1982), I was interested in understanding how the emotional demeanors of officers were constructed in relation to organizational discourses and micro-practices. The lion's share of past emotion labor research examines employee groups who, as part of their work product, labor to display a pleasant demeanor. These include studies of Disneyland employees (Van Maanen and Kunda, 1989), cruise ship activities coordinators (Tracy, 2000) and supermarket cashiers (Rafaeli, 1989). In contrast, the correctional officers' labor is expected to be unemotional, stoic, and tough as part of their job. Correctional officers likely face many of the same emotion labor hurdles as do police officers (Martin, 1999; Pogrebin and Poole, 1991; Stenross and Kleinman, 1989), and 911 call-takers (Shuler and Sypher, 2000; Tracy and Tracy, 1998). However, little is known about emotional issues among correctional officers—an occupational group that differs from others in having to deal with convicted criminals on a day-to-day, long-term basis. Furthermore, very little research has examined the mundane organizational practices that encourage and construct particular emotional outcomes among employees. Considering all of this, I entered the correctional field with several loosely structured research questions, two that I discuss here: (1) What emotional constructions are evident among correctional officers?, and (2) What organizational discourses normalize, encourage, and make sense of these emotional constructions?

Puzzling Performances

In the early stages of my data collection, I met with a number of "puzzling performances" or emotional stances among correctional officers that, on their face seemed strange, and in some cases, even irresponsible or deviant. While few officers explicitly discussed (admitted?) these emotional constructions, as I shadowed officers in their daily work and took part alongside them in training sessions, I observed officers projecting an us-them mentality, a literalistic attitude, a withdrawn demeanor, and a sense of paranoia.

Officers were generally disdainful of inmates; they called them the "scum of the earth," and "disgusting filth." They seemed cold and detached; oftentimes when inmates or members of the public asked questions, officers either avoided eye contact, or used eye contact as a power game—nonverbally daring others to stare them down. Likewise, even though officers were told that part of their job was to help rehabilitate inmates, they nevertheless evidenced an us-them attitude, displaying a distinct joy at busting inmates and learning they were doing something wrong. For instance, when officers found contraband during inmate strip searches, I heard them refer to it as a "pay-off." One said, "You want to make a bust so bad. It's a wonderful thing to find something." While I heard another exclaim after a search, "We *love* to catch 'em—we LOVE to! It's all a game—who's smarter, them or us." Likewise, in the booking room at Nouveau Jail, I observed an officer whose eyes glittered with excitement after he found a small amount of (what he thought to be) methamphetamine in an inmate's wallet. This officer asked another with anticipation, "Do you think it would be introduction of contraband?" He clearly hoped that he would be able to charge the inmate with this crime.

Furthermore, a fair share of officers seemed to evidence a literalistic, "just tell me what to do" attitude. Indeed, some officers felt as though organizational administrators actually desired unthinking, robot-like employees. One officer said:

> They want you to follow the rules . . . and if in the rule book there's a Y, you either go left or right. . . . The person that doesn't know how to get there is the person that they want, because . . . if you don't know what it is, look it up. It's right there. "What do I do?" It tells you what to do in every situation, so there's no room for you to think.

A number of officers echoed the idea that "thinking too much in this job can get you into trouble." One of the most interesting illustrations of literalistic thinking I observed involved a scenario in which a front lobby officer at Women's Minimum was serving as the facility gatekeeper. An attorney was attempting to gain entrance to visit his inmate client. In order to enter the facility, the lobby officer told the attorney, among other things, that he could not bring in dollar bills because "that's the rule." The officer did not explain the reason behind the rule: that paper money can be transferred easily as contraband to inmates. The frustrated attorney demanded that he be allowed to enter the facility with his dollar so he could use it in the (dollar-accepting) soda machine inside. The officer responded by robotically repeating different variations of, "No dollars allowed inside." I left the scene just as a supervisor emerged and (presumably) solved the dilemma. This situation illustrates how literalistic thinking precluded an officer's ability to consider, or at least articulate, alternative options. Obvious solutions included allowing the visitor to use the staff's soda machine in the adjoining break room or having the escort officer take the attorney's dollar and buy the soda after they all went inside the visitation area. However, the officer merely repeated the rule. Perhaps he did so in a desperate attempt to cling for a resource of power in the situation. Regardless, the incident serves to illustrate the literalistic construction that I observed to be common among a number of officers.

Throughout my research I was also struck by the *withdrawn*, complacent, and detached ways in which many officers approached their job. I observed in multiple training sessions that officers did not ask questions or interrogate problematic issues with supervisors. In one training session, for instance, officers did not complain or question the surprise announcement that no one would be allowed to take a vacation between Christmas and New Year's Day, something that countered ordinary policy. When the jail captain asked if anyone had questions, a couple officers grumbled to themselves and another yelled out sarcastically, "No questions 'cause we're so satisfied, sir!" The captain just laughed, shrugged his shoulders and proceeded in the meeting. This behavior was par for the course; in almost all the training sessions I attended, doodling was a far more popular activity among officers than discussing the issues or asking questions.

I also observed this withdrawn attitude among officers who failed to question or attempt to change organizational policies that appeared to be problematic. For instance, at Nouveau Jail I asked a tenured officer why it was fair that *medium*-security inmates were locked down in individual cells for the majority of the day, while *maximum*-security inmates were only locked down at night (and could spend the rest of the time hanging out with other inmates in the dayroom). She responded that being locked down was an incentive for the medium-custody inmates to go to life skills or G.E.D. classes. However, she did not attend to the issue of fairness and mentioned that it was not worth her time to pursue the issue with supervisors. In contrast, an officer who had been with the jail for just six months agreed with me about the unfairness issue and said he wondered the same thing. However, this officer also admitted that he had not asked colleagues or superiors about this seeming inconsistency, because he was still "learning the ropes" and did not want to be a "know-it-all." While the longer-tenured and shorter-tenured officers differed in their reasons, both believed they should keep their questions to themselves.

Officers also appeared suspicious and paranoid. As one officer explained in an interview, "You're constantly on the look-out. You're constantly wondering whether the inmates are going to have a bad day, react and jump on you." Indeed, when I hung out with officers, they rarely looked directly at me; rather their eyes roamed behind and around me, ready and waiting to spot trouble. Officer comments also suggested mistrust of colleagues and organizational administrators. One said, "You never know whether someone wants your job." Officer's watchfulness and suspicion stayed with them even when they left the doors of the facilities to go home. I held my officer interviews in various restaurants, and noted that 18 of my 19 interviewees chose a chair that faced *out* toward the restaurant during my interviews (rather than in toward the wall). One officer explained, "I'm always aware of where I'm sitting, where my back is. And that's something I've kept with me." Another said, "I find myself fighting to not be so paranoid. I'll go to the store . . . and I'll look at somebody and you'll think, he looks like an inmate. I have no idea where it comes from." Officers commented in interviews that their family perceived them to be overly protective. Several indicated that their paranoia negatively affected their marriage; one even thought paranoia played a role in his recent divorce. Indeed, I found myself to be increasingly paranoid and untrusting as I spent time in the correctional field, eyeing strangers with suspicion and even envisioning fictionalized encounters in which I might have to talk tough or get into a fight![2]

As discussed, correctional officers evidenced an us-them attitude, literalism, withdrawal and paranoia. A goal of my research was to make sense of these emotional demeanors. As I spent more time with the officers, and began analyzing my data, I realized that these emotional constructions, while puzzling prima facie, make sense in light of the organizational structures and emotional norms that shape the micro-practices of the work routines of officers.

Making Sense of Emotional Constructions Through Organizational Norms and Contradictions

From a Foucauldian viewpoint, discourse transmits and produces power, which in turn continuously produces and constitutes the self (Foucault, 1977, 1982). From this point of view, identity is constructed in relation to surrounding organizational discourses and norms. Through an interpretive analysis of data sources including training sessions, officer and administrator interviews, training manuals and correctional day-to-day behavior, several organizational "norms" emerged as integral to the construction of emotion among correctional officers. I use the word "norms" to refer to organizational expectations for officer behavior, rather than because they are accurate descriptions of the ways members usually behave (Bettenhausen and Murnighan, 1985). Organizational norms are communicated not only through supervisor mandates and official organizational messages (Sutton, 1991), but also through informal communication channels and peer control (Barker, 1993).

Probably the strongest and most often repeated organizational expectation for officers at both Nouveau Jail and Women's Minimum was that officers should continually suspect and mistrust inmates. In officer training sessions supervisors discussed how inmates were "game players" who sat around "24-7" looking for ways to "set you up" and "suck you in." A training manual warned that "inmates will use flattery and appeal to your ego," and in a session on "working with the female offender," officers watched a video called "con games inmates play," and took home an "employee susceptibility traits self-test."

Officers were also encouraged to *be tough* and *maintain detachment*. The "be tough" norm was infrequently espoused officially by organizational superiors; it rather served as an implicit message sent through physical training sessions and various correctional officer activities. For instance, hours of physical training taught officers how to hold, take-down, hit, kick, cuff, and apply pressure points to inmates. During these training sessions, officers also volunteered to be sprayed with mace or hooked up to inmate restraining/punishment devices so they could

"prove" to other officers that they could "take it." Officers reiterated the importance of toughness in their informal talk, saying things like a good officer is
"hard" and "not a chocolate heart." They would also occasionally engage in tough
banter with each other, telling dirty jokes, bragging about their latest sexual
exploits and making fun of inmates. Indeed, "talking tough" is a common social
ritual among criminal justice employees, serving, among other things, to serve as
a "social test" to ensure that coemployees can be relied upon to back each other
up in an emergency (O'Donnell-Trujillo and Pacanowsky, 1983).

Confusing the situation, however, was the fact that officers were also
expected to *respect* and *nurture* inmates. Espousing philosophies common to
supervisors at both facilities, the Women's Minimum volunteer trainer said,
"Speak [to inmates] as you want to be spoken to, just as we do with our kids,"
and the Nouveau Jail captain said, "Treat them like human beings, give them a
little dignity and respect." Officers manifest this norm in their talk, saying, for
instance, that officers should not "snub their noses" at inmates. Closely affiliated
with the respect norm, officers were also expected to nurture, listen to, interact
with, and protect inmates. Supervisors said that good officers, "have to believe
they can help," and training manuals maintained that "interacting with inmates is
essential for the development of a positive climate." Officers also discussed the
ways they should serve as a nurturer. For instance, many officers referred to
inmates in child-like metaphors, and explained how their role was to care for and
protect inmates.

Officers' work was also structured by norms about rule following. On the
one-hand, officers were expected to *follow the rules*, and be consistent in "writ-
ing-up" inmates and fellow officers for rule infractions. Indeed, supervisors and
line officers alike internalized, memorized, and continually repeated the organizational mantra that officers should be "firm, fair and consistent." However, at the
same time, officers received stronger and more frequent messages that they
should *be flexible*, use common sense, and treat cases and situations on an individual basis. I observed supervisors verbally denigrate officers who "wrote up"
inmates when a "good talking to" would have worked just as well. Likewise, officers said they preferred colleagues who were not "badge happy."

While most of the rules for officers directly dealt with their experiences with
inmates, officers' work was also marked by norms that structured their relationships with one another. First, officers often heard that they should *rely on each
other* for support and back each other in a crisis. For instance, trainers told officers that they should feel comfortable talking to one another or to institutional
counselors, especially if they were having trouble with a particular inmate. An
informal facet of this norm was that officers were unofficially supposed to *keep
officer problems among officers* and refrain from "running to the boss" about colleague missteps. Indeed, officers who "told on" each other were ridiculed by
inmates and officers alike, being called "snitches."

At the same time, officers were officially encouraged to *inform on each other* if they saw colleagues engaging in behavior that was against the rules. They were also told in various ways that they should not "be needy." The paramilitary organizational structure, separation of duties and physical layout of the facilities implicitly sent the message that officers should be emotionally independent. Organizational training sessions explicitly told officers that they should not turn to each other for personal support. For instance, one trainer said, "If you want to talk about your personal life, there's two times to do it—at role call and at home." Role call, saturated with employee announcements, usually lasted 10–15 minutes.

As I classified myriad data from interviews, shadowing, and training programs into "organizational norms," I began to see how the discourses that characterize correctional work life are largely contradictory and dilemmatic in nature. As outlined above, officers face organizational expectations Like the following: to respect inmates, nurture and protect inmates, suspect inmates, be tough and detached, follow the rules, be flexible, and rely on each other and not be needy. My analysis, organization and labeling of the norms purports a clear-cut representation of the organizational edicts—something that is far from the scattered fashion in which the norms were presented and absorbed in the correctional setting. Table 1 summarizes these contradictory tensions and the norms encompassed by each tension.

Table 1. Contradictory Tensions That Mark the Correctional Officer Job

Organizational Norms in Tension		*Contradictory Tension*
Respect inmates	Suspect inmates	Respect↔Suspect
Nurture inmates	Be tough	
	Maintain detachment	Nurture↔Discipline
Follow rules and procedure	Be flexible	Consistency↔Flexibility
Rely on others	Don't be needy	Solidarity↔Autonomy
Handle problems among officers	Inform on fellow officers	

When I articulated these contradictions to officers late in my research, many shook their head, smiled wryly and agreed. However, employees rarely explicitly acknowledged or discussed the contradictions. Organizational structures and training sessions obscured how much of correctional work is intrinsically paradoxical. For instance, when officers did inquire about contradictions, supervisors would often soothe their concerns by saying, "Well, just be professional." Despite the fact that officers did not explicitly discuss these norms, or the contradictions among them, I argue that they nevertheless played an important role in the construction of emotion among correctional officers.

First, consider the *us-them mentality*. Why would officers, who are supposed to be helping inmates get back on track in their life, be excited when inmates did something wrong? Although officers are supposed to nurture and empathize with inmates, the norm of suspecting inmates is even stronger. Furthermore, the central duty of correctional officers is to monitor inmates—which includes conducting strip searches, doing rounds, overseeing visitation, and simply watching. While these duties make up the primary share of correctional officer work, I found that officers only occasionally catch inmates in wrongdoing, and thus, officers rarely see tangible "fruits" of their monitoring efforts. As one officer said, "Unlike a carpenter or even a computer worker, at the end of the day, you have nothing to show for your work. Here the goal is to do as much as possible to *prevent* incidents." Considering this, it should come as no surprise that, just as street police officers strive to construct drama and excitement in their rather mundane work (Trujillo and Dionisopoulos, 1987), correctional officers likewise find a thrill in "catching" or "busting" inmates; it serves as "proof" to officers that their never-ending, monotonous monitoring routines are actually important.

The literalistic construction also make sense when we consider how officers have to balance contradictory organizational expectations, be consistent with the rules, yet act with flexibility. A small minority of officers were skilled at manipulating organizational rules in ways that allowed them to *feel* consistent while *maintaining* flexibility. However, others saw following rules "by the book" as a way to keep themselves out of trouble. Furthermore, rules served as one of few resources of power for correctional officers. Reconsidering the aforementioned officer's literalistic reaction to the attorney's request to take a dollar bill into the visitation area, the officer could appear to be respectful but still get his way by robotically repeating, "Sorry, those are the rules."

A *withdrawn* construction is also plausible and should be expected when we consider several organizational norms. First, when officers offered suggestions or asked questions during training sessions, supervisors often met them with bureaucratic explanations that discouraged further discussion. In fact, trainers directly rewarded non-question-asking by allowing trainees to leave early if they did not generate enough discussion. Furthermore, I found that officers felt stymied in their attempts to formally change organizational procedures or alert administrators about inmate problems. For instance, one officer told me that he was not going to write up inmates any more for rule infractions, saying, "It's frustrating because you write them up and then they [administrators] just let it go. And then the inmates just laugh at you." One way to avoid frustration was to withdraw from the process altogether.

Officers' withdrawn emotional construction also makes sense considering how "not caring too much" ironically assisted officers in their endeavors to attend to the organizational norm that they treat inmates with respect. Supervisors suggested, and officers seemed to agree, that by not learning the details of an inmate's (potentially heinous) criminal background, they could better treat inmates nicely. However, not knowing the history of inmates also made it easy for officers to actually ignore the fact that they were working with criminals altogether, and thus, in many ways, this situation encouraged a complacent and withdrawn emotional construction. By not caring too much, officers could avoid inmate hassles and attend to the organizational expectations that they should respect and nurture inmates.

The construction of *paranoia* also makes sense in relation to organizational discourses in the correctional field. For instance, while officers were told to follow the rules by the book, they also were told to be flexible. In order to achieve this mandate, a number of officers engaged in their own personal brand of creative rule following, a technique that was largely organizationally condoned. However, there was always some uncertainty in whether officers' creative solutions would be judged by supervisors as creatively *flexible* or as creatively *inappropriate*, and thus, managing the tension of Consistency vs. Flexibility may have led to an unintended emotional consequence of paranoia. Indeed, I experienced some mild paranoia myself due to this tension. During my orientations to the facilities, I was told in no uncertain terms that "gum-chewing" was not allowed because "gum can be used by inmates to jam locks." I fully expected to maintain consistency with this rule. However, during the course of my research, officers and supervisors alike offered me gum. I usually accepted, largely because I did not want to appear to be a "goody-goody" researcher. Nevertheless, I was simultaneously paranoid that they could use this as grounds for kicking me out.

A paranoid construction is also understandable considering the mandate that officers suspect inmates as well as the contradictory expectations about trusting colleagues on the one hand, but not being needy on the other. Indeed, a number of officers felt confused about whom they could trust and when they should trust. When officers admitted to colleagues that they were upset about troubling incidents with inmates (e.g., suicides, aberrant behavior, etc.), they often met with unfortunate ends. For instance, after one officer told several colleagues that she would be a "happy woman" if she never had to violently "take-down" an inmate again, she was summoned with a mental health referral herself—an action that suggested she was "just as crazy" as the inmate. Incidents such as these served to reinforce the norm that officers should be continually suspicious, not only around inmates, but also around each other.

Last, withdrawn, literalistic, and paranoid emotional constructions make sense when we consider the potential implications of continually facing contradictions in one's work. As detailed in table 1, officers face the contradictory tensions of Respect vs. Suspect, Nurture vs. Discipline, and Consistency vs. Flexibility, and Solidarity vs. Autonomy. Past research tells us that recipients faced with contradictions usually respond with some combination of confusion, displeasure, and anxiety (Putnam, 1986). Furthermore, family systems theory suggests that people who hear contradictions as *double binds* are susceptible to particularly debilitating emotional reactions. Specifically, people faced with double binds are hypothesized to respond by becoming over-analytical and paranoid, literalistic and/or withdrawn (Watzlawick, Beavin, and Jackson, 1967), feeling states that I also found to be evident among a number of correctional officers. In light of the norms and contradictions facing correctional officers, the puzzling emotional demeanors evidenced by correctional officers are not so puzzling after all.

Conclusion

In the preceding overview, my goal has been to illustrate key claims and arguments central to my research with correctional officers. In closing, I highlight several different ways in which participant observation was central for constructing the study.

First, it was through observation of and interaction with officers that I was struck with the puzzling performances of literalism, withdrawal, paranoia, and the us-them mentality. As one might imagine, these are not popular self-descriptors. I only became aware of them through hanging out in the field. My fieldnotes recorded not only participant behaviors and performances, but also the *absence of* particular behaviors and performances. This was of particular relevance for documenting withdrawn demeanor by officers. Indeed, participant-observation is as much about what is *unsaid* as it is about what is *said* (Denzin, 1997).

Participation also enriched interviews. I oftentimes prompted interviewees with certain organizational performances I had observed in the field. I would ask officers what they thought they were feeling at the time, or how they made sense of the situation. Furthermore, I used earlier participant-observation data to construct preliminary analyses that I then shared with interviewees. Our dialogue about my preliminary analyses provided additional data and took me out of the role of detached expert (Denzin, 1997; Martin, 1992).

Participation was also essential for understanding the ongoing social construction of emotion among correctional officers. By spending time in the field, I felt the construction of certain emotions in myself. For instance, as mentioned, I began to feel both more paranoid and tougher through my experience in the correctional setting. Throughout the research process, I included self-reflective memos in fieldnotes about my involvement and feelings in the scene (Lindlof, 1995). My feelings, and my consistent notations about them, allowed me to better understand and analyze the discursive construction of feelings among my research subjects.

Participant observation and interaction with officers was also key for understanding how particular emotional constructions made sense in light of the norms and contradictions of the job. In summary, the work of correctional officers is structured through organizational norms including: respect inmates, nurture inmates, suspect inmates, be tough and maintain detachment, follow the rules, be flexible, rely on others, and don't be needy. Together, these norms form contradictory tensions, including: Respect vs. Suspect, Nurture vs. Discipline, Consistency vs. Flexibility, Solidarity vs. Autonomy. I never found these norms or contradictions laid out neatly in a training manual or rattled off by an administrator. Rather, they emerged from bits and pieces of field data—from dialogues, stories, interviews, "bitch sessions," personal musings (of doubts, reflections, identity constructions), and eyewitness testimony. Through an awareness and understanding of the ongoing contradictions that construct the correctional organizational structure, researchers can make sense of seemingly strange or otherwise nonsensical emotional performances and officers may see possibilities for myriad responses to work expectations.

Notes

1. I logged a total of 171 research hours yielding 722 single-spaced, typewritten pages of raw data. Readers can refer to S. J. Tracy (2001) for more detail on data sources and analysis procedures.

2. I found these fantasies to be quite surprising and unlikely. I have never been in a physical or verbally threatening fight and am quite sure that I would not fare well if I were to actually get into one.

References

Barker, J. (1993). Tightening the iron cage: Concertive control in self-managing teams. *Administrative Science Quarterly, 38*: 408–437.

Bettenhausen, K. and Murnighan, J. K. (1985). The emergence of norms in competitive decision-making groups. *Administrative Science Quarterly, 30*: 350–372.

Cheek, F. E. (1984). *Stress management for correctional officers and their families*. College Park, MD: American Correctional Association.

Conover, T. (2000). *Newjack*: Guarding Sing Sing. New York: Random House.

Denzin, N. K. (1997). *Interpretive ethnography: ethnographic practices for the 21st century*. Thousand Oaks, CA: Sage Publications, Inc.

DiIulio, J. J. (1987). *Governing prisons: A comparative study of correctional management*. New York: The Free Press.

Fineman, S. (1993). An emotion agenda. In S. Fineman (Ed.), *Emotion in organizations* (pp. 216–224). London: Sage Publications, Inc.

— — —. (1996). Emotion and organizing. In S. R. Clegg, C. Hardy, and W. R. Nord (Eds.), *Handbook of organization studies* (pp. 543–564). London: Sage Publications, Inc.

— — —. (2000). Emotional arenas revisited. In S. Fineman (Ed.), *Emotion in organizations, 2nd edition*. London: Sage Publications, Inc.

Foucault, M. (1977). *Discipline and punish: The birth of the prison*. (A. Sheridan, Trans.). New York: Vintage.

— — —. (1982). The subject and power. In J. Dreyfus and P. Rabinow (Eds.), *Michel Foucault: Beyond structuralism and hermeneutics* (pp. 208–226). Chicago: University of Chicago Press.

Harré, R. (1986). An outline of the social constructionist viewpoint. In R. Harré (Ed.), *The social construction of emotions* (pp. 2–14). Oxford: Basil Blackwell.

Hochschild, A. R. (1983). *The managed heart: Commercialization of human feelings*. Berkeley, CA: University of California Press.

— — —. (1993). Preface. In S. Fineman (Ed.), *Emotion in Organizations* (pp. ix–xiii). Thousand Oaks, CA: Sage Publications, Inc.

Huckabee, R. B. (1992). Stress in corrections: An overview of the issues. *Journal of Criminal Justice, 20*: 479–486.

Lindlof, T. R. (1995). *Qualitative communication research methods*. Thousand Oaks, CA: Sage Publications, Inc.

Martin, J. (1992). *Cultures in organizations: Three perspectives*. New York: Oxford University Press.

Martin, S. E. (1999). Police force or police service? Gender and emotional labor. *Annals of The American Academy of Political and Social Science*: 111–126.

O'Donnell-Trujillo, N., and Pacanowsky, M. (1983). The interpretation of organizational cultures. In M. S. Mander (Ed.), *Communication in transition: Issues and debates in current research*. New York: Praeger.

Pogrebin, M. R., and Poole, E. D. (1991). Police and tragic events: The management of emotions. *Journal of Criminal Justice, 19*: 395–403.

Poole, E. D., and Regoli, R. M. (1981). Alienation in prison: An examination of the work relations of prison guards. *Criminology, 19*: 251–270.

Putnam, L. L. (1986). Contradictions and paradoxes in organizations. In L.Thayer (Ed.), *Organization↔Communication: Emerging perspectives 1* (pp. 151–167). Norwood, NJ: Ablex.

Rafaeli, A. (1989). When cashiers meet customers: An analysis of the role of supermarket cashiers. *Academy of Management Journal, 32*: 245–273.

Shuler, S., and Sypher, B. D. (2000). "Seeking emotional labor: When managing the heart enhances the work experience." *Management Communication Quarterly, 14*: 50–89.

Stenross, B., and Kleinman, S. (1989). The highs and lows of emotional labor: Detectives' encounters with criminals and victims. *Journal of Contemporary Ethnography, 17*: 435–452.

Sutton, R. I. (1991). Maintaining norms about expressed emotions: The case of the bill collectors. *Administrative Science Quarterly, 36*: 245–268.

Tracy, S. J., and Tracy, K. (1998). Emotion Labor at 911: A case study and theoretical critique. *Journal of Applied Communication Research, 26*: 390–411.

Tracy, S. J. (2000). Becoming a character for commerce: Emotion labor, self subordination and discursive construction of identity in a total institution. *Management Communication Quarterly, 14*: 790–827.

———. (2001). Emotion labor and correctional officers: A study of emotion norms, performances and unintended consequences in a total institution. *Dissertation Abstracts International, 6107A*: 2519. (University Microfilms No. AAI99-79409).

Trujillo, N., and Dionisopoulos, G. (1987). Cop talk, police stories, and the social construction of organizational drama. *Central States Speech Journal, 38*: 196–209.

Van Maanen, J., and Kunda, G. (1989). Real feelings: Emotional expression and organizational culture. In L. L. Cummings and B. M. Staw (Eds.), *Research in Organizational Behavior 11* (pp. 43–104). Greenwich, CT: JAI Press.

Walters, S. P. (1986). *Alienation, powerlessness, and social isolation among correctional officers*. Unpublished doctoral dissertation, University of Montana.

Watzlawick, P., Beavin, J. H., Jackson, D. D. (1967). *Pragmatics of human communication: A study of interactional patterns, pathologies and paradoxes*. New York: W. W. Norton and Company.

PART FIVE

Short Stories as
Expressions of Ethnography

CHAPTER 15

Hands

LISA M. TILLMANN-HEALY

Hands gripping the pay phone receiver, stretching the skin taut across my knuckles, I ask, "How bad is it?"

When my father hesitates, travelers' boots seem to cease clopping on the airport tile floor. "He could go today," Dad says.

Holding my composure, I tell him, "I'll meet you there."

"Okay. See you—"

"Dad?"

"Yeah?"

"I love you."

"I love you, too," he replies. "See you at the hospital."

I walk briskly to the ground transportation counter. "Hastings," I tell the man. "I'm in a hurry."

His double snap signals a driver, who nods and hustles over to grab my bags. The hailer opens a back door for me. Climbing in, I tell the driver, "Regina Hospital, please." We speed toward the airport exit.

As urban interchanges and road signs whiz by, I sit twirling and pulling dry skin from my lips. At last, we cross the bridge separating the Twin Cities from Hastings and ascend the long, steep hill whose summit holds Regina. The driver pulls up to the entrance and fetches my suitcases. I lay 55 dollars on his open palm and rush inside.

"Intensive care?" I query, moving past the receptionist.

"Third floor," she responds. I scurry to make the next elevator.

Once upstairs, I pass through double doors leading to the ICU. "Harry Tillmann?" I ask the staff nurse.

"Across the hall, 367."

I enter quietly, thinking he may be asleep. His weary eyes open immediately. "Oh, ooohhh, Lis," he says through a foggy oxygen mask.

175

I gently settle on the edge of his bed. "I missed the wild Wisconsin winter," I tell him, grooming his patchy white hair with my fingertips. "Florida's much too mild in January."

"Right," he says, smiling a bit. He blinks away tears, and we sit together, him gasping for breath with his fluid-filled lungs, me caressing his unsteady hand, sliding my fingers along the spaces between his.

I stare at the eighty years ingrained in my grandfather's hands. Culinary hands that kept enlisted men fed in the second World War. Supple hands that stroked my grandmother's raven hair. Strong hands that repaired the old dam restraining the eager Mississippi. Calloused hands that constructed my father's childhood home on Elm Street. Proud hands that cradled his three boys, and later, eight grandchildren. Paternal hands that carved holiday turkeys. Nurturing hands that cultivated the garden soil that burst open every spring in symphonies of crimson and marigold. Tired hands soothed by sweating glasses of lime Kool-Aid. Forgetful hands that rattled the cup of Yahtzee dice for one too many turns. Aging hands stained with the burgundy of exploded blood vessels. Incorrigible Parkinson's hands that played invisible pianos as he sat in his napping chair, watching "wrastling."

From behind me, I hear, "Lis?"

"Dad!" I respond, standing up.

My father approaches and pulls me to him. We then drag chairs to opposite sides of the bed and sit down, each taking one of my grandfather's quivering palms.

I glance across the bed. Neighboring the crooked pinky my father broke playing basketball, his $15.00 wedding band glistens under the florescent lights.

I look from his hands to my grandfather's to my own. Wide nails, unruly cuticles, short, stubby fingers, prominent veins—Tillmann hands, to be sure. No Sally Hansen models here.

My grandmother shuffles in. She leans down, and I kiss her waiting cheek. We steeple our palms and begin to pray.

— — — —

Four days later, I clutch the side of the mahogany bed as my father strokes the satin that envelops his father's body. Looking down, I see them. Scrubbed clean. Caked with foundation. Folded, one into the other, and wrapped with an onyx rosary. I reach over. Mine, atop my father's, atop his. Perfect, enjoined, hands.

CHAPTER 16

He Touched, He Took

CHRISTINE E. KIESINGER

She cannot say with certainty that it happened on this date, at this time, in this place, with this person.

The only thing she can say with certainty is that "it" happened.

*

" . . . what actually happened is not nearly as important as how you feel about what happened."

— Anne Sexton, *Searching for Mercy Street:*
My Journey Back to my Mother

*

The hazy, elusive quality of certain memories in her life make grasping them difficult, if not impossible. But they come to her again and again, disrupting the most peaceful of moments, calling into question everything she has thought to be true about her life.

Her desire to make sense of these fleeting memories brings her to this act of writing. Pen in hand, she vows to begin not from a stance of historical truth or fact, but from a space of raw emotion.

She will put language to the images and sensations as they come to her.

His breath, hot on her neck.
His scent — an odd mixture of dirt and lysol.
The feel of his hands, rough and calloused, as he places candy in her's —
soft and small.

She will write from her body and all that her body feels during this act of remembering.

177

A repulsion stronger than anything she has ever known.
A feverish longing, a quaking passion.
The desire to flee and kill him, and at the same time, wanting to pull him closer.

She will write with a trembling hand and a broken heart.

She will write with a great deal of sadness for the little girl she was, and for the woman she has become.

She will write with gratitude for her ability to write, with pride in her courage to confront and understand.

She will write with a fierce resolve to regain, what he took when he touched.
This is her story.

* * * * * * * *

He touched, he took . . .

The memories come like
a moving picture.

The scene:
A man,
a child,
a damp, dark basement.

A box of apples quietly spoiling in the far right corner—
their sweet, rotting odor filling the air.

The dirt floor
cool and uneven
under
my small feet.

The muffled sound of a television coming from the room above.

I am
chilled
wet
damp
flushed
repulsed yet . . .
shaking
energized,
confused,
eager

and
wanting.

These images—
move by so
rapidly . . .

(Ah, how powerfully the mind works to repress those things we are not yet prepared
to remember.)

But my body remembers,
my tissues,
my very cells
HOLD
these
memories
in vivid detail.
&
this is why I
shudder
when in his presence
&
this is why I grow
flushed
when I watch
his slippery fingers
grasping a coffee mug
&
this is why I
gag
when I smell the
warm,
pungent
odor
of his
breath.
*
He touched me "there."
You know,
in "that" place . . .

"that" place I am not to speak of,
"that" place I am not to acknowledge,
"that" place I am not to make my own.

He touched me "there,"
&
he took something from me . . .
something core,
fundamental,
something that was
MINE.

He touched me "there,"
&
he took something from me
and I have felt this loss,
an
emptiness,
&
I have lived my life
struggling
to fill this
void—
struggling
to make myself
WHOLE
&
FULL
*

On the day I began remembering, I realized that I allowed him to do what he
did for licorice.
Licorice . . .
mostly black, sometimes red.
Not the long, stringy shoelace kind . . .
Not the harder, stronger, longer pieces with deep ridges,
but stout, fat, round pieces
of licorice,
mostly black,
but sometimes red.

I held the licorice, (4 pieces, maybe 5) in the palm of my hand
until he finished &
when he went away,
I peeled open my palms—slowly.
Hot, sweaty, wet—the licorice I held stained my palms
a black-red.
I never really enjoyed the taste of warm, limp licorice. But I ate it anyway.

Imagine that—
imagine that I allowed him to do what he did for licorice.

As a child,
I thought only of licorice
when he took my hand
and led me to the basement.

Licorice always made me feel better . . .

a few pieces,
just a few
&
I was
momentarily
satiated
calmed
not
too
terribly
empty.

Years later food would become the means through which I would fill
the void and quell the emptiness I felt after he touched me—after he took
an important part of me.

Home alone.
Finally.
I eat like a wild animal
hurriedly
frenzied
but focused, as if in a trance.

I eat.
I cope.

My binges are private,
secret,
but
undeniably
self-expressive
acts.

In the binge moment—
my spirit SCREAMS:

"Fill me . . . that I may not fall through the hole in my heart!"

My body SHOUTS:

Fill me . . . that I might become soft & sedate
that I might go numb
and not feel this pain.

My mind COMMANDS:

"Fill me . . . that I might distract myself from what is real—
that I might distract myself from stumbling upon the truth of my experience."

In the binge moment the child within me is weeping
&
through her tears she whispers:

Feed me, fill me, save me
because I am
hurt & cold & abandoned
&
because

I AM SO HUNGRY
SO VERY HUNGRY

hungry for all of those things you took when you touched.

Food helps me to quiet the force of my memories and the feelings they evoke.
But the quiet is brief and the urge to release—to rid myself of the food—to rid
myself of him is overpowering.

Slam!
The bathroom door closes with force behind me.
The cool, slick tile feels familiar beneath my feet.
The muffled sound of a television coming from the room below is a sound I
welcome.

I purge.
I cope.

The purge . . .
UP & OUT.

Forceful. Shocking. Rocking.
Abrupt to the body.

Heaving . . .
a contraction
&
ah,
the blessed release . . .

My skin:
hot while heaving
cool while releasing.

Orange brown spray against white porcelain
disgusting
smelly
yet
so
utterly gratifying.

Particles of food cling to the toilet bowl,
but they are MORE than just particles of food.

They are pieces of me —
shards of my experience —
a tangible expression of
my rage, my pain, my memories.

Hovering over the toilet,
vomit
dripping from the corners of my mouth,
the adult in me whispers:

"I hate you."
"I hate what you did to me."
"Fuck you."
"I release you."
"I rid myself of you and of those things bad, ugly, and painful."
"You are shit."
"You are waste."

&
"I feel
so

POWERFUL
FLUSHING
you
away."

*   *   *   *   *   *   *   *

She cannot alter the past.

She cannot stop the memories from revealing a truth she is not sure she is prepared to own.

So, she eats to forget and then she flushes him away,
over & over & over again.

*

And this is how it has been for her.

The memories, followed by the binge, followed by the purge—

a dangerous cycle but a necessary one—

a survival strategy without any certain clarity about what it is she is actually surviving.

She has only her hazy memories, the feelings they evoke, and the truth they speak from which to begin understanding why she is who she is, and who she might become.

And so she continues to watch the moving picture in her mind carefully.

She continues to pick up her pen to put language to the texture of the images that move swiftly past her in the oddest of moments. The memories continue to come and her story fills out—grows plump, more vivid, more real.

She willingly rides the emotional roller-coaster when she is around "him," in an effort to "study" him—to watch him closely, as if in doing so she can find an answer to the one question she is certain she will never ask him:

WHY?

She writes from and through her memories with the hope of recovering what he took when he touched—with the hope of rediscovering what was fundamentally
her own.

CHAPTER 17

Happy to be Writing

PATRICIA GEIST-MARTIN

"Happy"

"Happy is gone!" Makenna, my eight-year-old daughter yelled in her high pitched voice of surprise as we pulled into our driveway.

"No, really? Are you sure?" I ask softly, feeling already the shock and devastation I hear in my daughter's voice.

It was dark. The flash of the car's headlights had already passed by the planter where our life-size scarecrow Happy, stood guarding our house since the first of October. After pulling into the garage, we both jumped out of the car to inspect the scene of the crime. Sure enough. No Happy. And no stake that held Happy in place in front of the cobwebs, ghosts, and spiders decorating the front of our house.

"Who would do this?" Makenna whispered. "Why?" "How could they do this?" "Did they take anything else?" "Why?" The questions streamed out with hardly a breath in between as tears began to well up in her eyes.

Later, we discovered that along with Happy, our U.S. flag was missing. My husband, J. C. and I tried to calm Makenna's fears that someone might return to steal other things by telling her that it was probably a teenage prank.

That night at bedtime, she is still struggling with the "Whys" and "How could theys" and so I tried once again to explain.

"Makenna, remember this feeling of loss you are having right now when you are a teenager. Imagine that you are with a group of friends and they say, 'See that scarecrow there. Let's see if you can get it.'"

"I dare you," Makenna chimes in with a devilish grin.

"Yeah, that's right, it is probably a dare. And you run as fast as you can, grab it, and run back to your friends and say 'I got it. I got it.'"

By this time Makenna is laughing and smiling and I am thinking, "Thank goodness, that worked."

Only a moment later, her laughter stops abruptly and her eyes and mouth form a very serious look as she proclaims, "It's still not right!"

"I know, I know," I said as I rubbed her back. I felt with her deeply what it meant to face this form of violation for the very first time.

In the morning, I woke up to find her dutifully making colorful illustrated signs which she insisted we put up all around the neighborhood.

So the two of us walked, talked, stapled, and taped ten signs to telephone poles just in case the pranksters threw Happy in the bushes and someone found her.

But no one called.

Makenna told me in a questioning voice, "that we should put an announcement on the Internet to find our missing "Happy."

She asked J. C. in a telling voice, "Daddy, do you think this might have anything to do with the terrorists?"

The answers don't come easily these days. So the very next day we picked out a new scarecrow. Makenna named her "Happier."

Now I write this story and read it to you, not because I see it necessarily as a good example of a new ethnography, or because I am launching a new ethnographic project on my daughter, or theft, or loss. Instead, it serves as a springboard for three ideas that I would like to offer for a discussion of *Writing the New Ethnography*. The impetus for these ideas are three standout quotes from Goodall's book that I feel best represent the method of new ethnographic writing. In this way, we may consider what it is about writing in ways that voice the self and privilege the writer's personal experience within a culture that actually shape methodological practice.

The first methodological imperative: "Descriptions of the outward world come from deep inside us" (Goodall, 2000, p. 95). The food for thought that engages our methodological spirit necessarily materializes from our own experience. Our methodological practices of interpreting and writing necessarily bring to bear what we know and feel deeply about the outward world within which we live. This is truly the stuff of any good writing. The methodological imperative is to produce in writing, representations that vividly portray meaningful moments, even those that occur in the seemingly mundane, routine course of the day.

I wrote the "Happy" story three days after it occurred. But over the course of those three days, I found myself relaying the story on four separate occasions. Each time, every time there would be this knowing moment of "thank goodness children can't comprehend the horror of what occurred last month." And at the same time, I know that deep within my daughter Makenna, Happy's theft was a horror. And I know that deep within me, I felt a horror in witnessing the beginning of the end of Makenna's age of innocence.

I

A second meaningful methodological imperative from Goodall's book: "The characters in your story have to learn something out about what happens to them. They must grow in understanding, make a realization, and maybe change. . . . Good writing, like conversation, is transformational" (Goodall, 2000, p. 41). As ethnographers, as researchers, as theorists, as teachers, as academicians, we are compelled to write in ways that our characters, (including us), learn something. As well, we are compelled to converse with others about this insight, this contribution. We do this through the stories we write. At times that change or transformation is joyous, but certainly it can be devastating or even simply tender or soothing.

In my "Happy" story it becomes increasingly clear that Makenna is indeed transformed by this single event in her life in ways she still is struggling to figure out. To move in just a few days from a view of the event as a one-time prank to perceiving it as possibly related to the recent terrorists' violence, represents an incredible transformation. As a reader (or listener), we know that she has learned something profound, but we also know that she is changed by learning something that was once inconceivable—that someone could steal someone else's dearly loved possession.

II

Finally, a third meaningful methodological imperative from Goodall's book: "A way of seeing is also a way of not seeing" (Goodall, 2000, p. 73). In my view, a methodological imperative for ethnographic writing is that it be critical. Our way of seeing is also a way of not seeing (Burke, 1935, p. 49). Our way of writing is a way of seeing what we haven't seen before—that which we have taken for granted as obvious or simply viewed as just the way things are. In the process of writing what we see (hear, smell, taste, touch, feel), we begin to learn what meanings and images are privileged or marginalized.

In writing "Happy" I saw so much of Makenna I knew to be true, but writing about her in this one story, I began to see what I hadn't seen or had taken for granted about my daughter: (1) that she could not fathom theft, especially of something so dear to her as Happy (realize that she took over 15 minutes to pick out Happy from the field of scarecrows for sale), (2) that she would take immediate action and make it her responsibility to get Happy back, (3) that she would sense the futility of putting up signs and instead view the Internet as a panacea for resolving the dilemma, and finally, (4) that taking action in this way helped her to move on. Even though in the moments surrounding the discovery of the theft, she couldn't imagine replacing Happy, after taking action she became more comfortable with replacing Happy with a different scarecrow. In a very short time, she has even grown to appreciate the unique features of Happier.

Writing the New Ethnography offers us other vital methodological imperatives that assist us in finding the story in the words we write and re-write and learning what we are becoming, and questioning who we are in this changed world we live in today. I am happy to be writing myself into making some sense of it all.

References

Burke, K. (1935). *Permanence and change: An anatomy of purpose,* (3rd ed.). Berkeley, CA: University of California Press.

Goodall, H. L., Jr. (2000). *Writing the new ethnography.* Walnut Creek, CA: Alta Mira Press.

CHAPTER 18

The Millennium Waltz

A Story in Three-Quarter Time

JULIE M. CRANDALL AND MARY HELEN BROWN

If such a thing exists, on a normal day in Las Vegas, time doesn't much matter. Food, drink, and entertainment are available constantly, 24–7. No clocks are present in casinos because the management does not want to distract the slot players and the players at the gaming tables from the business at hand. Of course, a show might start at a certain time, and one must place bets at the sports book at the right time, but for the most part, day runs into night and night runs into day without notice or comment. Tonight, December 31, 1999, however, time is everything.

I approach the Las Vegas Strip from the south and park in the free parking garage of the Luxor Hotel. I step on the Strip at 3:00 p.m. The casinos shimmer as the sun peeks between the buildings. I hear cheers and screams as I stroll down the strip. "Oh, yeah, 2000." "Only nine hours to go; let's party, baby." The people around me are young, their clothing baggy and loose, their hair a rainbow. They are trying to make a fashion statement although I'm not sure what kind. They speak in a mixture of slang and obscenities.

The streets are lined with small chain-link fences placed to keep revelers from darting into the streets. Police officers guard the fences and offer directions and information to the visitors. They seem tense as they observe the passing crowd. Occasionally, they search backpacks, duffel bags, and purses looking for any sort of contraband, mainly drugs and weapons. An agitated rent-a-cop asks three hookers to move along. They had made their business obvious by making an offer that was overheard by too many people.

I wander into a couple of hotels, the MGM Grand and New York, New York. Both reek of stale beer and cigarettes. Elevator music fills the air, and frenzy fills the table. Celebrity impersonators—Cher, Elvis, and Barbra—belt out their hits. The limits on the gaming tables are raised in honor of the occasion; the standard bet is $25. "Seven," yells a croupier. "Awww, crap," comes a response, "dammit, dammit, dammit." I walk past the slot machines. A klaxon sounds, a light flashes, and a small, frail looking elderly woman jumps and screams, "Yes, yes, yes!" She shows everyone her jackpot and proudly sits awaiting the pay-off. Her jackpot is high enough that it cannot be paid off by the machine. "Congratulations," I say to her, secretly despising her good fortune. I make my way back to the street party.

The sky is turning from orange to a deep purple. The millions of neon lights lining the boulevard flicker on. The neon buzzes as the lights heat up. A siren howls in the distance. Youngsters appear from adjacent streets, obviously dropped off for the experience. The Strip turns into Mardi Gras West, complete with bare breasts and beads. Money, kisses, beads, and sexual favors are offered for quick flashes.

I head down the Strip, but stop when I hear a muffled voice from a megaphone. A doomsday group preaches that the millennium marks the end of the world. Most carry signs, but one carries a megaphone and addresses the crowd: "God will destroy you in hell if you don't repent. Have you ever noticed the word SIN lies in casino? You go inside and you pray to God. 'Oh God, help me hit this slot.' Have you deserted God?" Members of the crowd respond to this and other similar messages. "John 3:16, jerk. Do you know what that says? For God so loved the world that he gave his only begotten son, whosoever believeth in him shall not perish from the earth, but have eternal life. You know that one, Jackass?" Others in the crowd shout out verses. One of the doomsday prophets yells: "You are a sinner for coming to Las Vegas, gambling and then reciting the Bible."

One young man proves to be a formidable opponent for the prophets. Andrew dresses in baggy jeans and a tight shirt. He discredits verses from the megaphone man by reciting them correctly. He lectures them on peace and understanding. He receives hoots of support from the crowd, but after several minutes, he realizes his cause is futile, takes a long drag off his cigarette, slams down a beer, gives his final regard to the millennialists, calls to his buddies to follow, and swaggers through the crowd receiving high fives from those around him.

I follow Andrew a while, amused by his efforts to attract the attention of every available woman on the Strip. He and his friends plan a competition to see who can kiss the most women before the clock hits midnight. After a while, a cross-dresser with cigarette in mouth walks up to Andrew asking for a light. At first, Andrew happily obliges until he notices that this beautiful woman is, in fact, a man. Andrew lights the cigarette, grabs his friends, and scurries away.

Frank wears tight leather pants and a pink tank-top. Accessories include a black leather shoulder purse, yellow boa, and seven strands of rainbow beads.

Frank revels in attention. A crowd gathers and encourages Frank to "show us your tits." Frank is obviously elated and eggs them on by rubbing the yellow boa all over her body. The display catches the attention of each person passing by and that of two female officers on horseback. Cameras flash and video cameras record the event. Frank lifts the beads off slowly, one by one. Removing the tank reveals a white lace bra. Then, quickly, Frank raises the bra and pulls it back. The crowd roars with cheers, whistles, and expressions of approval. People offer money and beads which Frank accepts eagerly. Frank scans the crowd, joins a group of young men, and they stroll away arm-in-arm.

Crowds filter through the trash-laden streets. People discuss the New Year and their hopes and dreams for the future. They also discuss computer crashes, bomb threats, and the end of the world. Still, for the most part, the evening is festive. It's getting colder, and I take refuge in the newly opened Bellagio Hotel to thaw out. I head to the bar and order a beer. The bartender comes back with a bottle of Bud Lite and says: "6.75." "You must be joking." "Nope, they told us to jack up the prices around New Years." Eight dollars later, after tip, I finish my drink, curse myself for paying so much, and savor the heat for a few more minutes.

I move along to the Mirage Hotel and watch a man lose $100 from an enormous stack of chips. Henry tells the dealer about his plans for the new millennium, to "win big in Vegas, find myself a pretty little wife, and celebrate the New Year." He sips his drink as his stack of chips dwindles. The cocktail waitress appears just in time to lay down another drink and receive a $5 tip for her trouble. Henry changes tables and grins from ear to ear as he wins a few times only to have his smile erased as his luck turns. He disgustedly shoves his chips in his pocket and strolls away. He wanders around the casino awhile, plays some video poker, more blackjack and pulls a few slots. He makes small talk with a newly married couple about hopes and dreams for the future. He buys them a drink of congratulations and heads to Treasure Island. There is an enormous crowd at Treasure Island, and it's so cold that I'm shivering. I glance down at my watch, not knowing how much time had passed. I'm surprised to see that it is 11:35.

I hurry to the Paris Hotel. By this time, walking is almost impossible, and I shove my way through the streets keeping my bearings by glancing skyward at the Eiffel Tower replica. I arrive with 15 minutes to spare. Voices are tense as the hour approaches. People talk of the world ending, the sky opening up, God appearing to take Christians to heaven, terrorists. With 10 minutes to go, a large boom sounds, and many scream in fear. We glance overhead and are relieved to see fireworks set off prematurely. Five helicopters hover; their searchlights illuminate the huge crowd and the whoomp-whoomp-whoomp of their blades mixes with the screams.

People chant as the seconds pass. The Paris Hotel's countdown clock can be easily seen. At two minutes, the partying increases, and the chanting is deafening.

A family next to me clutches each other not sure whether to cheer or to kiss each other goodbye.

With one minute to go, members of the crowd jump up and down and scream at the top of their lungs. Fifty-nine, fifty-eight, fifty-seven—the numbers tick away. Time almost stops; the numbers freeze before moving on. I don't know myself whether to close my eyes and pray or to keep them open and watch the millennium unfold. Forty-five, forty-four, forty-three—the seconds go by glacially, and the ear-splitting screaming inexplicably gets louder. People hug, hold hands, and kiss as the clock moves–thirty, twenty-nine, twenty-eight, twenty-seven. . . . A woman next to me sticks out her hand. I hold it tightly. Together we count down the last ten seconds of the only century we've known. Ten, nine, eight, seven, six, five—my stomach knots; I can't hear through the wall of sound; the woman squeezes my hand. Four, three, two, one . . .

"Happy New Year," the crowd roars in unison. Everyone grabs everyone they can. People kiss, hug, cheer, cry, and jump. Beer, confetti, and silly string fill the neon skies. We smile like idiots. A bungee jumper leaps from the Eiffel Tower bearing down on the crowd only to be snatched skyward. Two acrobats perform flips, somersaults, and handstands on a platform above us. I hug everyone within arms distance. We shout about the beauty of life, the happiness we feel, and the awesome celebration. The family next to me embraces in joy.

Confetti rains down. My face is wet with beer and who knows what else. My feet are cold and sore from walking all night, but nothing in the world can bother me. I stroll down the Strip basking in the feeling, congratulating those around me, hugging those who approach me, and smiling with everyone. Time resumes its rightful place.

PART SIX

Novels as Expressions of Ethnography

CHAPTER 19

Geocommunication

A Paradigm of Place

CATHERINE BECKER AND FREDERICK C. COREY

Fred: *An Introduction*

The material in this chapter has roots in two vastly different places. One of those places is a nineteen-year-old, working-class woman from Buffalo who rode a motorcycle 9000 miles in search of her birth mother, a connection to nature, and spirit. The second is a forty-year-old gay man from the expensive suburbs of the Midwest who found himself lost in a benevolent desert, geographic as well as cultural. We met by way of empirical fiction. Each of us was working on a novel; each was engaging a resistance to the adoration of "communication science"; each was in search of a meaningful explication of identity; interpersonal relationships, culture, and human communication. The editor of this volume convened a panel on ethnographic fiction in November 1999, and we met at the conference. We discovered we were drawing water from the same well.

In the pages that follow, we discuss our novels in the context of theoretical propositions that have informed our creative processes. During the collaboration, we discovered that while our theoretical frameworks were different, they were complementary. In our writing, we are drawing from social constructionism (Gergen, 1982; Shotter and Gergen, 1994), Speech Act Theory (Austin, 1975), intercultural communication (Martin, Krizek, Nakayama, and Bradford, 1996), gender studies (Becker and Levitt, 1990; Behar, 1995), performativity (Parker and Sedgwick, 1995; Pollock, 1998), aesthetic engagement (Berleant, 1991), and postmodern geography (Deleuze and Guattari, 1987, 1994). The processes are cyclical rather than linear; that is, neither of us started with theory and proceeded to fiction, nor did we begin with fiction and move toward theory. The creative processes described below are marked by simultaneity and a sense of "returning to" ideas, images, characters, experiences, and places.

Catherine: *Moving Between the Lines*

Its Saturday night, I am writing from my home that was built in the 1930s on an island that splits the Wailuku River, in the town of Hilo, on the island of Hawaii, in the middle of the Pacific. I hear the coqui frogs chirping outside. (I find I am tempted to share that there currently exists a movement to exterminate them by causing them to have a heart attack by overdosing them on caffeine because some people feel they are too loud. The Puerto Rican government has called for a reconsideration, because they are loved and considered a national symbol there. In a recent article in the *Hawaiian Island Journal,* a medical anthropologist discusses how our lack of adaptability is the problem, not the chirp of the frogs.) I am thinking that these details may be irrelevant for what I am about to write. I am thinking that I need to write these lines before I can address the ethnographic and communication implications of my novel, *Moving Between the Lines.* I must start in the present. I must start from a place.

In some hula halaus students must grapple with four crucial questions, Who am I? Where did I come from? What do I do here? How do I do it? Each of these questions is also crucial for the autoethnographic encounter. There is a fifth question that is also crucial, Where am I? For this question requires a consideration of how history, politics, culture, economics, and environment shape my construction of this place. Tonight, as the chirp of coqui surrounds my home, I know what it means to be home, to have found my place, to be engaged with an environment, a culture, and a community. But when I was nineteen and began the motorcycle trip that is the setting for most of the scenes in Moving Between the Lines, I did not.

Moving Between the Lines is a three hundred page novel about a nineteen-year-old, adopted, working-class woman from Buffalo, riding a motorcycle 9,000 miles across the United States, searching for her birth mother and a connection with nature and spirit. The trip leads the reader to encounter a variety of cocultures in the United States including working-class family life in the rust belt of the industrial North, the Roman Catholic Church, Fundamentalist-Christians, African Americans, Native Americans, bikers, strippers, Deadheads, communes, and others. These encounters are based on a solo trip that included twenty-two states and Mexico that I actually did take when I was nineteen.

The novel was developed from journals that I had kept throughout the early part of my life and while on the trip. It was written "secretly" in my "spare" time while I publicly grappled with the demands of a rigorous Ph.D. program that prides itself on being the "Communication Science" department. In my graduate school's culture, spare time and novel writing, although perhaps sanity producing, would have been perceived as consequences of cavalier behavior that probably indicated a lack of commitment to the study of communication at the graduate level. Consequently, the novel remained safely stored in the trunk of my car until the advent of autoethnography in our journals. For embedded within the novel are ethnographic moments, mini-descriptions of places, people, and conversations that evoke cultural context.

In the following excerpt, the main character, Kate, is leaving Buffalo on her motorcycle as she describes the place she seeks to escape:

Riding out of the city, I passed the tall, white grain silos. The smoke stacks of the mostly abandoned steel plants ran along for miles on both sides of the road. The shut-down factories free of adults and their pollution had once been an enchanted kingdom for my playmates and me. Following the railroad tracks into the grain elevators had been one of the most exciting discoveries during my childhood. We held contests to see who could break the most windows in the abandoned buildings. I had held the record with eighty-six. When one of the boys fell to his death from the shaky stairs on the eleventh floor, the media discovered our fortress. This led to a controversy on the fate of the structures. The historical preservationists argued they were a proud part of Buffalo's heritage and must be saved. Others said they were an eyesore on the skyline and needed to be demolished.

Riding past them, my mind transformed the desolate plants into an amusement park. The labyrinth of infinite conveyers would keep the visitors amazed for days, maybe lifetimes. My speed increased to 80 miles an hour. "It doesn't matter what they do with them, I'm oudda here. My kids aren't going to grow up playing in abandoned factories, and they won't be writing poems about pollution." Nevertheless, I couldn't help wondering what ever would become of the children of generations of faceless inhabitants who occupied the rows of soot covered houses which surrounded the factories. Did they ever dream of escape as I had? Did any of them ever make it? Or did they grow up just to take their place on the line, like their parents, and their parents before them.

The novel is and contains communication—conversations and dialogues that offer glimpses of meaning making in action. The following excerpt provides an example of communication with and about "others."

I managed to get a part-time job at a downtown athletic club. Teaching aerobics, and selling memberships. It was a poshy prestigious place and as those places usually are, sexist and racist as hell. The membership consisted mostly of men wearing yellow ties with grey spots and secretaries in hot pursuit of men wearing yellow ties with grey spots, and few other people in between. I was the first woman they ever had on staff.

One Saturday afternoon, when I was working by myself, two huge men, who happened to be black, walked into the club wearing camouflage clothes. They had that certain something that allows one to identify them as Vietnam Vets. I can always spot them, there's just something about them, as if somehow innocence, lost too soon and forever, shows on their faces, leaving in its place only traces of their shared terror, their brotherhood of pain. After giving them a "tour" around the athletic club, we sat down in the closing booth and discussed membership fees. They had told me that they wanted to join the club to try and break out of the rut they had been in. They both were interested in joining the basketball team, playing co-ed volleyball, and using weights. I signed them up on a month dues plan and scheduled their introductory appointment.

When they walked in two days later, my boss took one look at them and all the color drained from his already white face. You could cut the tension like a ribbon. People didn't stare, they didn't move away, they simply averted their eyes. They pretended they didn't see them at all. You know, they didn't give them the same look that people give cripples, or beggars, or pregnant women. As soon as they left, the boss paged me on the intercom and told me he wanted to see me right away. I walked into his office. He sat in front of a huge square desk. He was direct and to the point,

"Look, you're one of the best salesmen we've ever had, even if you are just a girl. And I want you to know that I am not prejudice or anything but I'm warning you, if you ever let any of those types in here again, you're fired!"

I wanted to quit immediately but after spending every cent I had and then some that summer, I really needed the money. And jobs in Buffalo are not easily come by. I held my breath and decided to think it through over a drink at the bar downstairs from the club. It was an exclusive place; as I was sitting on a stool and sipping wine that evening, I looked around to see who was excluded.

Things in Buffalo were pretty much the same.

By sharing, *Moving Between the Lines,* publicly with other communication scholars and ethnographers, I find myself standing at a juncture in my career where I have been presented the opportunity to interweave the seemingly disparate identities of "scientist" and "novelist," and perhaps overcome the sort of schizophrenia that these public and private selves produce. Perhaps their intermingling will offer answers to the ethnographic question, "what is going on here?" Perhaps their intermingling will help reveal just what we gain by studying communication as the making of meaning.

As I consider the role a work such as *Moving Between the Lines* plays in my research agenda, I feel the vulnerability that comes by what seems like a move in another and almost opposite direction from my more "scientific" writing. But I have been trained to look for patterns, and this is no exception. I begin to see that all of my "scientific" research examines the possibilities that emerge from a social constructionist approach to the study of culture and communication (Shotter and Gergen, 1994; Gergen, 1984). A social constructionist approach assumes that culture is created through shared symbols and overlapping meanings (Barnett, 1998; D'Andrade, 1984). Therefore, from a social constructionist perspective, communication is the central process by which we come to know and interact with the world. Therefore, communication is the force that reproduces or transforms current cultural creations and power relations within them. Most of my research applies rigorous scientific methods to identify patterns in cultural constructions so that these patterns can be altered in ways that will alleviate the suffering that comes from cultural constructions that are oppressive to groups or particular individuals (Becker, 2001; Becker and Levitt, 1999; Becker, 1998; Becker, Levitt, and Moreman, 1998; Becker, 1997a; Becker, 1997b). My ethnographic writing, in this case, in the form of a novel, also has the same intention.

The following excerpt comes from a scene that takes place on a reservation at a Native American powwow. Kate goes there with Kayandra, a half-white, half Native American, woman she picked up hitchhiking. In this scene, communication between the members from the different cocultures begins to reveal how each constructs the other.

Some of the men were drumming and chanting magical songs, in a language that was struggling to survive. Most of the young people there couldn't understand a word, neither could I. The schools and the missionaries had done their job well. Yet, their songs remained, reminding. The tones, the eerie crying chants, curved through the air like the wind. So strange, so foreign, so familiar.

I am.

I exist.

I shivered.

So, who am I?

If I could only feel connected. These people as diverse from one another as they were, were definitely connected. Chet had asked me earlier if I was from the nation of Wannabes.

"Who are the Wannabes?"

"The Wannabes are white hippies who wannabe Indians."

Or more accurately, want to be their romanticized images of them. I understood what he meant. I had had my fantasies of finding a brave who would sweep me off on his horse and adopt me into his tribe. After two days witnessing the drunken despair on the reservation I felt embarrassed for having such thoughts.

How ignorant I was.

Of their language, of their pain, of their history.

I didn't even know my own.

But Chet had been right. I did wanna BE. BE familiar with my history. BE connected to my people. I wanna BE part of a culture whose values I could identify with and respect. A world where wanting to be was respected more than wanting to HAVE.

The wondering was winding up again.

Who am I? What am I doing here? Where was SHE?

I listened to them sing. It was as if the answers to my questions were all in their song, if only I could understand it.

A few minutes later Chet overhears a philosophical conversation between Kate and Kayandra's grandmother on the nature of power and of silence. Irritated by the discussion he interrupts,

"You ladies talk this way in front of the wrong people and they'll think you are crazy fools."

Grandmother replies, "That is very true, grandson. And if we talk this way in front of the right people, they will think we are very wise."

The next excerpt takes us across the line of sexual taboo as Kate first explores sexual intimacy with Kayandra. They have just had their first kiss when the main character sees a vision of a rock rolling back from the entrance of a cave. There is an explosion of orange light.

In the distance voices murmur. The murmur grows louder until words can be heard coming from the darkness beyond the orange light.

"Lesbian."

"Freak."

"Abnormal."

"Sick."

"Sinner."

Following the voices are images of the past as I'm whisked back into watching myself relive all the disappointments I'd encountered in my search.

Lies.

Laws.

Lines.

Once again we cross a line between what is forbidden, and find, not damnation, but release.

Line crossing can be pretty scary business.

Their discussion later that evening also offers some insight:

"Kayandra, what happened tonight was beautiful and powerful but part of me still feels like maybe we sinned."

"Sin in Spanish means without. Did you feel like something was missing, love or intimacy or spirit?"

"No."

"I think I know the feeling you were having, I use to feel that way, kind of like guilt?"

"Do you think I've been brainwashed into feeling guilty about sex?"

"Sure. If people can be convinced that something powerful is bad, then they lose touch with that power. Say shit is dirty, and they won't use it to grow food.

Say sex is dirty, and they won't get in touch with the energy behind it. They use sex to keep us apart, instead of to bring us together. They use fear the same way."

"How?"

"Once you control someone's fear, you control their life. People build or support the building of weapons because they are afraid of war. Kind of ironic, isn't it? Lots of people allow religion to control their lives because they are afraid of hell. They're so afraid of hell or being punished or rejected by some big DaddyO in the sky, that they walk around terrified to try anything other than what the controllers say they should do, think, and even feel. Pretty effective huh?"

"So you're saying that fear keeps us from crossing whatever lines that have been drawn around us?"

"By keeping us from drawing our own lines, controllers enslave the hearts and the minds of the controlled. Anyhow, whatever way one does it, moving beyond the lines lets you see other possibilities. Seeing other worlds is one of the first lessons of power."

"I feel like I'm waking up, but I don't feel fully awake yet."

"You cannot draw your own lines without first crossing the lines of fear and guilt."

"Kayandra, what's on the other side of the lines?"

"Beyond the lines one discovers an eternally changing view and infinite lines to choose from."

"I'm afraid of getting so tangled up I'll never be able to find my way out."

"Once you move beyond the lines of your fear you can never get caught again."

I wanted to learn how to go beyond the lines, but I didn't have any idea how to begin to overcome the overwhelming sensation that a world of infinite choices would be as terrifying as a world with no choices at all.

Later in the novel Kate has a vision in which the spirit of a Native American grandmother encourages her to continue crossing lines in spite of her fear.

Her voice ran along with the sound of the river; she was speaking in her native tongue, and yet somehow I understood her.

"Now that you have crossed the bridge over the Rio Vista, you must create your own lines."

"How do I do that?"

"Creating lines of your own is much more difficult than moving between the lines that others have created."

"How shall I know what lines to create?"

"By putting yourself on the line."

"By putting myself on the line?"

"Putting yourself on the line means complete commitment and great risk."

"I'm scared."

"Scared is only a step away from sacred," she said.

And she was gone.

Awareness of the nature and process of social construction can lead to sentiments, expressed in the novel, that are not unlike those I am experiencing right now.

I am real! I want to roar it to the world. Can anyone understand the discipline, the dedication, the determination, the drive, the loneliness, the perseverance that this takes? It is a thankless task, is that why I do it? Do I want to be thanked? Thank you for suffering so. Is this an offering to nail myself to a cross? Is the cross my own? Who is this for? There is no denying that this journey takes me to myself. It transforms nothingness into creation. Creativity needs to be shared. Because as grandmother said many chapters ago, a vision nobody shares is the product of a sick mind. But does that mean that the process of creation is sick? And when is creation considered healthy? Only if it is shared? Only then am I to be freed? For a creation once born and released into the world beyond the creator, has a life of its own. It is both connected and disconnected from its creator. But maybe I am wrong in this analysis. I do not create this by myself, it is our creation. For, even now, you are creating me, participating in me, facilitating in the process of bringing me to life. You are doing so at this very moment, as we share these lines.

As the process of construction becomes conscious, boundaries blur and the space between the lines explodes with potential. Form collapses and takes identity along with it.

Call me crazy.
To be called crazy is a very freeing thing. If you feel like dancing you dance. If you feel like singing, you sing. If you want to wear two different colored socks, that's O.K. too. And if you want to ride a 400 Honda across the United States, people will just say, "It's that crazy Kate again. If you can't relate to what you read then perhaps it is because you aren't crazy. Sane people always know exactly who and where they are, or at least they pretend to. Pretending is a necessary component of sanity. So-called sane people just love to call people who are different from them crazy. Somehow that seems to assure them that they aren't crazy which is very important to sane people. . . . Chances are, you just might find that you are probably crazy too. In which case it's likely you'll recognize some of yourself here. That's because I am you. And you are me. But then you're you too. And I am me. But you're out there somewhere and I'm somewhere in here. Or are you here and am I out there? At this moment, I probably am out there somewhere, but then again I'm here too, with you, of course, where I always am.

Since I have been looking backwards in order to go forward, not only with *Moving Between the Lines* but with all of my communication scholarship, perhaps a meaningful place to end this discussion would be with one of the novel's final passages:

Line,
a unit in the rhythmic structure of verse,
a straight or curved geometric element that is
generated by a moving point and that has extension only along the path
of that point,
to come into the correct relative position,
the course or direction of something in motion,
a system of transportation,
the principle circuits of a power system,

pipe for pumping a conveying fluid,
a source of information,
a state of control,
a course of conduct,
a general plan,
a group of individuals tracing descent from a common ancestor,
a family,
a cord,
a boundary,
a division,
a contour,
a limit,
a calling,
an action,
a thought,
an insight,
a horizontal row of printed characters on a page.

Epilogue: These lines may help you find out who you are. You can accept or reject any that you choose. These lines cross and connect with the lines of others. It is not certain what will happen if you accept these lines, or any others. These lines may assist, entertain, enrage, or ensnarl you. Lines are all this creation offers. The best we can ever do is to follow them, move between them, leave them behind, or create lines of our own. For you and I are only fiction, but the lines are real and true.

Fred: *Bitter Becomes Us*

If anyone asked, Andy said he moved to Phoenix for the weather. The truth was far more Andy. A year after his mother died, he met a sweet guy with a sensitive sexiness about him. They became lovers, Andy thought; they slept together, ate breakfast together, called each other with nothing in particular to say; and when this sweet guy said he had to leave Chicago and return to Phoenix, Andy decided that he, too would live in Phoenix. Andy had no idea this sweet, sensitive guy was being kept by a rich, older gentleman in Carefree.

On January 1 of the year I would turn forty, I contemplated my accomplishments, lost desires, plans for the future, and a list of things I always wanted to do but never did. First on that list was a novel. I took to telling people I was an "aspiring novelist." A middle-aged man, it seemed to me, was well-suited to be aspiring. It gave him something to look forward to, a future. Instead of marking myself as a history or stagnant present ("I have worked hard all my life," or, "I am a professor"), I wanted to identify myself as something forthcoming. "I am an aspiring novelist" spoke to a future I was willing to enter.

This writing process started with a character, Andrew Johns, his brother, Randy, and my ongoing interest in writing about gay culture from the subject position. From a literary perspective, the two brothers would serve as simple contrast. Both defined themselves in terms of their relationships, but while Andy wanted to have a loving, interpersonal romantic relationship with another man, Randy wanted to be at the forefront of the collection of men who defined "gay culture." Andy wanted a simple life with another individual, and Randy wanted to embody the norms, values, customs, and habits of the emerging social system of "the tribe." As I crafted the text, I wanted to explore *place*, a complex fold in gay identity. Contemporary writing about gay culture takes as its point of departure New York or San Francisco. Identities, discourses, and communication systems have been defined by these two cultural hubs. What, I asked, are the nuances of "other" locales, and would it be possible to explore geographical dimensions of gay life outside the center?

> Andy had moved, furniture, silverware and all, to the Valley of the Sun; he moved to be in a relationship; (he defined himself in terms of his relationships); and he found himself in Phoenix with no identity at all. Andy felt he was, simply put, just another transplant from the frigid Midwest. To worsen matters, he discovered that in Phoenix he had minimal cultural capital. In Phoenix, gay men wanted at least one of five things: a big chest, a big wallet, a pretty face, extreme youth, or an enormous personal endowment. A guy with two of the five was quite marketable, but a guy like Andrew Johns, a guy with none of the above, was simply there, and there was no *there* there.

Sexuality and Performance

Andy needed a boyfriend, and in the first sixty pages of the novel, I created an absurd scenario, farce in which he would snare a man named Matthew Van Boven. The scene reads well but has no intellectual or cultural value. Andy saw Matt and decided "they stood in the path of time," and he was determined to snare Matt in spite of the fact that Matt was engaged to be married. Andy passed himself off as straight and invited Matt to a dinner party, a spoof on heterosexuality during which Andy would seduce the husband-to-be. Andy convinced his best friend, Bonnie Lopez, to play the role of his pregnant wife, and he persuaded Randy to seduce Matt and deliver him into the arms of Andy. Randy brought a flamboyant friend, Cha Cha Martinez, to play his wife. By the end of the evening, Bonnie was drunk and dropped the baby, Cha Cha was confused and called the police, Randy was exasperated with his brother's feeble attempts to find a boyfriend, Matt's fiancé was suspicious of her future husband's sexuality, and Andy had, indeed, captured Matt's fancy.

As the story developed, I desired an infusion of theoretical perspectives related to human communication, art, and the study of culture. The idea of two men having sex is, for many, an extremely uncomfortable proposition. Would it be possible, I asked, to call upon theoretical principles of performative writing and aesthetic engagement in order to create text that evoked sexuality and invited the reader to participate in the pleasures of intimacy? Performativity is based largely in Austin (1975) and Speech Act Theory, and in recent years, scholars in literary and performance studies have focused on "performative writing." Performative writing is, in part, creative writing with heightened relevance. The author may engage traditional tropes, including metaphor, synecdoche, hyperbole, or metonymy; the text may be replete with sensory appeals; the reader may appreciate a rhythm or cadence; the words may be self-reflexive and referential; the collected words, composed through the great literary traditions of form, may be expressive of human feeling. In her essay "Performing Writing," Della Pollock (1998) speaks of performative writing as evocative, metonymic, subjective, nervous, citational, and consequential. Pollock pursues a nuanced advancement of Austin's performativity in Speech Act Theory, and her writing offers a theoretical enrichment of the "performativity" explored in *Performativity and Performance* (Parker and Sedgwick, 1995). From these writings, we might surmise that performative writing is, at its foundation, "good" writing, but it is more: Performative writing is the explication of a cultural phenomenon from the subject position; subject and object are a fluid composition; the reader becomes compelled to respond to the cultural text in a visceral as well as cognitive mode; the interaction with the text is transformative and, as Pollock (1998) writes, performative writing "is for writing, for writing ourselves out of our-selves, for writing our-selves into what (never) was and may (never) be" (p. 98).

I turned as well to Berleant (1991) and his theoretical reformulation of art and aesthetics. Berleant brings to the forefront "aesthetic engagement," and this engagement presents an invitation not unlike the allure of performative writing as a practice, and, further, the expressive attributes of performative writing as a product. From Berleant's (1991) perspective, aesthetic engagement "joins perceiver and object into a perceptual unity" (p. 46), and three attributes of this process are continuity, perceptual integration, and participation. As both practice and product, performative writing can be aesthetic engagement. Performative writing is an embodied continuity of cultural experience. Like a work of art, performative writing "is assimilated into the full scope of individual and cultural experience without sacrificing its identity as a mode of experience" (Berleant, 1991, p. 46). The writer and the writing express cultural, social, political, and spiritual values, not as isolated or fleeting phenomena, but as citational discourses of reflection and experience. The notion of perceptual integration is a more immediate effect of this continuity, and in performative writing, we find a unified procession of experience. Berleant (1991) speaks of the blurring of traditional distinctions, an integration of "the creator of art, the aesthetic perceiver, the art object, and the performer" (p. 47). This blurring is a dynamic characteristic of performative writing, so much so that *doing* the act is as much a process pursued by the perceiver as the writer. Both writer and perceiver are the performance initiators; both *engage* the aesthetic process. My question, then, is not who participates, but rather *in what* do the creators and perceivers participate? There are the likely suspects—experience, language, identity, form, culture, analysis, memory, or emotion—but could we not engage a specific communicative act between creator and perceiver? Could I create scenes based in a relational, communicative dynamic that are passionate, nervous, and vulnerable?

> Andy was sprawled across the bed, flat on his back, staring at the ceiling. "I brought you food," Matt said, "bagels and cream cheese and tomato slices and . . ." He sat down on the edge of the bed and leaned over Andy, placing his hands on either side of Andy's shoulders. Matt's face was all of eight inches from Andy's, and when Andy closed his eyes, he felt Matt's face move close. Breathing became a part of breathing, lips part of lips, and, as Matt slowly unrolled the bedcovers, Andy felt the crisp air move slowly down his shoulders, chest, nipples; the crisp air was followed by the gentle touch of Matt's lips, through the sternum, between the ribs, and along the hairs rising from the naval. Matt paused and nibbled, ever so slowly and gently, and then continued his journey, unrolling, kissing, unrolling, kissing, until Andy felt himself risen into the crispness of the air and the sudden warmth of the mouth. Andy pulled his legs from under the covers and draped them over Matt's shoulders. Andy's pelvis rose from the bed and surged in a slow, pulsing rhythm guided by the palms on his thighs. Now deep inside, enveloped in moisture now intermingled, Andy felt from deep within, deep within the core, a rearrangement of his entire body, a sure and profound shift in everything that made him alive, a now unstoppable surge, a thrust, a push, a rising force, and with a slight gasp he released and collapsed. Matt crawled over Andy and buried his face in this newfound space.

Perils of Whiteness

A cultural text that does not address questions of race would seem to be lacking a self-reflexivity. The ongoing negotiations of identity often involve ethnicity, cultural affiliation, and powers that are bestowed or denied individuals based on skin color. I am especially fascinated by what Martin, Krizek, Nakayama, and Bradford (1996) outline as the invisibility of whiteness, and I tried to discuss that in the context of Matthew's inability to identify himself:

> Yet, for Matthew, extreme whiteness did seem to be at the root of his troubles. He was tall. He was male. He was Protestant, a vague Protestant, a Methodist when he was young, but a Presbyterian while he was a teen, in large part because the Presbyterian Church was more lovely. He came from good stock. His father had money, and his mother had grace. And he was white, so terribly white. "We are not anything," his father would say, "except American. American through and through." For the Van Bovens, race was about other people, people not quite so white.
>
> "The Orientals are smart," Shirley would say, ever so kindly, "especially at math."
>
> "The Negroes could have jobs if they wanted them."
>
> The Van Bovens were Republican, of course, but more specifically, they were *not* Democrats. Lyndon Johnson was a socialist, and what the country needed was a great leader. One can only imagine how pleased the Van Bovens were when Richard Nixon was elected President. Nixon would protect the Americans from the Communists, pinkos, and, be it needlessly added, the homosexuals.
>
> Shirley and Hal Van Boven would never be so gauche as to utter the word homosexual in their home. But life in Orange County was different from life in Clare, Michigan. Whereas Andy's parents would see homosexuals on the television news, would hear a broadcast about the homosexual riot outside a bar in New York City, and cast the scene as something very far away, Matt's parents recognized homosexuals as all-too close. San Francisco, after all, was in California, and someone told someone who told Shirley that there was actually a group of homosexuals living openly in Los Angeles, a place not so very far away from Orange County. The homosexual danger was on the Van Boven doorstep. To say the word was to invite danger inside the house. Homosexual. They would walk around the word, insinuate, construct a sentence but leave the word out, thereby creating presence through absence. A person was "that way," or, "you know," or a forced clearing of the throat. On that rare occasion when an image of the homosexual would appear on the evening news, Hal would watch in frozen silence, and Shirley would "st" her tongue. They never made idle death threats, and they never spewed hate. Instead, they offered their sophisticated and gracious disapproval. A lowering of the eyes, wrinkle of the brow, sound of the tongue, this was all: but this was enough to establish social

order. The Van Bovens had the right, the cultural capital, the power to cast their judgment on others. They were not mystified or confused as the Johns were. They understood homosexuality well enough, and they were at liberty to judge.

Shirley and Hal voted firmly for the Briggs Amendment, without comment.

How to Do Things

Speech Act Theory (Austin, 1975) is an intriguing framework for the articulation of expression and possibility of human action. Austin focuses primarily on language, but is it not possible to push Speech Act Theory into other forms of communication? Andy enjoyed Los Angeles. He would travel to visit his brother, park himself at a café table jammed up against the wall on an impossibly narrow sidewalk, and contemplate culture. How, in the spirit of Austin, might we do things with jeans?

Santa Monica Boulevard through West Hollywood was its own little world, plopped down and popped up closer to the Mormon Temple than downtown, cleaner than Hollywood but not as charming as Melrose, easy to find but hard to maneuver. The sidewalk was narrow and the street was wide, but the action was on the walk. The walk was the performance. The single guy walked and cruised. Two guys walked hand in hand, as though that in itself were a reason for living. The hungover guy walked around and around the block looking for his car, which was towed away hours ago. The old guy walked and turned, walked and turned, walked and turned, until the sight alone of his neck hurt.

But the jeans displayed the nuances. To Andy, a well-phrased pair of jeans did not make a statement. They initiated action. The hold around the waist, glide around the hips, fall down the thighs, flex with the knees, drop to the ankles, and then, as though rising and falling were two actions in one step, play returned upward, from the ankle to the calf, up slowly and gracefully to the crotch, around and with the loins, riding along the butt, and dancing in and around the pelvis: each move, twist, fall, and return from the paved earth spoke of an impending moment. A well-phrased pair of jeans did not report on the covered flesh, did not offer a jejune analysis of strengths and weaknesses. No, a well-phrased pair of jeans was not a simple report on the sexy man's body. A well-phrased pair of jeans spoke of forthcoming felicity. Mystery. Pain. Jealousy. Pleasure. Ecstasy. Self-doubt. Jubilation. Andy's

eyes followed the well-phrased pair of jeans, for they called him
onward. The well-phrased jean was a call to action.

Bump

A controversial topic in contemporary gay culture is the use of drugs, particularly
in the context of the "circuit parties," weekend parties that attract thousands of
gay men from the United States, Canada, England and Australia. One of the
largest circuit parties is The White Party, held on Easter weekend in Palm
Springs, California. I attended The White Party in 1996, and the following passages are based on my "participant observation" of that spectacle.

And what Andy would never understand, not in the early days of
Los Angeles, and not in the later days of wretchedness, was the use and
subsequent abuse of drugs. "You," Randy said, "do not understand a
good high." The drugs started out easily enough. A big night at the
Probe, The White Party in Palm Springs, the Tea Dance at the San
Diego Zoo, or a journey to Hotlanta would be enhanced with a bump
of ecstasy, a hit of Special K, or an appointment with Carol. Someone
would ask for Carol, and a little bag of cocaine would appear like a
long, lost friend.

"We'll see you in Palm Springs," Randy said. "Don't be late, and
don't be down."

To no one's surprise, Randy was late. He arrived amidst an
entourage of flash: a BMW convertible, a forest green Seville, a bright
red Infiniti with tan leather interior, and someone from New York
rented a Lincoln Town Car. They had synchronized the music; each car
pierced the air in synchrony with the Master Beat mix from the previous year's affair. The talk of drugs started almost immediately. The
comments were small, ranging from "party favors" to accessories," but
poolside—how they shone, with a Lycra suit to highlight a particularly
taut abdomen, boxers to point to refined calves, a tank suit to accentu-
ate an attractive package—the talk was more direct: "Pace yourself."
"Where's my pouch?" "Save some." "What if we run out?" "Bouzakis
is here, anyway, someplace." Body oil glistened on the flesh. A body
entered the water and emerged, pectorals rising. A dip in the water was
an audition, and the best would find each other before the weekend
drew its last, bitter breath.

Los Angeles and its environs had become the domain of the
Buffed Out Gay Adonis, the BOGA culture, a territory governed by the
Sports Connection, a 24-hour gym also known as the Sex Connection.

Daily regimes were marked by free weights, pills, and low-calorie blender drinks. And, like the mythical figure, the Adonis prototypes appeared once, twice, possibly four times a year, stunning flowers in bloom, bloodred, dancing with the queen of death, seducing the patrons of love and lust.

[*At the dance party*]: Andy and Matt made their way into the thick mass of flesh, sweaty, strong, pulsing, groping. A group of guys were in a circle, dancing together, having sex? Andy was compelled to look closely. Yes, they were having sex. The music slowed, and the Evian water bottles from the back pockets, waistbands, and the floor. Andy went to the bathroom. A guy was in the stall. Vomiting. His friends, or maybe they were strangers who cared, were pulling him by the arms. "You're sick, man. You're sick. You gotta get home."

"I'm not sick," the guy said, and he projectile vomited. Andy ducked to the left. The oral shit flew past him and hit the wall. "I'm not sick. You're sick." He was hunched. His stomach curdled. He lifted his head. Andy stared. "What are you looking at?" He was not a bad looking guy, Andy thought. Under other circumstances, he would have been the kind of guy Andy fantasized over. "What are you staring at?" Andy tried not to look at him, and he cast his gaze toward the urinal. "I am a temple of beauty and power," the guy said, and he collapsed.

Geographical Exposition

Throughout the novel, a recurrent theme is the explication of place, identity, and culture. In contemplating these issues, I turned to the writings of Gilles Deleuze and Félix Guattari (1987; 1994). In *A Thousand Plateaus*, Deleuze and Guattari (1987) open the way to philosophical interrogations of nomadic science, language, the body, and territoriality. An ongoing metaphor throughout the book is the *rhizome*, the life-supporting root system that is marked not by its beginning or end, but rather by its imbeddedness. The rhizome travels beneath the surface and sprouts life—or, in this case, a place in the world—as constituent propositions. A *rhizome*, write Deleuze and Guattari (1987), "connects any point to any other point, and its traits are not necessarily linked to traits of the same nature; it brings into play very different regimes of signs, and even nonsign states" (p. 21). One such nonsign state was, for Andrew Johns, an elm tree that graced the window of his childhood bedroom:

Andy developed a deep admiration for this tree, this lonely survivor. Before Dutch elm disease, elms appeared at the turn of every day in the American Midwest. The elms were not stately and sturdy like the oak, nor did the elm have the curvaceous, rambunctious oak leaf. The elm was not dignified like the maple tree, and the leaf could never compete with the maple's autumnal fire. But then the elm was not obnoxious like the weeping willow, selfish and self-serving, the ruin of sewers, and the elm was not sickly like the birch, with its flaky bark and call for constant attention. The elm, when the time came, was merely tagged and quickly removed.

Our relationship with place and territoriality remains, for me, a mystery. In *What is Philosophy?*, Deleuze and Guattari (1994) posit "geophilosophy" as a continuation of the rhizome, and in so doing, they ask of relationships between the *who, where,* and *when* of human thought. "In what sense," they ask, "is Greece the philosopher's territory or philosophy's earth?" (Deleuze and Guattari, 1994, p. 86).

Although Andy had no particular affinity for the earth, and although he did not particularly enjoy nature, or trees, or mountains, or the sea, he believed he was somehow connected to the ground upon which he stood. His was not a spiritual connection. He never, for example, communed with nature. If he hugged a tree, it was only for the irony and phallic pleasure. No, he did not ever feel a mutual bond between himself and the earth. But he felt connected. He believed that who he was, how he felt about himself, and how he shaped his way of being in the world, was linked inextricably to the territory that grounded his experiences. The gay man living in the desert was not the same gay man who lived in Chicago, and he would have become a very different gay man had he never left Clare, Michigan.

Andy attended to the vernacular. What people said, how people walked, the ways people gardened, all this was of simple fascination. He would never understand or command his geography. A pair of jeans, a geranium on the shelf, a gecko on the desert stone: these were the details that etched themselves into his memory. He liked local histories, stories of bars that are no more, people who had since died or moved away. But his was a passive enactment of inscription. Territories happened to Andy. He never happened to territories.

Who I am is deeply connected to where I am. A legitimate question, then, is: Where am I now? My eyes dart. I want to avoid that question, or slip past the locale with a simple, "I am in the desert."

I have "finished" the novel, and I sent it off to a few literary agents who offered kind rejections. In truth, I want not to be finished with the novel. The manuscript has become, for me, a cornucopia of ideas, images, places I have (never) been and people I have (never) met. My novel is an expression of a culture still evolving, growing, hurting, and struggling. I extract and expand on those ideas whenever I write, and should the novel itself never be "published," I will not be sad. I find pleasure in aspirations.

Catherine: Synthesis and Conclusion

In our introduction, Fred observed, "we were both drinking from the same well." In the conclusion of this essay, I will explore the nature of this well from which we both drink. The well from which we both drink is American culture. Both novels take place in a context that reveals a sense of placelessness that is common in the American experience. In a country that is comprised of conquerors, immigrants, transplants, and others, place is often a contested and difficult concept to locate. Andy resides on the margins of the gay world in a place that seemingly has no center, while Kate whisks us along on her search for utopia through territories that are almost its antithesis.

Both novels contain scenes where sexuality is performed in such a way that new communicative possibilities are presented. Both characters attempt to find or create ways of meeting others that is beyond popular American cultural conceptions of romantic love and sexuality. Both novels contain scenes that explore homosexual sex. In Fred's novel, that exploration is part of his focus as his gay main character searches for love. In Catherine's novel, her gay sexual encounter is only one experiment on her road to self-discovery and liberation. Although different in focus and intent, both of their sexual performances move us from separateness toward connection.

Another theme that appears in both novels has to do with "whiteness." Both authors wrestle with whiteness and its implications for communication. Fred's excerpt demonstrates the role whiteness plays in forming identity and the character's relation to his family. Catherine's excerpts describe racism as it manifests through exclusion and exoticizing of the other. Additional excerpts related to whiteness that could have been included here are a scene in her novel that invites the reader to share her internalized racism through her first encounter with an African American in her childhood; another is an indictment of racism in the Christian church that eventually leads her to cut its tethers from her psyche.

Both novels take place in the aftermath of the sexually liberating and psychedelic period following the sixties and seventies in the United States. Therefore, both novels not only address sex, but also drugs. Fred's excerpt entitled, "Bump" confronts head on the drug infused hedonistic world of sexual and sensory stimulation that exists in gay culture. In a part of her novel not presented here, Catherine explores the alternative culture that surrounds the rock band the Grateful Dead and the psychedelic aspect of the counterculture of the Deadheads. Both of these sections of the novels were generated from participant-observation.

Both authors describe their experiences from the margins of the margins. Both are in the position to report on a cultural phenomenon that is seldom discussed in academic circles. Because of their controversial nature, both authors reveal their participant observations of these passionate experiences with nervous vulnerability. Consequently, Catherine chose to exclude an excerpt about this cultural experience; Fred found the courage, the conviction and perhaps the social position to be able to include it. Sometimes, what we don't say, is as important as what we do say. For what is considered an appropriate topic for research is also a consequence of culture.

Conclusion

It is another evening, about a month after Fred and I began this journey together. I am at home. The coqui are still chirping. As a result of our conversations with one another, we have developed a clearer understanding of the importance of place. We have explored the sometimes subtle and not so subtle ways that place shapes communication and communication shapes place. Through our communication with one another, we have carved this place that we now share with you. And as a result of our being here together, we may leave this place changed. Thanks for coming. Aloha.

References

Austin, J. L. (1975). *How to do things with words*. (2nd ed.). Cambridge: Harvard University Press.

Barnett, G. A. (1998). Communication and organizational culture. In G. M. Gold-haber and G. A. Barnett (Eds.), *Handbook of organizational communication* (pp. 101–130). Norwood, NJ: Ablex.

Becker, C. (2003). Data-driven, dynamic models (3D) for intercultural communication training in organizations. In G. Barnett and G. Cheney (Eds.), *International and Multicultural Organizational Communication*. Cresskill, NJ: Hampton Press.

Becker, C. and Levitt, S. (1999). Perceptions of power: Women and leadership in organizations. In P. Salem (Ed.), *Organizational Communication and Change* (pp. 273–288). Cresskill, NJ: Hampton Press.

Becker, C. (1998). The ways that communication may foster or inhibit socialization: The case of Brazilian immigrants in Japan. In G. Gumpertz and S. Drucker (Eds.), *The Huddled Masses* (pp. 301–308). Cresskill, NJ: Hampton Press.

Becker, C., Levitt, S. and Moreman, S. T. (1998). Women's perceptions of computers and new information and communication technologies. In G. Barnett and L. Thayer (Eds.), *Organizational Communication: Emerging Perspectives V* (pp. 117–139). Norwood, NJ: Ablex.

Becker, C. (1997a). An analysis of organizational culture as a thermodynamic process. In G. Barnett and L. Thayer (Eds.), *Organizational Communication: Emerging Perspectives V* (pp. 121–139). Norwood, NJ: Ablex.

– – –. (1997b). Toward an ethical theory for comparative political communication based on the coherence between universal human rights and cultural relativism. In A. Gonzalez, and D. Tanno, (Eds.), *Politics, Communication and Culture* (pp. 76–89). Sacramento: Sage Publications, Inc.

Behar, R. (1995). Introduction: Out of Exile. In R. Behar and D. Gordon (Eds.), *Women Writing Culture* (pp. 1–32). Berkeley, CA: University of California Press.

Berleant, A. (1991). *Art and engagement*. Philadelphia: Temple University Press.

D'Andrade, R. G. (1984). Cultural meaning systems. In R. A. Shweder and R. A. LeVine (Eds.), *Cultural Theory: Essays on mind, self, and emotion* (pp.88–119). Cambridge, UK: Cambridge University Press.

Deleuze, G., and Guattari, F. (1987). *A thousand plateaus: Capitalism and schizophrenia*. (B. Massumi Trans.) Minneapolis, MN: University of Minnesota Press.

– – –. (1994). *What is philosophy?* (H. Tomlinson and G. Burchell Trans.) New York: Columbia University Press.

Gergen, K. J. (1982). *Toward transformation in social knowledge. New York:* Springer-Verlin.

Martin, J. N., Krizek, R. L., Nakayama, T., and Bradford, L. (1996). Exploring whiteness: A study of self labels for white Americans. *Communication Quarterly, 44*: 125–144.

Parker, A., and Sedgwick, E. K. (1995). *Performativity and performance*. New York: Routledge and Kegan Paul.

Pollock, D. (1998). Performing writing. In P. Phelan and J. Lane (Eds.), *The ends of performance* (pp. 73–103). New York: New York University Press.

Shotter and Gergen, K. J. (1994). Social construction: Knowledge, self, others, and continuing the conversation. In S. Deetz (Ed.), *Communication Yearbook 17* (pp. 3–33). Thousand Oaks, CA: Sage Publications, Inc.

PART SEVEN

Artifacts as Expressions of Ethnography

CHAPTER 20

"Reality Ends Here"

Graffiti as an Artifact

DEAN SCHEIBEL

The original graffito is now gone. It was painted over. Then it reappeared. However, eventually they tore down the old film school and built a new one. And yet, the graffiti lives on. The graffiti has been transformed. But it will never die. The graffiti has taken on new forms, in new contexts, and means new things to the students and professors at the film school. This study is about a piece of graffiti, and its life as an artifact.

Artifacts are the products of people and are phenomena "ripe with human meanings" (Jorgensen, 1989, p. 92). Artifacts include such things as tools, art works, clothing, buildings, official records, personal documents, business reports, and videotapes (see Dipert, 1993; Hodder, 2000; Jorgensen, 1989; Stohl, 2001). Although typically encountered in the course of doing participant observation, artifacts "serve as a distinctive basis for inquiry in and of themselves, not just as a source of support for other findings" (Jorgensen, 1989, p. 93; see also Dipert, 1993; Hodder, 2000). Thus, artifacts can be considered as central to ethnographic research as other types of data.

In discussing the significance of artifacts, Stohl (2001) states that "all organizational artifacts are seen as communicative manifestations of culture" (Stohl, 2001, p. 346). Yet Stohl also questions the value of artifacts, stating that the "microanalytic focus [of artifacts] . . . does little to help us understand the links between culture, organization, and communication" (p. 347). In contrast, the current study assumes that artifacts are invaluable when interpreted in the context of other artifacts, and in conjunction with data gathered through participant observation and interviewing.

219

As artifacts, written texts are particularly important to the study of communication, and various types have been examined, including corporate "house organs" (e.g., Cheney, 1983), "fake IDs" (e.g., Scheibel, 1992), policies and brochures (Clair, 1993), and, of central concern to the current paper, graffiti (e.g., Conquergood, 1994; Rodriguez and Clair, 1999; Scheibel, 1994). Graffiti are artifacts. As such, graffiti are "mute evidence" that "endures physically and thus can be separated across space and time from its author, producer, or user" (Hodder, 2000, p. 703). Such texts are valuable to qualitative research in that "the information provided may differ from and may not be available in spoken form, and because texts endure and thus give historical insight" (Hodder, 2000, p. 704).

To interpret artifacts, such as graffiti, it is necessary to understand them "in the contexts of their conditions of production and reading" (Hodder, 2000, p. 704). Thus, "as the text is reread in different contexts it is given new meanings, often contradictory and always socially embedded. Thus, there is no 'original' or 'true' meanings of a text outside specific historical contexts" (Hodder, 2000, p. 704). The interpretation of artifacts is complex and multifaceted in that artifacts are not only capable of being manipulated and altered, but also of "being used and discarded, reused and recycled" (Hodder, 2000, p. 704). This is important in that the interpretation of graffiti texts and other artifacts may implicate and reflect issues of "ownership."

The idea of context itself is problematic. Clearly, artifacts must be interpreted within contexts that they are found, and those contexts change. We as researchers decide on the boundaries of context when we interpret artifacts. Thus, the interpretation of artifacts may rest in "situating [artifacts] within varying contexts while at the same time entering into a dialectic relationship between those contexts and the context of the analyst" (Hodder, 2000, p. 705).

The current study of an artifact that came to life via graffiti is framed by an "ethnography of expression" perspective (Clair, 1996, 1998). This perspective

> embraces the communicative and expressive practices as central. Moving freely from place to place, ethnographies of expression "displace" the practices that were once viewed as tied to a specific location. ... Meanings and practices change, develop, disappear, and reappear as they strain, struggle, squeeze, slip and slide among the practices that create cultural meanings, and the meanings that create, sustain, and sometimes challenge the practices. (Clair, 1996, pp. 9–10)

Thus, the current study examines a single expression that is a piece of graffito that is an artifact. In so doing, the emphasis is on the phenomenon, not the organization in which the artifact is embedded. However, the artifact and the organization—text and context—are inseparable.

Graffiti at the University of Southern California

Graffiti at USCs film school has always had special significance. The incorporation of the word "graffiti" into the title of George Lucas's film, *American Graffiti* (1973) is not inconsequential if one considers Lucas' history as a student at USCs film school. Lucas' film, "glorifying youthful friendships . . . sought to immortalize the comradeship nourished in [Lucas'] film school days" (Farber, 1984, p. 34). During Lucas' school days at USC—and for a number of years afterward—the writing of graffiti took place in a somewhat dilapidated "graffiti-covered wooden barracks built from surplus World War I lumber" (Harmetz, 1981, p. 16). The success of *American Graffiti* and other Lucas movies (e.g., *Star Wars*) eventually moved George and Marcia Lucas to donate money which made it possible for USC to construct the George Lucas Instructional Building and the Marcia Lucas Post Production Building. In the process, however, the original film school, alternately called "the stables" and, less frequently, "the barracks"—the name itself is contested—was torn down. Ironically then, the impoverished yet convivial conditions which inspired a successful movie, became a factor in its own destruction. When tearing down the graffiti-covered walls in 1984, sections of walls from the old film school were auctioned off to various individuals, including George Lucas.

Minimally we can say that the linking of graffiti, the buildings on which the graffiti was written, and film, provide historical contexts for interpreting the culture of USCs film school. In writing about these things, I use the historical facts about George Lucas, his history at USCs film school, and "the stables" and their graffiti to create a historical and organizational context that will inform the current analysis. The significance of graffiti and the film school is also evidenced in a documentary artifact entitled *The First Fifty Years* (1990), which traces the history and development of USCs School of Cinema-Television. *The First Fifty Years* ends with a depiction of the graffiti on the walls of the deserted buildings, and then the demolition of "the stables." This points to the interplay of artifacts, in this case, graffiti and film. *The First Fifty Years* was produced under particular conditions, by people who know how to use technologies (e.g., cameras and editing equipment); these people made artistic decisions about representing graffiti within an artifact that is itself a representation of institutional history. Moreover, the highlighting of graffiti in the film's images suggests that graffiti was accorded a special place in the representation of the institution, by the institution.

The following analysis will interpret an artifact that is ethnographically expressed in a particular piece of graffito. The interpretation will first follow the artifact as it develops and changes at one university over twenty-five years. Following that analysis, the interpretation of the artifact examines how the meaning of the artifact becomes problematic when the piece of graffiti moves to a different university.

The First Graffito. In the mid-1970s, the artifact finds expression in a piece of graffito that is linked with a USC film student, Rick Redeman, who was shooting his "480" film ("480" refers to the course number within the film school's curriculum). Although no one ever admits writing the graffito, according to one professor, Redeman was "the likely candidate or [he] had someone [else]" put up the graffito. The graffito appears above the portal leading into the film school:[1]

REALITY   ENDS   HERE

There are a number of interpretations that can be made about the original artifact. One interpretation is that the graffito is a metacommunicative comment that frames the complex, sometimes adversarial interactions between student film crews and the USC film school faculty. One theme in Howard Lavick's film[2] is Redeman's film crew's recurring problem of skirting getting official approval for "tying in" to power sources for electricity to run their equipment—with the outcome being that the film crew blows electrical fuses at a couple of locations on USCs campus. These mishaps would eventuate in an awkward confrontation between the film crew and the faculty, which Lavick also filmed. In a scene following this meeting, during which Redeman had apologized for circumventing rules governing film crews, Redeman's comment implicitly questions the "reality" of the meeting:

> [A professor] said, "You guys are in big trouble," when really, we weren't [in big trouble], you know. I mean what he said to me, he says, "you fuckin' guys have *got* to learn how to play the game. You know. And that was the whole thing. What we saw in there today [i.e., the meeting], was *the game*. Getting along. And it was a real education. Just realizing that. They [i.e., the faculty] don't want to deal with it. We [i.e., the film crew] don't want to deal with it. But it's something everyone has to, you know, play their roles.

In reflecting on those days, a USC film professor's description of those meetings as "rough and tumble" also suggests the contested nature of interactions between film students and faculty. There is a sense that Redeman's graffito may have been, perhaps in part, an "expression of resistance" in the sense that the organizational rules for making his film, were, in part, rules to be broken (Hodder, 2000, p. 706). So perhaps the graffito comments on the tension between creating a film while dealing with organizational problems engulfing the making of that film.

A second interpretation of the graffiti is as an expression of identity and nonconformity.

The persistence of "REALITY ENDS HERE" is attributable, in part, to the linguistic brevity and equivocality that is inherent in its language, particularly when juxtaposed with contexts of academia. For many, the academy is marginalized as not being in the "real world"; that is, academia is something more artificial, something less real. However, given that the film school is already physically situated "within" the university setting, the graffito suggests that the film school setting is qualitatively different than its immediate surroundings. And this was so, in the sense that the stables were somewhat squalid when set against the more elegant structures that grace the USC campus. Thus, the graffito also suggests that, as one former USC film student stated, "you are entering into a world that has no connection to the meaning and reality of USC." Thus, we need to consider the university as physical context, which would include the university's student body: when the graffiti was first written, the film school was a place for artists and oddballs. Only later, *after* the successes of film students like George Lucas, Ron Howard (e.g., *Backdraft* and *Cocoons*), and John Milius (e.g., *Big Wednesday* and *Conan the Barbarian*), were film schools being interpreted as "the gateway to the new American Dream" (Latham, 1992, p. 107).

A third interpretation of the graffito is that the artifact serves to mark off the physical boundaries of the film school, and to declare their space as somehow being metaphorically outside the confines of the physical universe. That is, the artistic expression of making films is a reality that film requires some imagination to construct reality in a way so as to get one's film accomplished. In this sense, the graffito REALITY ENDS HERE may also be interpreted as a strategic move, in the sense that the film school defines itself as the arbiter of declaring what is real. Thus, the rules of the physical universe are made problematic in that, as one professor commented, "making films doesn't follow the rules." Such an interpretation works well with the nature of filmmaking, whose stock-in-trade is playing with our sense of reality. For example, consider the name of George Lucas' special effects organization, Industrial Light & Magic. Thus, in one sense the idea that REALITY ENDS HERE creates the possibility for entering a distinctively different kind of place, one above and beyond our everyday sense of reality. Along the same lines, within film production, the common phrase "painting with light" (from the title of legendary cinematographer John Alton's [1949] book) is an ontological metaphor that privileges a certain occupational niche with an ability to imaginatively recreate the physical universe in a way beyond the abilities of mortals. In this sense, the proclamation that REALITY ENDS HERE marks film school as being a place where people can become artists, by applying different rules and aesthetics in the creation of art that transcends everyday reality. That is, REALITY ENDS HERE, as one professor states, suggests that "you are now subjecting yourself to cinematic laws that are different than reality."

The Second Graffito. The demolition of USCs old film school did not kill REALITY ENDS HERE. In writing this article, I drove down to USCs School of Cinema-Television and walked around the buildings, looking for the graffito. I found the graffito on a short, slightly arched concrete bridge that links the George

Lucas Instructional Building with the Marcia Lucas Post Production Building. The words are etched into the concrete. The words measure about nine inches in height and total approximately six feet in length, which is only slightly less that the width of the bridge itself. "REALITY ENDS HERE!" The addition of an exclamation point is probably an embellishment on the original graffito. I say "probably" because some of the USC professors believe that an exclamation point was also part of the original graffito in one of its incarnations on the old film school building (although the exclamation point is not evidenced in Lavick's film). However, what is most interesting is that the new context has attempted to retain some of the spirit of the original graffiti. That is, the placement of "REALITY ENDS HERE!" on a bridge carries a doubled sense of the ethos of change and transition, in the sense that bridges are places to cross, suggesting transition. Further, however, the graffito has also managed to retain the essential graffiti character of the original. The writing of the words was crudely done, as if someone had sneaked onto the bridge and carved the words into the still wet cement with a stick. We need to remember that the writing of graffiti is typically a secretive, clandestine activity. And the words on the bridge carry that ethos. We pause and consider the tension between the graffiti and the opulent buildings in which the graffiti text exists. Was the graffito recreated surreptitiously, under the cover of darkness? Or, was the graffito recreated with that idea in mind?

Photograph by Brian Moss

When the new film school was built, many people expressed a desire to keep a connection with "the stables." There was, as a professor states, "a concern to create a continuity of that spirit." In fact, George Lucas took pains that the architectural form of the old film school—a central rectangular courtyard surrounded by buildings, somewhat stables-like in construction—was recreated. The new film school's buildings retain this basic form. According to one former professor, Lucas had the new buildings surrounding the inner courtyard designed and built with different heights, so that it would not be possible to later connect roofs of the various buildings and thus turn the courtyard area into office space. To that end, faculty members attempted to retain artifacts from the old film school and incorporate them into the new film school. For example, a red-flowered bougainvillea plant was transplanted from the old courtyard into the new one; but its growth couldn't be controlled and so the plant was removed. Further, wooden beams from the old film school buildings were kept, with the intention of building them into the ceiling of the new Marcia Lucas Post Production Building. However, the beams were discovered to be so termite-infested that they could not be used.

And the graffito? There are various stories about how the graffiti came to be inscribed on the bridge. One professor suggests that any story told about the graffiti is likely "one of many legends." I've been told that originally a student scrawled REALITY ENDS HERE, but had written it so badly that it was smoothed over and later redone by a USC film school faculty member, who scrawled the graffito under the cover of darkness. The identity of the faculty member remains a matter of speculation. According to one professor, "the university was irritated" that the brand new facility had been marred by the graffiti. However, I was told that many of the students and faculty members—though not all—of the film school were pleased. And let's face it, if there had not been considerable support for the continued existence of the graffito, it would have been removed in short order. An interpretation of the artifact in its second appearance suggests a tension between, on one hand, a desire for creating a spirit of continuity with the free-spirited past and, on the other, a move toward a "professional" ethos that would eradicate the graffiti.

The Third Graffito. Another USC film school alumnus from the stables' era is director Robert Zemeckis (e.g., *Forrest Gump*). Not too far from the main cluster of buildings of USCs School of Cinema-Television is the Robert Zemeckis Center for Digital Arts. Zemeckis has also had the graffito recreated. Again, the graffito's physical placement—set in concrete on the ground in front of the door leading into the facility—suggests the ethos of transition from one world into another. In contrast to the original graffito and its recreation on the bridge between the Lucas buildings, this time REALITY ENDS HERE has been expertly done, embodying an aesthetic quality not found in the other graffiti. The four-inch high letters are perfectly uniform, designed to resemble a Times Roman type face, have been stamped into a white concrete background such that there is a uniform indentation; they are colored a golden brown that is a few shades darker than tan. While the linguistic content has been retained, to refer to *this* REALITY ENDS HERE as graffiti becomes more problematic. According to one member at the Robert Zemeckis Center for Digital Arts, REALITY ENDS HERE had become a school "motto" by the time it was set in concrete in February 2000, which was a month before the building officially opened. Significantly, the understanding that REALITY ENDS HERE has become a "motto" speaks to the interpretation of the graffiti as now expressing a "principle, goal, or ideal" (Boyer, Ellis, Harris, and Soukhanov,1983, p. 447). Nonetheless, the appropriating of the graffiti—aesthetically and otherwise—suggests an institutionally approved meaning.

Photograph by Brian Moss

At USCs new film school, the graffito REALITY ENDS HERE has taken on new, institutionally co-opted and commodified forms. It was stamped on a commemorative coin celebrating the film school. It has been emblazoned on merchandise that has been sold through the film school. Clearly, these new contexts also suggest the transformation of a cultural artifact. As an expression of resistance, the graffito is becoming a dim memory for some, and unrecognizable as such to new members. Clearly, the graffito has been appropriated by those "in charge," and has become an expression of something else. But what? I would argue that the graffito functions in several ways. First, the graffito is a symbolic device for retaining a sense of continuity in the face of organizational change. The USC film school is the oldest in the country; its inception may be traced back to the early days of the movie industry. Along these lines, the graffito is one of the last links with the "stables"—which, despite having been destroyed—has taken on meaning as an artifact meaningful in its own right, both to those who experienced that context firsthand or have reconstructed the history of the USC film school in watching the films.

The circular clustering of the main buildings of the new School of Cinema-Television is very nest-like in its architectural construction. And at the center of the nest is the graffito, REALITY ENDS HERE, etched into the soft curve of a bridge's egg-like trajectory. Thus, the physical placement of the graffito also suggests that the ideal had become metaphorically centralized, and protected. Mostly, however, the graffito is a self-reflexive comment about the nature of filmmaking. As a USC professor pointed out, the graffito represents film school as inhabiting a place beyond reality. It hides as reality; and this is similar to filmmaking, which appears to be constructing reality, but is really a fantasy, constructed by a different reality.

"REALITY ENDS HERE" Comes to Loyola Marymount University

The analysis thus far has offered interpretations as the artifact has changed over time. Although the graffiti has also changed in its physical placement, those changes have all been within the confines of a particular university. However, in now interpreting the graffiti as it moves to a different university, we are changing the context not only spatially, but also institutionally.

A number of professors at Loyola Marymount University's film school were themselves educated at USCs old film school, and were intoxicated with the ethos of the stables. Like George Lucas, these professors carry fond memories of the graffiti-covered walls and the comradeship that comes with creating works of art in dilapidated conditions. As a professor at Loyola Marymount University, Lavick has taught film production courses, including LMUs "460," the senior film project that is in most ways, the equivalent to USCs 480 course, which had been the focus of Lavick's ethnographic film while a USC film student. While teaching the 460 course at LMU, Lavick shows his students *The 480 Experience*—often in the first week of the course—which served to illustrate the logistical and artistic problems that students may encounter while making their films, including the artistic tensions between students and professors (Scheibel, 1994). These students, then, in watching the film, and in talking with their professors, are made aware of the history of USCs graffiti-covered film school; they too, are exposed to "REALITY ENDS HERE." Given their exposure to the graffiti in Lavick's film—now serving as artifacts of socialization—it is not surprising that for many years, the basement film editing rooms were covered in graffiti. Although the graffiti was repeatedly painted over—typically at the end of a school year, after students finished editing their films—it reappeared. At LMU, a number of professors tacitly supported the graffiti; further, at least one professor actively tried to keep the graffiti from being painted over. There has been a sense among the faculty that the basement editing rooms had inherited the ethos of USCs "stables," and that such conditions were not antithetical to the creation of art, but in fact, might be a good thing. Thus, Lavick's film, with its lingering focus on a single piece of graffiti, became, in part, the impetus for stimulating the production of graffiti in the LMU film editing rooms. Again, we see here the interplay of artifacts.

During the early 1990s, LMU film students started creating and manufacturing film school-related clothing in the form of hats and T-shirts, inspired perhaps by a desire to express their own identity as LMU film students. An early T-shirt was composed of images appropriated from other artifacts. On the front of the T-shirt was a lion wearing a beret, symbolic of the Loyola Marymount University Lions and also the image used by Metro-Goldwyn-Mayer at the beginning of their films. However, the back of the black T-shirt stated, in bright yellow block letters:

REALITY
STOPS
HERE

The LMU film school faculty's reaction to the T-shirt—at least those who had gone to film school at USC—was one of distaste.[3] First, the T-shirt smacked of artistic plagiarism. Less obviously, the appropriation of the original graffito by students who had not attended USC, and who had not been of "the stables," was a violation of the meaning and attachment that certain faculty members held for that graffito. Further, the use of symbolism by the students so closely associated with USCs film school was embarrassing, in the sense that LMUs film school competes with USC for students, for awards, and for recognition. Thus, the use of USC's symbolism was interpreted as a self-imposed strike against LMU's desire to maintain its own identity as a film school that competes with USC and other local film schools. Not surprisingly then, REALITY STOPS HERE . . . stopped there. The graffito could not be successfully altered, transformed, or reused in this case (Hodder, 2000). The context defined the text's existence, and the text was found wanting.

Conclusion

We can see the tensions between text and context and the problems and opportunities these create (Hodder, 2000). Texts and contexts serve to define each other, with the meanings changing as the text is reread, sliding through time and place (see Clair, 1996; Hodder, 2000). In the current study, the graffito was inscribed on buildings, photographed for films and research purposes, and manufactured on coins and clothing. The meaning of the expression REALITY ENDS HERE changed with the context in various ways. The physical representation of the expression on buildings is an obvious example, but provides an illustration of how the creation and transformation of meanings are instantiated through expressive practices. Thus, changes in the context may create tensions that challenge the practices by which the artifact is brought into being.

An ethnography of expression (Clair, 1996) allows for an interpretation of meaning as the text and context change across time and place (Clair, 1996). As an artifact, the graffito REALITY ENDS HERE has been an expression of student resistance, an administrative expression of organizational continuity, a "motto" reflecting the principles of an art form, a problem of artistic integrity and organizational identity, and a locus for mystery and legend. In examining the artifact in its various appearances, we interpret the changes and fluctuations in meanings, forms, and functions as the expression slides through time (Clair, 1996). And as such, we note that the artifact is always, *always*, a problem of interpretation.

In the course of writing this article, I went down to the film editing rooms, looking for graffiti. I found none. Of course, it is very early in the fall semester, and students won't start editing their films for a month or two. Perhaps graffiti will again appear. I hope so. I would be disappointed to have it end here.

Notes

1. My drawing of the graffiti is based on repeated viewings of Howard Lavick's film, *The 480 Experience*. I used a freeze-frame feature on the video-cassette player, then attempted to sketch the graffito.

2. Howard Lavick's ethnographic film was filmed by Lavick when he was a USC film student. Lavick's film captures director Rick Redeman and his crew while they attempt to shoot Redeman's film.

3. While studying film students in the early 1990s, I saw and heard a professor voice disapproval over the article of clothing.

References

Alton, J. (1949). *Painting with light*. New York: Macmillan.

Boyer, M., Ellis, K., Harris, D. R., and Soukhanov, A. H. (Eds.) (1983). *American heritage disctionary* (2nd college ed.). New York: Dell.

Cheney, G. (1983). The rhetoric of identification and the study of organizational communication. *Quarterly Journal of Speech, 69*: 143–158.

Clair, R. P. (1998). *Organizing silence: A world of possibilities*. Albany: State University of New York.

— — —. (1996, May). *Methodologies for organizational communication researchers in the 21st century*. Paper presented at the annual meeting of the International Communication Association, Chicago, IL.

— — —. (1993). The bureaucratization, commodification, and privatization of sexual harassment through institutional discourse: A study of the "Big Ten" universities. *Management Communication Quarterly, 7*: 123–157.

Conquergood, D. (1994). Homeboys and hoods: Gang communication and cultural space. In L. R. Frey (Ed.), *Group communication in context: Studies of natural groups* (pp. 23–55). Hillsdale, NJ: Lawrence Erlbaum.

Dipert, R. R. (1993). *Artifacts, art works, and agency*. Philadelphia: Temple University Press.

Hodder, I. (2000). The interpretation of documents and material culture. In N. K. Denzin and Y. S. Lincoln (Eds.), *Handbook of qualitative research* (2nd ed.) (pp. 703–715). Thousand Oaks, CA: Sage Publications, Inc.

Farber, S. (1984, June). The USC connection. *Film Comment, 20*: 34–39.

Harmetz, A. (1981, November 25). U.S.C. breaks ground for a film-TV school. *The New York Times,* p. C16.

Howe, J. (Director). (1990). *The first fifty years* [film]. Los Angeles: School of Cinema-Television, University of Southern California.

Jorgensen, D. L. (1989). *Participant observation: A methodology for human studies.* Newbury Park, CA: Sage Publications, Inc.

Latham, A. (1992, October). SRO and Movie U. *M,* pp. 107–113.

Lavick, H. (Director). (1975). *The 480 experience* [film]. Los Angeles: Department of Cinema-Television, University of Southern California.

Rodriguez, A., and Clair, R. P. (1999). Graffiti as communication: Exploring the discursive tensions of anonymous texts. *Southern Communication Journal, 65*: 1–15.

Scheibel, D. (1994). Graffiti and "film school" culture: Displaying alienation. *Communication Monographs, 61*: 1–18.

— — —. (1992). Faking identity in clubland: The communicative performance of "fake ID." *Text and Performance Quarterly, 12*: 160–175.

Stohl, C. (2001). Globalizing organizational communication. In F. M. Jablin and L. L. Putnam (Eds.), *New handbook of organizational communication: Advances in theory, research, and methods* (pp. 323–375). Thousand Oaks, CA: Sage Publications, Inc.

CHAPTER 21

Sense-Making Artifacts on the
Margins of Cultural Spaces

AMARDO RODRIGUEZ

Graffiti are universal communicative artifacts. For example, epigraphologists used the graffiti found on the walls of the city of Pompeii, which was destroyed by a volcano in A.D. 79, to accurately reconstruct many cultural features of the people who inhabited the city (D'Avino, 1964; Lindsay, 1960; Tanzers, 1939; Varone, 1991). No doubt, most peoples and cultures throughout the world anonymously write, draw, and paint on walls and other surfaces. These acts are inherently social. As Bruner and Kelso (1980) astutely observe, "although [often] written in the privacy of a toilet stall, the writing of graffiti is an essentially social act. . . . To write graffiti is to communicate; one never finds graffiti where they cannot be seen by others" (p. 241). Yet graffiti remain relatively absent in communication inquiry and ethnographic research (for exceptions see Conquergood, 1994; Rodriguez and Clair, 1999; Scheibel, 1994). Communication scholars and ethnographers seem to still assume that graffiti have no communicative value. It is supposedly the doing of deviant and delinquent minds (Abel and Buckley, 1977; Dundes, 1966; Gaylin and Jennings, 1996; Klein, 1974; Opler, 1974).

But these negative views of graffiti are no longer seen as either constructive or heuristic. Rodriguez and Clair (1999) contend that graffiti reveal how relations of power are being contested, what issues are worthy of being contested, and with which groups graffitists align themselves. Moreover, "graffiti provide an outlet for people to express their attitudes with regard to race, gender, and sexual orientation" (p. 2). Indeed, we now consider graffiti a highly structured communication medium that deserves attention and serious study (Bonuso, 1976; Boyd, 1980; Bruner and Kelso, 1980; Bushnell, 1990; Cole, 1991; Conquergood, 1994; D'Angelo, 1976; Durmuller, 1988a, 1988b; Feiner and Klein, 1982; Gumpert,

231

1975; Jones-Baker, 1981; Kohl, 1972; Kostka, 1974; La Barre, 1979; Long-necker, 1977; Melhorn and Romig, 1985; Newall, 1986-1987; Nierenberg, 1983; Reisner and Wechsler, 1974; Rodriguez and Clair, 1999; Scheibel, 1994; Spann, 1973).

In this paper, I discuss how attention to nontraditional communicative arti-facts like graffiti is important to strengthening the integrity of our scholarship and research. In the case of graffiti, its unique and compelling communication fea-tures allow cultural members to use it to facilitate the communication of ideas and concerns that communities censor (Rodriguez and Clair, 1999). In this regard, graffiti offer communication researchers and ethnographers valuable insights to important subterranean conflicts and tensions. I also discuss how viewing graffiti as a communication opportunity uniquely expands and deepens communication inquiry and ethnographic research. Finally, I propose a few theoretical and methodological solutions to a few of problems that graffiti and other such non-traditional communicative artifacts inherently present to communication researchers and ethnographers. The paper ends with a discussion of how graffiti expands our understanding of *naturally occuring discourse*.

Graffiti as Sense-making

Graffiti represent a communicative opportunity that offers valuable insight to the concerns, conflicts, and other discursive behaviors of cultural members. As Rodriguez and Clair (1999) observe, what distinguishes this opportunity from others is the fact that it functions both personally and openly. Personally, graffiti allow the key benefit of anonymity, that is, protection against any form of retri-bution. Any person can say whatever, however, and whenever, to whomever. In fact, graffitists acknowledge this benefit: "it's a chance to vent frustrations—to say things you wouldn't dare speak up about" (Fraser, 1980, p. 258), ". . . because sometimes you feel like letting the whole world know how you're feeling w/out giving yourself away" (p. 260). The result being that graffiti tend to reflect an honesty and openness that is rarely found in other kinds of public discourses (Boyd, 1980; Bruner and Kelso, 1980; Cole, 1991; Hentschel, 1987; Rodriguez and Clair, 1999).

The lack of explicit rules and protocols also allow graffitists to express themselves without the fear of social punishment that arises from any kind of vio-lation (Rodriguez and Clair, 1999). Accordingly, graffiti level the playing field by getting past all of the factors—such as social status, hierarchial position, educa-tion, access, familiarity with rules, expertise, communication competence—that advantageously privilege and benefit certain members against others. It is the only rhetorical form that affords such egalitarian and democratic virtues. Graffiti therefore represent an equal opportunity rhetorical form—arguably, the only rhetorical form that affords such equality for all discussants. Indeed, when various public discourses are officially and oppressively muted by government officials, graffitists consistently resort to public walls to hold such discourses (Chaffee, 1989). Simply put, the rhetorical features of graffiti are unique and compelling. Thus, attending to graffiti adds to the arsenal of means (e.g., metaphor and story analysis) to understand sense-making actions by members of varied cultures. In doing so, however, communication researchers and ethnographers need to be mindful that using graffiti as a source of interpretive material possesses a few inherent problems. These problems, however, are by no means insurmountable. In the following sections of this paper I explicate these methodological and theoretical problems and offer different solutions.

Methodological Problems and Solutions

Methodologically, graffiti are unobtrusive communicative artifacts and, as such, come with the pluses and minuses that come with such artifacts. From a plus standpoint, unobtrusive measures afford a source of data in environments where the audiences and persons being evaluated may be reluctant to provide the research team with the genuine information. Also, since the types of data that constitute an unobtrusive measure already exist, like graffiti, the cost of data collection are usually significantly lower than the cost of other more conventional measures (Terenzini, 1986). Moreover, Webb, Cambel, Schwartz, and Sechrest (1966) contend that unobtrusive measures counter a major weakness of other traditional methods—dependence upon language. As Webb and Weick (1979) point out: "Heavy prior reliance on self-report has excluded crucial populations from organizational inquiry, postponed cross-checking of propositions, . . . and imposed a homogeneity of method which raises the prospect that the findings are method-specific" (p. 221).

Unobtrusive measures direct the researcher to the primary source of data, bypassing the language which respondents can deliberately or inadvertently use to distort the data. This distortion constitutes silence, provision of inaccurate information, deliberate omission of data, and the inability to effectively articulate the desired information. For example, Klofas and Cutshall (1985) found that graffiti provided a unique source of data with which to examine issues raised with other methods. Ley and Cybriwsky (1974) also posit that graffiti are potential indicators of attitudes, behavioral dispositions, and social processes in environments where direct measurement is problematic. As such, graffiti often offer an accurate (and unobtrusive) index of a community's political and behavioral temper (Deiulio, 1978; Webb and Weick, 1979).

On the other hand, unobtrusive measures have a few minuses that ethnographers need to note. Although Lincoln and Guba (1985) advocate the use of unobtrusive measures, they acknowledge that these measures suffer certain weakness: (1) they are sometimes heavily inferential; (2) they are serendipitous; (3) they cannot be directly interpreted; and (4) it is difficult to establish their trustworthiness in either conventional or naturalistic terms. Moreover, Bates (quoted in Greenberg, 1979, p. 268) admits: "We don't know who writes it [graffiti] or whether the attitudes are representative of those of the general population, or even of [the graffiti-writers] themselves." Klofas and Cutshall (1985) also mention this limitation. They also posit that graffiti are incapable of providing the breadth of information afforded by other traditional data collection procedures. In addition, Klofas and Cutshall (1985) contend that graffiti provide few clues to subcultural adaptations in environments where such phenomena are common.

The minuses that come with graffiti are indeed significant. On the other hand, however, we need to also note that all measures and techniques that ethnographers use to gain "thick" descriptions of cultures have different limitations that are equally problematic. Ethnographers therefore need to use graffiti in conjunction with others measures and techniques. We should strive to use a variety of techniques—e.g., in-depth interviews, participant observation, metaphor analysis—so as to make for triangulated insights and understandings.

Triangulation always makes for deeper understandings (e.g., Polkinghorne, 1983; Webb, Campbell, Schwartz, and Sechrest, 1966; Webb and Weick, 1979). The effectiveness of triangulation rests on the premise that the weaknesses inherent in different methods will be counterbalanced by the strengths inherent in other methods. In other words, triangulation purports to exploit the assets and neutralize the weaknesses in each method. Polkinghorne (1983) introduces the concept of *syncretic research* to extend the capability of methodological triangulation. Syncretic research requires the data from the multiple methods be combined and integrated into a unified and integral result. In this regard, enthnograhers can use insights gained from their investigation of graffiti in their in-depth interviews with cultural members to gain a deeper sense of how and where and from whom the members are using to achieve sense-making and understanding. For example, Bruner and Kelso (1980) placed an interview protocol pertinent to graffiti on an electronic bulletin board to assure anonymity to respondents. They assumed that the face-to-face interview process probably inhibited self-disclosure. Also, Rodriguez (1994) found in a series of in-depth interviews that organizational members do indeed use graffiti for enculturation purposes. Enculturation refers to those processes by which organizational members acquire the social knowledge and skills necessary to behave as competent members. It emphasizes those communicative performances in which the newcomer learns the social knowledge and skills of the culture. Many interviewees in Rodriguez's study believed that graffiti provided more accurate insights to organizational life ("I read everything [graffiti]. Gives a feel of the people in the environment.") than traditional organizational media.

Theoretical Problems and Solutions

Ezrahi (1988, p. 137) raises an interesting question: "Is the writing on the wall only graffiti?" Indeed, a major theoretical problem with previous graffiti research is that many scholars view all wall inscriptions as either possessing communicative value or lacking communicative value. Various theoretical perspectives fail to make any meaningful distinction between different wall inscriptions which is either empirically or theoretically useful. For example, Chaffee (1989) makes a distinction between graffiti and wall painting. Warakowski (1991) posits that there are "genuine graffiti" and others not so genuine. Reisner and Wechsler (1974) make a distinction between wall inscriptions that are significant and others that are insignificant, banal, and sheer defacement. Blume (1985) advances a topology based on communication functions that exclude graffiti that perform mnemonic functions. This topology includes mass communication, categorical communication, individual communication, and reflexive communication.

Durmuller (1988b) warns against relying on intuition when making categorical distinctions among wall inscriptions. Instead, Durmuller (1988b) advises that researchers consult cultural members for their interpretations before making any determination. "This seemed especially important with regard to assigning graffiti texts to sociocultural domains, and to the reading of these texts as speech acts" (Durmuller, 1988b, p. 179). Absent from most of the proposed distinctions are theoretical frameworks to consistently make sense of wall inscriptions. As a result, applying these proposed distinctions empirically is problematic. What is required is a theoretical framework that embraces an interactional perspective on human action, such as symbolic interactionism, critical theory, and feminist theory. In my view, a symbolic interactionist perspective could prove to be quite useful in addressing many of the theoretical nuances that graffiti present to communication researchers and ethnographers.

Wolf (1992) posits that the symbolic interactionist perspective demands that the field of communication refine the conceptualization of rhetorical forms to include nonverbal rhetorical forms as the Tlinget basket (an artifact of the Eyak Indian nation) and a variety of other social acts. "I would argue . . . that what the field of rhetorical criticism has deemed rhetoric is unnecessarily limiting" (p. 13). Wolf (1992) argues that "Reconceptualization allows other people's experiences to be accounted for. Additionally, recoceptualization allows for the inclusion of rhetorical forms previously overlooked or discounted" (p. 2). In other words, Wolf (1992) believes that prevailing standards of what constitutes rhetoric ignores the rhetoric of people who are victims of oppression and use their rhetoric to challenge the dominant system. This criticism has much currency. Indeed, the inclusion of nontraditional communicative artifacts often affords the inclusion of voices of peoples and groups that have long been marginalized in communication inquiry (Conquergood, 1994; Rodriguez and Clair, 1999; Bruner and Kelso, 1980).

A symbolic interactionist perspective gives a constructive framework to work with nontraditional communicative artifacts. The reason being is that it directs us to focus on both context and meaning. It also provides a useful and heuristic framework to describe and explain communicative behaviors. McQuillen and Quigley (1989) contend that a symbolic interactionist perspective naturally contributes to the understanding of communicative phenomena, because it is directly and concretely interwoven with the process of human communication from internalization to societal interaction. In addition: While providing a perspective from which to examine communication, symbolic interactionism avoids the major faults of alternate theories. Interactionism is neither too abstract nor too concrete. It is directly linked to communicative behavior, and thus is not guilty of imposing an inappropriate mechanism on the discipline to create a quality or sophistication and maturity at the expense of potentially rich avenues of exploration. . . . Symbolic interactionism, in its essentials, is the sole communication perspective that is not a begged, borrowed or stolen mechanism; it is a valuable point from which to view and explore the myriad aspects of the discipline. (p. 6)

Human beings are considered a symbol creating, using, and misusing species who construct their reality through the negotiation of meanings that they assign to their symbols (Burke, 1966; Langer, 1951). According to Johnson (1982): "The importance of language in symbolic interactionism must be stressed, for it is through language (symbolic action) that man [*sic*] acquires the meanings necessary for functional social behavior" (p. 11). With respect to graffiti, chain responses to an original graffito compellingly demonstrate both interpretation of meaning and social interaction. The responses concretely indicate that respondents have indulged in the act of interpretation and have derived meaning from the graffito. As Bruner and Kelso (1980) explain: "A new person coming to a toilet stall who chooses to write a graffito must take account of what has previously been written, even in the minimal sense of choosing an appropriate location on the wall" (p. 241). It is indeed quite common for a new graffitist to weave an arrow through a thick maze of other graffiti to target a particular graffito (Rodriguez and Clair, 1999).

A symbolic interactionist perspective invites communication researchers and ethnographers to view graffiti as social interaction. It positions graffiti as another type of communication practice that members use to construct and display their understanding of life. In sum, a symbolic interactionist perspective offers a heuristic framework to view graffiti as communicative acts that inform, recreate, and sustain members' sense-making actions.

Conclusion

Communication researchers and ethnographers are increasingly being encouraged to look carefully at the *naturally occuring discourses* found in their research environments so as to better understand how cultural members are negotiating sense-making. The implicit suggestion is that such discourses are inherently face-to-face. But graffiti push our definition of naturally occurring discourse. In doing so, graffiti reveal to us that culture exists in the absence of face-to-face interaction, and cultural interaction transcends social/human interaction (naturally occurring discourses). In other words, graffiti reveal that cultures remain active and interactive in the absence of physical human/social interaction. What this means is that communication researchers and ethnographers now have to focus on *Where are cultural members' sense-making experiences occurring?* Directing our attention toward the varied forms of communication practices should open onto new vestiges of understanding culture

References

Abel, E. L., and Buckley, B. E. (1977). *The handwriting on the wall*. New Heaven, CT: Greenwood Press.

Blume, R. (1985). Graffiti. *Discourse and Literature, 3*: 137–148.

Bonuso, C. A. (1976). Graffiti. *Today's Education, 65*: 90–91.

Boyd, S. R. (1980). The cultural differences of female graffiti. *Journal of the Metropolitan Washington Communication Association, 9*: 25–38.

Bruner, E. M., and Kelso, J. P. (1980). Gender differences in graffiti: A semiotic perspective. *Women's Studies International Quarterly, 3*: 239–252.

Burke, K. (1966). *Language as symbolic action*. Berkeley, CA: University of California Press.

Bushnell, J. (1990). *Moscow graffiti*. London: Unwin Hyman.

Chaffee, L. G. (1989). Political graffiti and wall painting in Greater Buenos Aires: An alternative communication system. *Studies in Latin American Popular Culture, 8*: 37–60.

Cole, C. M. (1991). "Oh wise women of the stalls . . ." *Discourse* and *Society, 2*: 401–411.

Conquergood, D. (1994). Homeboys and hoods: Gang communication and cultural space. In L. R. Frey (Ed.), *Group communication in context: Studies of natural groups* (pp. 23–55). Hillsdale, NJ: Lawrence Erlbaum.

D'Angelo, F. J. (1976). Fools' names and fools' faces are always seen in public places: A study of graffiti. *Journal of Popular Culture, 10*: 102–109.

D'Avino, M. (1964). *The women of Pompeii*. Naples, Italy: Loffredo.

Deiulio, A. M. (1978). Of adolescent cultures and subcultures. *Educational Leadership, 35*: 518–520.

Dundes, A. (1966). Here I sit: A study of American latrinalia. *Kroeber Anthropological Society Papers, 34*: 91–105.

Durmuller, U. (1988a). Research on mural sprayscripts (Graffiti). In A. R. Thomas (Ed.), *Methods in dialectology* (pp. 278–284). Clevedon: Multi-lingual Matters.

———. (1988b). Sociolinguistic aspects of mural sprayscripts (Graffiti). *Sociolinguistics, 17*: 1–16.

Ezrahi, S. D. (1988). Considering the apocalypse: Is the writing on the wall only graffiti? In B. Lang (Ed.), *Writing and the Holocaust* (pp. 137–153). New York: Holmes and Meier.

Feiner, J. S., and Klein, S. M. (1982, Winter). Graffiti talks. *Social Policy, 12*: 47–53.

Fraser, B. (1980). Meta-graffiti. *Maledicta: The International Journal of Verba Aggression, 4*: 258–260.

Gaylin, W., and Jennings, B. (1996). *The perversion of autonomy*. New York: The Free Press.

Greenberg, J. (1979). Off the wall at Umass. *Science News, 116*: 268.

Gumpert, G. (1975). The rise of uni-comm. *Today's Speech, 23*: 34–38.

Hastings, R. (1984). Juve is majic: The anglicisms of Italian football graffiti. *Italian Studies, 39*: 91–102.

Hentschel, E. (1987). Women's graffiti. *Multilingual Journal of Cross-Cultural and Interlanguage Communication, 6–3*: 287–308.

Johnson, K. S. (1982). Phenemenology and symbolic interactionism: *Recommendations for social science research* (Report No. SO 016 669). University of Alabama (ERIC Document Reproduction Service No. ED 259 971).

Jones-Baker, D. (1981). The graffiti of folk motifs in Cotswold Churches. *Folklore, 92*: 160–167.

Klein, F. (1974). Commentary. In L. Gross (Ed.), *Sexual behavior: An interdisciplinary perspective* (pp. 87–88). New York: Spectrum.

Klofas, J. M., and Cutshall, C. R. (1985). The social archeology of a juvenile facility: Unobtrusive methods in the study of institutional cultures. *Qualitative Sociology, 8*: 368–387.

Kohl, H. R. (1972). *Golden boy as Anthony Cool: A photo essay on naming and graffiti*. New York: Dial Press.

Kostka, R. (1974). Aspects of graffiti. *Visible Language, 8*: 369–371.

La Barre, W. (1979). Academic graffiti. *The International Journal of Verbal Aggression, 3*: 275–276.

Langer, S. (1951). *Philosophy in a new key*. Cambridge, MA: Harvard University Press.

Ley, D., and Cybriwsky, R. (1974). Urban graffiti as territorial markers. *Annals of the Association of American Geographers, 64*: 491–505.

Lincoln, Y. S., and Guba, E. G. (1985). *Naturalistic inquiry*. London: Sage Publications, Inc.

Lindsay, J. (1960). *The writing on the wall: An account of Pompeii in its last days*. London: Mueller Company.

Littlejohn, S. W. (1989). *Theories of human communication*. California: Wadsworth.

Longnecker, G. J. (1977). Sequential parody graffiti. *Western Folklore, 36*: 354–360.

McQuillen, J. S., and Quigley, T. A. (1989, April). *Theoretical Practicality: A Functional Taxonomy of Speech Communication*. Paper presented at the Southern Speech Communication Association Annual Convention, Louisville, KY.

Melhorn, J. J., and Romig, R. J. (1985). Rest room: A descriptive study. *The Emporia State Research Studies, 34*: 29–45.

Misic, D. (1990). Fan identity symbols. *Kultura, 88–90*: 147–158. (From *Sociological Abstracts*, 1993, Abstract No.9303176).

Newall, V. (1986–1987). The moving spray can: A collection of some contemporary English graffiti. *The International Journal of Verbal Aggression, 9*: 39–47.

Nierenberg, J. (1983). Proverbs in graffiti: Taunting traditional wisdom. *Maledicta: The International Journal of Verbal Aggression, 7*: 41–58.

Opler, M. K. (1974). Commentary. In L. Gross (Ed.), *Sexual behavior: An interdisciplinary perspective* (pp. 86–87). New York: Spectrum.

Pacanowsky, M. E., and O'Donnell-Trujillo, N. (1982). Communication and organizational culture. *Western Journal of Speech Communication, 46*: 115–130.

Patton, M. Q. (1980). *Qualitative evaluation methods*. Beverly Hills, CA: Sage Publications, Inc.

Polkinghorne, D. (1983). *Methodology for the human sciences*. Albany: State University of New York Press.

Reisner, R. (1974). Commentary. In L. Gross (Ed.), *Sexual behavior: An interdisciplinary perspective* (pp. 85–86). New York: Spectrum.

Reisner, R., and Wechsler, L. (1974). *Encyclopedia of graffiti*. New York: Macmillan.

Rodriguez, A. (1995). *Graffiti as organizational communication: An extension of organizational culture theory at an American urban university*. Unpublished doctoral dissertation, Howard University, Washington, DC.

Rodriguez, A., and Clair, R. P. (1999). Graffiti as communication: Exploring the discursive tensions of anonymous texts. *Southern Communication Journal, 65:* 1–14.

Scheibel, D. (1994). Graffiti and "Film School" culture: Displaying alienation. *Communication Monographs, 61*: 1–18.

Spann, S. (1973). The handwriting on the wall. *English Journal, 62*: 1163–1165.

Starr, M. (1990, November, 26). The writing on the wall. *Newsweek*, p.64.

Stern, K. S. (1990). *Bigotry on campus: A planned response* (Report No. HE 024 094) American Jewish Committee (ERIC Document Reproduction Service No. ED 328 108).

Tanzers, H. H. (1939). *The common people of Pompeii*. Baltimore, MD: John Hopkins Press.

Terenzini, P. T. (1986, October 25). *The case for unobtrusive measures*. Paper presented at the forty-seventh ETS Invitational Conference, New York, NY.

Varone, A. (1991). The walls speak. *Archaeology, 11*: 30–31.

Warakowski, J. (1991). The humor of graffiti. In G. Bennett (Ed.), *Spoken in jest* (pp. 279–289). Sheffield, England: Sheffield Academic Press.

Webb, E. J., Campbell, D. T., Schwartz, R. D., and Sechrest, L. (1966). *Unobtrusive measures: Nonreactive research in the social sciences*. Chicago: Rand McNally.

Webb, E., and Weick, K. E. (1979). Unobtrusive measures in organizational theory: A reminder. In J. Van Maanen (Ed.), *Qualitative Methodology* (pp. 209–224). Beverly Hills, CA: Sage Publications, Inc.

Wolf, E. (1992). *The Tlingit basket as a rhetorical alternative form*. Paper presented at Southern Communication Conference, Chicago, IL.

PART EIGHT

Genealogy and Postcolonial Identities as Expressions of Ethnography

CHAPTER 22

Genealogy as an Ethnographic Enterprise

JASON E. COMBS[1]

Ask any family historian who has roots in the Coal Fields region of eastern Kentucky, and she or he likely will know of George "Goldenhawk" Sizemore, an allegedly one-half or three-fourths Cherokee resident of the area during the early to mid-1800s. As one newspaper article in the Salyersville area argues, Goldenhawk remains a legend of sorts to many people in the region, as many colorful stories continue to be told about his adventures (Mueller, 1999, June 7). The article recounts one story regarding Goldenhawk's remarkable fertility:

> About the same time, 1860, Goldenhawk was indicted for bigamy in Floyd County, Henry Sizemore said. According to minutes from the hearing, the judge said, "Mr. Sizemore, I understand you have about 50 children." . . . Goldenhawk said, "I guess you're right. But, judge, if I'd been half as pretty a man as you are, I'd had more than that." (Mueller, 1999, June 7).

A similar story appears in the notes of my grandmother, Gwen Combs, which she gave to me one summer while I was a boy. She identifies Goldenhawk as the father of 52 children, through seven wives. "He would have had 62 had they all lived," she adds (Gwen Combs, personal communication, ca. 1985). Although written nearly fifteen years and seventy miles apart from each other, these two accounts demonstrate the importance for many people of understanding their roots, for through the recounting of each, the teller understands her or himself in relation to her or his ancestors, in these cases, one that lived over 150 years ago.

Today, genealogy thrives as a popular pastime. Although people pursue it for different reasons, writers agree that, for many, it comprises one way through which they strive to understand themselves (Lichtman, 1978; Stryker-Rodda,

1987; Wright, 1995). I have been a practicing genealogist for seven years. Over fifteen years ago, my grandmother gave to me several scraps of paper on which she copiously had written notes. "This is the family history," she told me. "I want you to keep it and pass it on, for when the old people are gone, there may be no way to ever get it again." I was ten years old then, and although I understood little of the importance of what my grandmother had given to me, I did as she told me to do. Nearly a decade later, five years after my grandmother's death, I found those same notes that had been sitting in the recesses of my desk and realized what my grandmother had entrusted to me. Since then, I have continued her initial work far beyond the rough ancestry that she had chronicled. After years of corresponding with others, sifting through government records from around the country, and conducting numerous interviews with family members, I have produced a genealogical account of our family that spans over five hundred years. Regarding some branches of our ancestry, it reaches even to earlier times.

Like many other genealogists, I have learned through trial and error, first-hand efforts, or from consulting various genealogical aids. To help novices to learn about genealogy in more economical and less frustrating ways, a wealth of literature has been published regarding genealogical methods, strategies, and techniques. Despite the necessity and value of this knowledge, these sources present an incomplete model of the genealogical enterprise: they emphasize technique at the expense of a more holistic understanding of what research entails. These sources conceptualize genealogy as a "science"; however, as they employ it, this metaphor ignores some of the more interpretive and social dimensions of genealogy. I suggest that "ethnography" offers a more fitting and insightful metaphor, one that recognizes these dimensions and thereby incorporates a more organic and personal appreciation for genealogical research. Reconceptualized in ethnographic terms, genealogy offers much promise to all researchers regarding the family, including those in academe.

Genealogy as the "Science" of Ancestry

I will begin with an explanation of what constitutes genealogy. Although one certainly can find subtle differences among different definitions, most of them share key ideas. Doane and Bell (1992) define genealogy as, "the study of family origins and the ways of individuals; individuals and families help to make history" (p. 15). Greenwood (2000) offers a slightly different definition: Genealogy is "that branch of history which involves the determination of family relationships" (p. 3). Certainly, these two definitions differ. Nevertheless, they share two common assumptions: the family constitutes the principal object of study, and that the study of that family intertwines substantially with the study of history.[2]

For many authors, this dual focus upon history at large and the history of specific persons constitutes the essence of genealogy. From this perspective, Stryker-Rodda (1987) argues:

Genealogy and history are now recognized as inseparable. The historian deals with masses of people and massive events, while the genealogist is specific about a person in the mass affected by massive events. Through information found in personal letters, diaries, and minutiae discovered in family searches, the genealogist becomes a historian contributing new knowledge to the history field. (p. 43)

In such a way, genealogists constitute a particular brand of historian: one who focuses upon the events of history in a more microscopic way (e.g., Doane and Bell, 1992; Greenwood, 2000; Lichtman, 1978; Wright, 1995). Although they are concerned with specific families as those families evolve through time, they do not view those families as existing within a vacuum. In the actions of family members, one can see the workings of history en masse. In this sense, genealogy is the study not only of familial relationships, but also of social relationships of various kinds, as the lives of family members intertwine with those of others across the vastness of time-space.

In attempting to develop some account of one's family across many generations, genealogists must draw upon "methods" that originate in the traditional social sciences. Stryker-Rodda (1987) suggests that in their study of families, genealogists often must draw upon practices from a great variety of disciplines, including law, religion, geography, and history. They often must consult old maps, legal documents, religious records, and historical writings. One of the most central "methods" of genealogical research, the biographical interview, has its roots in psychological, sociological, and anthropological studies (see Dollard, 1971; Langness, 1965; Mandelbaum, 1973; Watson, 1976; Watson and Watson-Franke, 1985). Whether genealogists are conversing with others about their experiences or those of someone else, they often are employing methods that derive from the study of social relationships in the traditional social sciences.

For these various reasons, many writers qualify genealogy as a "science," not unlike the traditional social and physical sciences. Stryker-Rodda (1987) argues:

Today genealogy is recognized as a science. It uses all of the techniques that any other science employs: research to discover what has been previously proved; building on that to discover new data; analysis of old and new research to discover weaknesses and strengths; synthesis to pull old and new together to complete the product. (p. 10)

Greenwood (2000) speaks towards a similar view. He charges that, when properly practiced, genealogy bears a "systemized" quality, characteristic of much work in the traditional sciences (p. 8). In his view, research should proceed more or less according to specific steps, many of which involve the same kind of interpretation, analysis, and theorizing that professional scientists do in their work. Genealogy is "a 'how-to' subject," in which one "must actually learn to *do* the research" (Greenwood, 2000, p. 4, italics added). One who adopts this view begins to view genealogy as a predominantly *technical* enterprise: the successful doing of it depends almost wholly upon developing sound skills and strategies.

Certainly, there is some value to such an approach. In much of the genealogical enterprise, if one does not have sound skills and strategies, then one will *not* succeed. The field of sources from which researchers must gather their information is fraught with various whirlpools and rapids that one must negotiate: inaccurate and incomplete census records, contradictory accounts of the same people and events, genealogies that presume to give the "truth" regarding certain ancestors but support themselves with little evidence, and documents that were written in a language that only vaguely resembles today's English. If one does not have a proper methodological base in the pursuit of one's ancestors, then one easily can become lost in the dizzying maze of grappling with these sources. The problem with most genealogical handbooks and aids is not that they focus upon the technical aspects of genealogy; it is that they focus *exclusively* on these aspects. Although many of these handbooks discuss how to *do* genealogy, they do not address how to *think* about genealogy. Therefore, although many genealogists might know their way around particular records quite well, they have little insight regarding what they are doing as a whole beyond the simple compiling of information and drawing of trees.

I suggest that this focus exclusively upon the technical aspects of one's research stems from the centrality of "science" as a metaphor for the genealogical enterprise. As writers in genealogy use it, "science" denotes a kind of *systematizing of method*. The assumption that if one masters the methods, then one masters the effort as a whole informs much of what various authors regarding genealogy say. With this assumption, one cannot help but to see both the genealogist and the genealogical enterprise largely in mechanistic terms. As the recipient and emulator of proper methods, the genealogist "does" genealogy through the gathering, sorting, and compiling of data in proper ways. The family tree that results is understood essentially as something that is "discovered" through the employment of these methods.

Something is lost in such a conceptualization. Genealogy consists of much more than the methods that genealogists use in researching the past. I suggest that a new master metaphor is necessary, which can reframe genealogists' understandings of what they are doing as they employ those methods: a metaphor that emphasizes the more personal and organic aspects of the genealogical process, and recasts specific methods as modalities through which these qualities continuously exist.

Genealogy as an Ethnographic Enterprise

"Ethnography" provides us with such a metaphor. Indeed, throughout the whole of the genealogical enterprise, a particular vector runs through it that embodies what many scholars in the social sciences associate with ethnographic research. Definitions of ethnography vary as much as, or even more than those of genealogy. However, despite some of the more subtle differences between them, many scholars closely identify ethnography with the direct observation of social events in their natural setting (e.g., Agar, 1996; Burawoy, 1991; Emerson, 1981; Goffman, 1989; Gubrium and Holstein, 1997; Jackson, 1996; Lincoln and Guba, 1985; Lofland and Lofland, 1995; Rawlins, 1998; Schwartzman, 1993). Often, such examination of social events is methodologically dubbed "participant-observation" (Agar, 1996; Burawoy, 1991; Gubrium and Holstein, 1997; Lofland and Lofland, 1995). Despite his hesitancy to define it in very concrete terms, Agar (1996) describes participant-observation as embodying "the assumption that the raw material of ethnographic research lies out there in the daily activities of the people you are interested in, and the only way to access those activities is to establish relationships with people, participate in what they do, and observe what is going on" (p. 31).

Although participant-observation does constitute a kind of method for studying social life, I suggest that most ethnographers would recognize that it involves much more than the enactment of any specific techniques. Ethnographers often do point to specific strategies and approaches that they and other researchers conventionally have adopted in their own work, and writers about ethnography often do explicate these "methods" for the benefit of readers who might be seeking insight regarding the doing of ethnography for themselves (e.g., Agar, 1996; Bantz, 1993; Goffman, 1989; Lofland and Lofland, 1995; Schwartzman, 1993; Strauss and Corbin, 1998). Nevertheless, in most of their writings, there is an implicit, sometimes *explicit* understanding that ethnography consists of more than the employment of these "methods." Indeed, as Agar (1996) suggests, ethnography does not lend itself well to training. It has an organic quality, a "complex flow" (Strauss and Corbin, 1998, p. 29) that largely depends upon the one who practices it, the people whom one studies, and the site where one's research occurs. Ethnographic writings often emphasize the robust, firsthand quality of ethnographic study. The research literally becomes both a part of the field that he or she is studying and the medium through which that studying occurs. In this sense, the experiences of the ethnographer in "doing" the ethnography are paramount.

As such, ethnography consists of "technique" only in a very holistic sense. The entire person of the researcher becomes relevant to the enterprise, and in drawing conclusions about the particular "field" that one is studying, one cannot divorce that person from the act of observing, except artificially. As one considers the "data" that one has collected, one must take into account one's own ideas, insights, opinions, emotions, hopes, fears, doubts, strengths, and weaknesses (Agar, 1996). In fact, one often makes an account of these qualities, for in some sense, they *are* the "data." The ethnographer is the instrument through which the "data" exists in the first place. Without the ethnographer as a questioning, interpreting, hypothesizing, theorizing, and account-making experiential being, there is no "data"—only parts of the social world waiting to be observed.

At the heart of any genealogical effort, one finds the same goals that mobilize ethnographic study. Like ethnography, genealogy is fundamentally a study of social life. However, the social worlds that genealogists explore are specific families. In its most skeletal sense, genealogy involves only the mapping of relationships among various members of that group, as these members develop associations with other families and those associations change and evolve from generation to generation. In such an effort, the primary principle informing one's study of these relationships is one of "bloodline," the genetic descent of particular human beings from other human beings through time. Nevertheless, no genealogist restricts his or her concern simply to the "blood ties" among family members, for there is always an implicit awareness that these relationships consist of more than mere genetic propagation. Like families now, the family of one's ancestors was a unique and complex *social world* (Bennett, Wolin, and McAvity, 1988; Jorgenson, 1989; Patterson and Garwick, 1994; Rawlins, 1989; Reiss and Oliveri, 1980; Wolin and Bennett, 1984; Yerby, 1989), which to some degree, every genealogical effort strives to understand.[3] Questions regarding marriage, parentage, occupation, burial, military service, religion, migration, land ownership, education, and citizenship explore the social aspects of one's life, regardless of whether or not the one in question still is living today.

Often, the members of that social world no longer exist in any immediate sense. Much of what genealogists explore concerns the lives of people who lived generations before their own time. In such cases, unlike the ethnographer, the genealogist cannot enter the world of those people and participate in it as one might in studying some living organization, tribe, or community. Nevertheless, this is not to say that she or he cannot "enter" that world in any sense of the word. What writers call "sources" for one's genealogical data are actually parts of that world that extend into the present. They are *artifacts* of the people who lived in that world. For them, these "things" had significance and function within the context of their everyday lives, and through them, genealogists have access to the worlds in which those people lived.[4]

In examining these artifacts, genealogists can induce not only what relationships might have existed genetically among particular persons, but also ones that existed socially, politically, and economically. Ethnographers engage in this same kind of "induction" as they draw conclusions about the living social groups whom they observe (see Bantz, 1993; Lofland and Lofland, 1995; Strauss and Corbin, 1998). In some sense, they do not have direct access to the meanings of the people whom they observe any more than genealogists do, regardless of how much or how little time separates them from the people they study. As Kenneth Burke (1973) suggests, there is *always* a gulf between the experiences of different human beings: what he calls the "principle of individuation" (pp. 265–266). Regardless of whether or not the person in question stands physically before us, we do not escape the need for interpretation in our efforts to understand him or her as a subject of experience (Burke, 1973; see also Husserl, 1973; Merleau-Ponty, 1945/1962). Throughout their respective efforts, ethnographers and genealogists only can infer the unobservable aspects of the social worlds that they study from the observable materials before them. They never can "know" those aspects in any absolute, unmediated manner.

Nevertheless, we should remember that the limited ability of genealogists to enter the social world of their ancestors is not always a condition of their research. In many circumstances, genealogists can encounter members of a particular social world while they are living. Interviews, particularly the biographical interview, often play a crucial part in genealogical efforts. Known variously as the oral history or life history, this method involves motivating a member of a particular social group to talk extensively about his or her experiences. It differs from other forms of interviewing in that the primary topic of the interview is the *life* of a person (Langness, 1965). The participants in the interview attempt to explicate and describe a human life in high relief, with much rich and often intimate detail. In this manner, it can differ both substantively and experientially from conversing about some issue, event, or phenomenon.

Especially in its incorporation of these methods, genealogy is a fundamentally social activity. In order to experience the world as particular family members experience it, ethnographers must become a part of that social world. Methodological writings regarding ethnography (e.g., Agar, 1996; Lofland and Lofland, 1995) often emphasize the various challenges that ethnographers face in creating and maintaining relationships with the people whom they are studying: the need to build rapport, coping with emotional stresses that accompany maintaining particular relationships, gaining access to certain "parts" of the social world, managing one's own identity in the social world, and various ethical concerns about what to say and about whom. Genealogists face similar challenges; however, in genealogical efforts, the "field" of relationships that one must maintain throughout the course of the research is often the members of one's own living family. Unlike in ethnography, entrée is not a typical concern in genealogical research, for in most cases, one is already an accepted member of the family. As such, one may move about it and converse with various members about various topics as one pleases. Nevertheless, even in the most ordinary cases, there are often "parts" of the social world of the family to which only certain members have access. Genealogists often require information that exists in the hands of only a few members, some of which those members ordinarily would not share with others. In eliciting this information, the genealogist's efforts can alter the family as a whole in very consequential ways.

My own genealogical work has spawned noticeable changes in the way that my family understands itself. I recall many stories that members of the elder generations told when I was a boy regarding the family's past. Since my research began, I have observed many *new* stories: ones that derive primarily from the information that I have shared with the family. For instance, on many occasions, I have heard my father talking proudly with some of his friends about one of our ancestors who fought as a Tory, a supporter of the British, in the Revolutionary War. Although he typically adds details of his own, the basic "facts" of the story derive from what I have told him regarding my research. Before I began the project, my father, a staunch patriot, likely would have criticized the views of anyone who did not support wholeheartedly anything that he and others might consider to be traditionally American. However, as his own storytelling indicates, his conceptualization of the family has changed, as well as, to some degree, his appreciation for what *is* American. Indeed, one could say the same for me: that my understanding of the family and myself as a member of it have changed as my research too has changed. The story about my Tory ancestor is not only the story of a man who lived over two centuries before my birth; it also is *my* story in the living present. In some sense, *experientially, I become a Tory with him*, regardless of my present views about American government and society.

This is a very important point, for we should recall that in noncommercial genealogy, the group that the genealogist is studying is almost invariably his or her own family. In such a case, separating the genealogist from what constitutes the group in which he or she has an interest may be an impossible task, especially when the genealogist considers the two to be largely the same. In most cases, genealogical research involves a process of *identification* (see Bullis and Tompkins, 1989; Burke, 1950, 1967, 1973; Combs, Rosback, and Aamodt, 2000, May; Cheney, 1983a, 1983b, 1991; Cheney and Tompkins, 1987; Papa, Auwal, and Singhal, 1997; Scott, Corman, and Cheney, 1998) on the part of the researcher towards the people whom he or she is researching. Burke (1973) describes identification as a sense of "we" that one feels in regard to another: "Thus, a person may think of himself as 'belonging' to some special body more or less clearly defined (family, race, profession, church, social class, nation, etc., or various combinations of these)" (p. 268). Through identification, to some extent, one does not differentiate rigidly the other person or group from oneself. One punctuates the identity of that person or group in a way that incorporates, rather than distinguishes one's own being.

On this point, one finds a significant difference between ethnography and genealogy. In traditional ethnographies, the ethnographer and the "field" that she or he studies are considered to be somewhat distinct from each other, much as the world of the genealogist and the world of his or her ancestors, as I have discussed them so far. To study a particular group, the ethnographer must negotiate entrée into that social group and find a "place" within the everyday affairs that constitute social life for its members, from which she or he, as a relative "outsider," can make observations (Agar, 1996; Bantz, 1993; Goffman, 1989; Gubrium and Holstein, 1997; Lofland and Lofland, 1995). Identification may occur; however, it probably would not occur in any extreme manner. However, for the genealogist, a question arises regarding precisely where the boundaries of the group that one studies actually exist in the first place. As Wright (1995) suggests, one's self is continuously implicated in the research that one does. The identification between ourselves and our ancestors underlies the entire genealogical effort, for in understanding our ancestors, we believe that we are understanding ourselves: "Who am I? Where did I come from? It is the search for the answers to these questions that [. . .] pushes us to trace our ancestors' footsteps through life. Somehow we feel our identity is linked to our ancestors" (Wright, 1995, p. 1). What one learns as one sifts through yellowed archives and diaries of people who long since have died turns back upon one's appreciation of the family in the present. The distinction between genealogist and genealogy, family of the present and family of the past becomes muddled, if not at times, lost altogether.

From such a perspective, one appreciates how the "doing" of genealogy involves a crafting of both one's own and the family's identities, as the two continuously intertwine. The "science" metaphor, so pervasive in conventional genealogical literature, ignores the highly complex manner by which identity and research organically converge. Indeed, it arguably may obscure that convergence overall. Understood as an ethnographic enterprise, genealogy can offer much insight regarding how a family and its members experience themselves, both now and in the distant past.

Conclusion

In this chapter, I have argued for a reconceptualization of genealogy that recognizes its fundamentally "ethnographic" qualities. Traditional sources about genealogy predominantly emphasize its technical aspects: the specific skills, methods, strategies, and knowledge that genealogists require to do the research. These sources metaphorically portray genealogy as a "science," an activity which they understand to be fundamentally technical. This metaphor ignores many of the more organic and personal dimensions of "doing" genealogy. For that reason, a new metaphor is necessary: namely, genealogy as "ethnography."

Understanding genealogy as an ethnographic enterprise sensitizes us to these dimensions and positions us in ways that allow us to think about genealogy in a more holistic sense. In doing so, we come to understand genealogy as more than merely the tracing of bloodlines and the drawing of trees. Genealogy becomes the study of social worlds, including ones that may have existed centuries before our own time. Understanding those worlds can help us to understand not only the family in its various incarnations throughout time, but also the countless social events and processes that somehow interweave with it. Furthermore, we begin to appreciate the coreflexive nature of family and self, whereby members and the group that they constitute fold into each other in complex ways. Genealogy provides much insight regarding this interfolding in one of the most important ways that one can understand it: through the eyes of the people who live it. As such, genealogy offers interpretive scholars of communication and other disciplines a promising avenue for grappling with many questions regarding social life. Future studies of social phenomena that relate to the family in any way can benefit greatly through genealogical study, particularly when it actualizes itself as an ethnographic enterprise.

Notes

1. I would like to dedicate this chapter to my late grandmother, Gwen Hall Combs, whose creativity, love, and effort have inspired an entire legacy of genealogical concern.

Correspondence regarding this chapter can be sent to Jason E. Combs, Department of Communication, Purdue University, West Lafayette, IN, 47907-1366.

2. The term *family* is a slippery one, which one can apply validly to innumerable configurations social and genetic relationships. Although most genealogists probably focus upon tracing their genetic origins, many also concern themselves with other kinds of relationships, such as adoption, foster relations, in-laws, partners, and even friends. I purposefully have avoided giving any definition of family, for with Jorgenson (1989), I suggest that how one defines it is ultimately a matter of personal choice. Indeed, the definition of family among a particular group of persons may be of significant interest to researchers, in addition to any people or relationships that one groups under that term.

3. In academe, some authors have undertaken projects that incorporate an understanding of their family's heritage and history into their scholarly goals (e.g., Clair, 1997; Nakayama, 1994; Tanno, 1994; see also Trujillo's chapter in

this collection). Such projects exemplify many of the ideas that I am articulating in this chapter.

4. There is a corpus of work within the social disciplines that specializes in the study of *past* social worlds. Called *ethnohistory* (e.g., Chance, 1996; Henry, 1998; Hoxie, 1997; Loren, 2000; Rasmussen, 1999), this methodological tradition couples an ethnographic perspective to understanding past groups and social phenomena. As such, it may provide additional insight to inform genealogical efforts beyond that which I suggest here.

References

Agar, M. H. (1996). *The professional stranger: An informal introduction to ethnography* (2nd ed.). San Diego, CA: Academic Press.

Bantz, C. R. (1993). *Understanding organizations: Interpreting organizational communication cultures*. Columbia, SC: University of South Carolina.

Bennett, L. A., Wolin, S. J., and McAvity, K. J. (1988). Family identity, ritual, and myth: A cultural perspective on life cycle transitions. In C. J. Fallicov (Ed.), *Family transitions: Continuity and change over the life cycle* (pp. 211–234). New York: Guilford Press.

Bullis, C. A., and Tompkins, P. K. (1989). The forest ranger revisited: A study of control practices and identification. *Communication Monographs, 56*: 287–306.

Burawoy, M. (1991). Introduction. In M. Burawoy et al. (Eds.), *Ethnography unbound: Power and resistance in the modern metropolis* (pp. 1–7). Berkeley, CA: University of California Press.

Burke, K. (1950). *A rhetoric of motives*. Berkeley, CA: University of California Press.

———. (1967). Rhetoric—Old and new. In M. Steinmann, Jr. (Ed.), *New rhetorics* (pp. 59–76). New York: Scribner's Sons.

———. (1973). The rhetorical situation. In L. Thayer (Ed.), *Communication: Ethical and moral issues* (pp. 263–275). London: Gordon and Breach Science Publishers.

Chance, J. K. (1996). Mesoamerica's ethnographic past. *Ethnohistory, 43*: 379–403.

Cheney, G. (1983a). On the various and changing meanings of organizational membership: A field study of organizational identification. *Communication Monographs, 50*: 342–362.

———. (1983b). The rhetoric of identification and the study of organizational communication. *Quarterly Journal of Speech, 29*: 143–158.

———. (1991). *Rhetoric in an organizational society: Managing multiple identities*. Columbia, SC: University of South Carolina Press.

Cheney G., and Tompkins, P. K. (1987). Coming to terms with organizational identification and commitment. *Central States Speech Journal, 38*: 1–15.

Clair, R. P. (1997). Organizing silence: Silence as voice and voice as silence in the narrative exploration of the Treaty of New Echota. *Western Journal of Communication, 61*: 315–337.

Combs, J. E., Rosback, K., and Aamodt, E. (2000, May). *Identification and the structuration of organizational ethics: A response to Redding's call to action*. Paper presented at the Sixth Annual National Communication Ethics Conference, Gull Lake, MI.

Doane, G. H., and Bell, J. B. (1992). *Searching for your ancestors: The how and why of genealogy* (6th ed.). Minneapolis: University of Minnesota Press.

Dollard, J. (1971). *Criteria for the life history: With analyses of six notable documents*. Freeport, NY: Books for Libraries Press.

Emerson, R. M. (1981). Observational fieldwork. *Annual Review of Sociology, 7*: 351–378.

Goffman, E. (1989). On fieldwork. *Journal of Contemporary Ethnography, 18*: 123–132.

Greenwood, V. D. (2000). *The researcher's guide to American genealogy* (3rd ed.). Baltimore: Genealogical Publishing Company.

Gubrium, J. F., and Holstein, J. A. (1997). *The new language of qualitative method*. New York: Oxford University Press.

Henry, J. (1998). From *Acadien* to *Cajun* to *Cadien*: Ethnic labelization and construction of identity. *Journal of American Ethnic History, 17*(4): 29–62.

Hoxie, F. E. (1997). Ethnohistory for a tribal world. *Ethnohistory, 44*: 595–615.

Husserl, E. (1973). *Cartesian meditations: An introduction to phenomenology* (D. Cairns, Trans.). The Hague: Martinus Nijhoff.

Jackson, M. (1996). Introduction: Phenomenology, radical empiricism, and anthropological critique. In M. Jackson (Ed.), *Things as they are: New directions in phenomenological anthropology* (pp. 1–50). Bloomington, IN: Indiana University Press.

Jorgenson, J. (1989). Where is the "family" in family communication?: Exploring family self-definitions. *Journal of Applied Communication Research, 17*: 27–41.

Langness, L. L. (1965). *The life history in anthropological science*. New York: Holt, Rinehart, and Winston.

Lichtman, A. J. (1978). *Your family history: How to use oral history, personal family archives, and public documents to discover your heritage*. New York: Vintage Books.

Lincoln, Y., and Guba, E. G. (1985). Postpositivism and the naturalist paradigm. In *Naturalistic inquiry* (pp. 14–46). Beverly Hills, CA: Sage Publications, Inc.

Lofland, J., and Lofland, L. H. (1995). *Analyzing social settings: A guide to qualitative observation and analysis* (3rd ed.). Belmont, CA: Wadsworth Publishing Company.

Loren, D. D. (2000). The intersections of colonial policy and colonial practice: Creolization on the Eighteenth Century Louisiana/Texas frontier. *Historical Archaeology, 34*(3): 85–98.

Mandelbaum, D. G. (1973). The study of life history: Gandhi. *Current Anthropology, 14*: 177–196.

Merleau-Ponty, M. (1962). *Phenomenology of perception* (C. Smith, Trans.). New York: Routledge and Kegan Paul. (Original work published 1945)

Mueller, L. (1999, June 7). New gravestone planned for Magoffin father of 50 [Electronic Version]. *The Salyersville Herald-Leader*. Retrieved October 7, 2001, from http://genforum.genealogy.com/sizemore/messages/569.html

Nakayama, T. (1994). Dis/orienting identities: Asian Americans, history, and intercultural communication. In A. González, M. Houston, and V. Chen (Eds.), *Our voices: Essays in culture, ethnicity, and communication* (pp. 12–17). Los Angeles, CA: Roxbury Publishing.

Papa, M. J., Auwal, M. A., and Singhal, A. (1997). Organizing for social change within concertive control systems: Member identification, empowerment, and the masking of discipline. *Communications Monographs, 64*: 219–249.

Patterson, J. M., and Garwick, A. W. (1994). Levels of meaning in family stress theory. *Family Process, 33*: 287–304.

Rasmussen, S. J. (1999). The slave narrative in life history and myth, and problems of ethnographic representation of the Tuareg cultural predicament. *Ethnohistory, 46*: 67–108.

Rawlins, W. K. (1989). Metaphorical views of interaction in families of origin and future families. *Journal of Applied Communication Research, 17*: 52–70.

— — —. (1998). From ethnographic occupations to ethnographic stances. In J. S. Trent (Ed.), *Communication: Views from the helm for the 21st century* (pp. 359–362). Boston: Allyn and Bacon.

Reiss, D., and Oliveri, M. E. (1980). Family paradigm and family coping: A proposal for linking the family's intrinsic adaptive capacities to its responses to stress. *Family Relations, 29*: 431–444.

Schwartzman, H. B. (1993). *Ethnography in organizations*. Newbury Park, NJ: Sage Publications, Inc.

Scott, C. R., Corman, S. R., and Cheney, G. (1998). Development of a structurational model of identification in the organization. *Communication Theory, 8*: 298–336.

Strauss, A., and Corbin, J. (1998). *Basics of qualitative research: Techniques and procedures for developing grounded theory* (2nd ed.). Thousand Oaks, CA: Sage Publications, Inc.

Stryker-Rodda, H. (1987). *How to climb your family tree: Genealogy for beginners*. Baltimore, MD: Genealogical Publishing Company.

Tanno, D. V. (1994). Names, narratives, and the evolution of ethnic identity. In A. González, M. Houston, and V. Chen (Eds.), *Our voices: Essays in culture, ethnicity, and communication* (pp. 30–33). Los Angeles, CA: Roxbury Publishing.

Watson, L. C. (1976). Understanding a life history as a subjective document: Hermeneutical and phenomenological perspectives. *Ethos, 4*: 95–131.

Watson, L. C., and Watson-Franke, M. (1985). Life history research in anthropology. In *Interpreting life histories: An anthropological inquiry* (pp. 1–29). New Brunswick, NJ: Rutgers University Press.

Wolin, S. J., and Bennett, L. A. (1984). Family rituals. *Family Process, 23*: 401–420.

Wright, R. S., III (1995). *The genealogist's handbook: Modern methods for researching family history*. Chicago: American Library Association.

Yerby, J. (1989). A conceptual framework for analyzing family metaphors. *Journal of Applied Communication Research, 17*: 43–51.

CHAPTER 23

In Search of Naunny's Ethnicity

An (Auto)Ethnographic Study
of a Family's Ethnic Identity

NICK TRUJILLO

Grandma always used to say she was Spanish. I mean, around here [in Los Angeles], everybody's Mexican. But Grandma heard me say that I was Mexican one time, and she said, "No you're not Mexican. You're Spanish."

—Great Grandson, Age 35

When my sisters and I were little kids, my father, who was born in Los Angeles in 1930, referred to himself as "Mexican." Our grandmother, whom we called "Naunny," used to tell us that we were not Mexican but were "Spanish." She said that no one in our family was from Mexico, though no one seemed to be from Spain either. Naunny herself was born in southern Colorado, and her ancestors had lived in New Mexico for generations, long before it was part of the United States. My sisters and I never really knew the difference between Mexican and Spanish, but Spanish sounded better to us, so we used that label whenever classmates asked us what nationality we were.

Introduction

I was devastated when my grandmother died several years ago at age eighty-six. As a tribute, I have been conducting research for the last few years on how relatives have assigned meaning to her life and death (see Trujillo, 1998; Trujillo, 2002). In this chapter, I examine the role that she played in shaping our family's ethnic identity. Several researchers have pointed out that grandparents are very instrumental in influencing a family's sense of culture and ethnicity. For example, Tinsley and Parke (1984) wrote that grandparents transmit "values, ethnic heritage, and family traditions" (p. 172). Similarly, Gutmann (1985) described grandparents as our "wardens of culture" (p. 181). Facio (1996) found that grandmothers in particular are expected to be the "cultural teachers" of the family (p. 94).

Methodologically speaking, this chapter is part of a larger study based on ethnographic interviews conducted with over fifty family members about the meaning of my grandmother's life and death. For that larger study, I conducted in-depth, semistructured interviews, asking a variety of questions to these family members about my grandmother, including, among others: What is your first memory of Naunny? What do you remember most about Naunny? Can you describe the last time you saw her? (What did you do? What did you say to each other?) How would you describe her defining qualities? What will you miss most about her? This chapter about my grandmother's ethnic identity is based on answers to a subset of interview questions including, among others: What did Naunny tell you about her ethnic background? How did she describe her ethnic identity? Did she ever call herself "Spanish"? Did she ever call herself "Mexican"? (What is the difference?) Did she ever use another label to describe her ethnicity? What label do you use to describe your ethnic background? (Why do you use that label?)

In addition, as a member of this family, my own memories influenced my interpretation of these family accounts; as such, my own perspectives about my ethnicity are part of this analysis as well. Accordingly, this paper is partly *autoethnographic* in nature. Denzin (1997) described autoethnography as "a turning of the ethnographic gaze inward on the self (auto), while maintaining the outward gaze of ethnography, looking at the larger context wherein self experiences occur" (p. 227; see also Communication Studies 298, 1997; Crawford, 1996; Ellis, 1997). I would not characterize this entire study as an autoethnography, however, because the focus of this project has been on the accounts of *other* family members. Obviously, though, as a member of this family my own views are part of this study and undoubtedly shaped how I interpreted these family accounts. Thus, I have put parentheses around "auto" in the word "ethnographic" in the title, and I have added my own parenthetical reflections about my grandmother's—and my own—ethnic identity throughout the paper.

At different times in my life I have filled out forms for job applications, for financial aid, for surveys, and for other miscellaneous matters. Whenever the forms asked me to indicate my ethnicity, I was always confused. After all, I am a mixture of ethnic groups, because my mother is Polish and my father is Hispanic. Unfortunately, most of these forms made me pick a single ethnic group. I usually selected the Hispanic label because my last name—that is, my father's last name—is

Hispanic. In addition, since we lived in Las Vegas, Nevada, my family spent a lot more time visiting my Hispanic grandmother and other relatives in East L. A. than my Polish grandmother and other relatives in Chicago, so I always identified more with the Hispanic relatives.

Even though I identified more with the Hispanic side of my family, I was never sure what ethnic label to use on the various forms, because I was never sure if we were "Spanish" or "Mexican." In addition, it seemed that the labels used to indicate Hispanic changed every few years: sometimes it was "Latino," sometimes it was "Chicano," sometimes it was "Mexican" or "Mexican-American," and sometimes it was "Hispanic." No matter what I checked off on these various forms, I always felt a little uneasy about the choice and about not knowing exactly what I was.

The Nature of Ethnic Identity

Hecht, Collier, and Ribeau (1993) defined ethnic identity as the "perceived membership in an ethnic culture that is enacted in the appropriate and effective use of symbols and cultural narratives, similar interpretations and meanings, and common ancestry and traditions" (p. 30). They also argued that ethnic identity is important to one's overall sense of identity. As they concluded: "By figuring out who you think you are, you decide how you want to be treated by others, whom you want to interact with, and how you will treat others" (p. 19)

Gans (1979) has argued that for many Americans, especially for later generations of European Americans in the United States, ethnic identity is largely symbolic. He noted that such symbolic ethnic identities have expressive rather than instrumental functions because they establish the uniqueness of the group in question without requiring individuals to actually participate in those groups because the allegiance is to the symbol and not to the actual ethnic group. As Waters (1990) put it, "symbolic ethnicity persists because it meets a need Americans have for community without individual cost" (p. 164).

These and other scholars have recognized that the key component of an individual's symbolic ethnic identity is the *label* used to signify membership in an ethnic group (see Acuña, 1996; Cole, 2001; Fairchild, 1985; Fairchild and Cozens, 1981). As Hecht, Collier, and Ribeau (1993) wrote, "Due to social categorization and stereotyping processes within U.S. culture, ethnic identity seems particularly focused on labels that provide a frame or anchor for naming identities and are thus useful for identity maintenance and management" (p. 68). Fairchild (1985) concurred, noting that "research in racial and ethnic attitudes has well documented the fact that one's attitude toward a particular racial group is, in part, a function of the racial or ethnic label associated with that group" (p. 48).

Given the importance of racial or ethnic labels, it is not surprising that the labels used to identify various racial and ethnic groups have changed over time. For example, Acuña (1996) pointed out that "identity has always been problematic among the 'other' in U.S. society—and it is no different among Chicanos, who especially since the 1960s have hotly debated what to call themselves" (p. xi). Indeed, the labels "Mexican," "Chicano," "Latino," and "Hispanic" have been used at different points in United States history (see Fairchild and Cozens, 1981) as have the labels "Negro," "Black," "Afro-American," and "African American" (see Fairchild, 1985). This recognition of the importance of labeling prompted me to examine the ethnic labels that my grandmother and other relatives have used to characterize my family's ethnic identity.

> I played baseball in college. One day before the season started, the head coach asked me about my last name. "Are you Italian?" he asked.
> "No, I'm Spanish," I said nervously, wondering why the head coach, a rather arrogant Anglo who had spoken very little to me during the winter months of practice, was asking about my ethnicity.
> "Spanish?" he said with a sarcastic tone of voice. "Is that Mexican?"
> "Yeah, I guess so," I said, tentatively.
> "I guess I'll call you Tortilla, then," he said and laughed. "Now go hit some fungoes to the outfielders, Tortilla."

From that point on, the head coach continued to call me "Tortilla." I am certain that he did not use the label affectionately. In fact, every time he yelled out "Tortilla," most of my teammates, except one Mexican player, laughed. A few of them also started calling me "Tortilla" as well. I felt uncomfortable every time someone yelled out "Tortilla," but was reluctant to criticize anyone for doing so because the head coach had coined the nickname. I remember wishing that I had told my coach that I was Italian, but then realized that he probably would have called me "Tortellini" or something else to make fun of my ethnic background.

In Search of Naunny's (and My Own) Ethnic Identity

> I remember one time somebody in the family said that we were Mexican. And Grandma said, "Why are you saying we're Mexican? No one in our family is from Mexico. We have never been from Mexico. We're *Spanish*." She said that we were descendants of the conquistadores. I thought, "Okay, that sounds fine. We're Spanish then."
>
> —Granddaughter, Age 49

With the birth name of Juanita Eloysa Martinez, my grandmother was a descendant of an extremely long line of Martinez people from New Mexico well before this area was part of the United States. Indeed, it was quite frustrating to try to determine the exact Martinez lineage because the name "Martinez" is one of the most common Spanish surnames in the world. In fact, I was only able to trace Naunny's paternal lineage back four generations, but after that I was overwhelmed by the thousands of Martinez names I came across as I conducted my genealogical research.

Although I did not determine the exact Martinez lineage, it is very likely that Naunny was a distant descendent of Hernan Martin Serrano. Martin Serrano first came to the area of what is now New Mexico in 1598 with colonist Juan de Oñate, over 100 Spanish conquistadores, and an unspecified number of women, children, and servants.[1] But whether or not Naunny's ancestors were descendants of the Martin Serrano family, they definitely lived in what is now New Mexico for many generations. According to historians, life in this region remained relatively unchanged for centuries after the Spanish conquest, because it was so far from Mexico City, the capital Spanish new world. Espniosa (1985) argued that this relative detachment from Mexico meant "the Spanish colonizers who entered New Mexico . . . lived a more independent and isolated existence than any other group of colonists of the old Spanish Empire in America." (p. 234).

Naunny's Martinez ancestors lived in northern New Mexico for many generations until the 1870s, when her grandparents and their children—including Naunny's father who was a very young boy—homesteaded to the village of San Miguel near the town of Trinidad in what is now southern Colorado.[2] By the time Naunny's grandparents settled in San Miguel, however, the region had undergone major changes. Indeed, while the eighteenth century might have been similar to the seventeenth century for the Hispanos of New Mexico, the nineteenth century was radically different than the eighteenth century. Mexico gained its independence from Spain in 1821, so New Mexico and southern Colorado had become part of the newly established Mexican nation and its citizens were officially "Mexicans." One year later, the Sante Fe Trail opened, leading to an explosion of trade between Mexico and the United States and to the era of Anglo fur trappers and "Mountain Men." Then, less than thirty years later, New Mexico and southern Colorado became part of the United States following the Mexican-American War, which began in 1846 and ended in 1848 with the Treaty of Hidalgo; in 1856, the United States and Mexico agreed to the Gadsden Purchase which established the current boundaries between the two countries.

The outcome of these events meant that the native Hispanos of New Mexico, whose families had lived there for generations, were now officially "Mexican Americans." By the 1870s and 1880s, American Anglos and immigrants from Italy, Poland, Greece, Ireland, Mexico, and other lands had arrived in droves with the advent of railroads, lumber mills, coal mines, and commercial agriculture and herding ventures. These changes dramatically disrupted—and, in many cases, ended—life in the Hispano villages. As Abbott (1976) concluded:

By the turn of the [20th] century . . . the development of coal mining and timber industries and the influx of European immigrants to work for the new companies accelerated a slow displacement of [Hispano] farmers. . . . In the early 1900s, many of the old plazas were abandoned by inhabitants who moved to coal camps or to Walsenburg and Trinidad to earn wages from the Anglos. (p. 49)

These and other historical changes also led to adjustments in the ethnic identity of the native Hispanos, adjustments that are still prevalent in New Mexico and southern Colorado to this day. Specifically, the native Hispanos started to refer to themselves as "Spanish" or "Spanish-American," and they tried to integrate into the new American nation by taking on an "Anglo" way of life. As someone who was born and raised in this area soon after these changes in ethnic identity were made, Naunny made these adjustments and passed them on to her children and grandchildren.

One day in college my girlfriend and I were walking across campus, talking about our families. I had mentioned earlier when we started dating that I was "Spanish," but on this walk I said that my dad was "Mexican."

"*Mexican*?" she said in a surprised and strangely offensive tone. "I thought you were *Spanish*."

"Spanish, Mexican," I replied, "what's the difference."

She paused. "It's no big deal," she said. "I just didn't know you were Mexican."

We broke up about a month later.

"Spanish," not "Mexican"

If you go to New Mexico and Colorado today, most people still consider themselves *Spanish*. Grandma always used to say, "We're Spanish." I've heard this in New Mexico a hundred times. They're obviously Mexicans. There's no doubt about it. But they all thought they were different from Mexicans. They say, "Nobody in my family has ever been born in Mexico." They were born in Colorado and New Mexico, not in Mexico, and their ancestors were from Colorado and New Mexico. But if you go back far enough, Colorado and New Mexico were part of Mexico. So, of course, they're Mexican. What's the difference anyway? Mexicans are Spaniards and Indians mixed up.

—Grandson, Age 52

In many ways, it is not surprising that Hispanics in New Mexico called— and still call—themselves "Spanish." As noted earlier, New Mexico was settled by Spanish conquistadores, many of whom were born in Spain. As Gonzalez (1967) explained:

> The New Mexico-phile will be quick to point out that the local brand of Latin culture goes back directly to the original Spanish *conquistadores*. Some of the more fervent also claim that the really important Spanish-Americans are in fact direct descendants, with unbroken "pure" Spanish lineages, of these first settlers, who are usually assumed to have been purebred Spaniards. This idea, based upon some truth and much fiction, has today become part and parcel of what might be called "the New Mexico legend," which is, in turn, part of the total cultural pattern that distinguishes this state from all the others. (p. x)

Other researchers have argued that the differences between New Mexicans and Mexicans are not as substantial as "the New Mexico legend" suggests, especially in terms of race and ethnicity. In fact, Nostrand (1992) argued that "the concept of being Spanish seems not to be a holdover of 'Spaniard' from the Spanish period, but instead stems from contact with Anglos" (p. 15). He pointed out that during the period of Mexican occupation of New Mexico following independence from Spain (1821–1846), Hispanos actually "called themselves 'Mexicans,' and they probably thought of themselves as not different from other Mexicans in Mexico" (p. 15). Nostrand argued that it was not until the American takeover, and especially the development of Anglo industries in the 1870s and 1880s, that the terms "Spanish" and "Spanish-American" came into favor.

With the advent of the railroads, mines, and other trades, tens of thousands of "Mexican" immigrants from Mexico came to the area for work along with immigrants from many countries in Europe. Deutsch (1987) wrote that most of the Anglo Americans in this changing region considered Mexicans to be of a much lower class than other ethnic groups, and, as such, these Mexicans suffered from much prejudice and discrimination in the Anglo-run industries. Not surprisingly, then, the Hispanos, who were born and raised in New Mexico, not Mexico, tried to make a distinction between themselves and these immigrants. Thus, the labels "Spanish" and "Spanish-American" came into favor, and, as Nostrand (1992) explained, "the aim for those who used [these labels] was to escape from the subordinate status of being Mexican, and as larger numbers of Mexican immigrants arrived, the aim also became one of disassociating oneself from those who were generally of a lower socioeconomic class" (p. 16). As Lozano (1976) put it bluntly, "the Hispanos in New Mexico and Colorado were driven to denying their Mexican origins by the prejudice held against Mexicans." (p. 200). Unfortunately for them, Anglos did not make the distinction between "Mexican" and "Spanish," and both groups suffered from discrimination.

As members of the native Hispanos of New Mexico, Naunny's relatives adopted these new labels, along with the "New Mexico legend" of their Spanish heritage. For example, the brother of one of Naunny's nephews (age 77), who, like Naunny, grew up in southern Colorado, told me: "The people on my mother's side called themselves 'Spanish.' They were actually from the original settlers who came from Spain." A niece (age 67), whose mother [Naunny's sister] also grew up in the region, echoed the same views, though she expressed ambivalence about the label yet, at the same time, revealed its lasting influence: "My mother also said we were Spanish. But I never knew what the difference was. I always heard that people who were Spanish with Indian blood were Mexican. And we're Spanish with Indian blood. So I don't know why everyone said we were Spanish? But I still say I'm Spanish, because that's the way I was raised."

Unfortunately, in the process of using the label "Spanish" to distance themselves from Mexican immigrants, some of Naunny's relatives—and no doubt many native Hispanos—may have developed some of the same prejudicial views of Mexicans held by Anglos. As Naunny's son (age 75) recalled: "I remember when I was in Colorado [as a young boy], and one of my cousins said, 'The Spanish-Americans live over here, and on the other side of the tracks is where all the Spics live.' I said, 'What's a Spic?' She said, 'They're the Mexicans.' I guess that's what her parents had told her." As González (1967) put it, "The old stigma of Indian ancestry has been replaced by a condescension toward those presumed to be of Mexican, as opposed to New Mexican, descent" (p. 78)

When Naunny and her new husband Charles left southern Colorado in 1924 and moved to Los Angeles, they took the "Spanish" label with them and continued to use it to characterize their ethnic identity. However, although California, like New Mexico, had been settled by Spanish colonists, the labels "Spanish" and "Spanish-American" never caught on in California, even with those who could legitimately claim to be descendents of the original Spanish colonists. In California, all people of Hispanic descent, whether born in California or Mexico, were called "Mexicans," so neither Anglos nor California Hispanics were aware of any special identity or distinction for Hispanics that were born in New Mexico and Colorado. In fact, California Mexicans resented the term "Spanish."

As Naunny's son (age 75) said, "My mother always told us that we were Spanish, but in Los Angeles, if you said you were Spanish, the first thing they asked you was, 'Are you ashamed to be a Mexican?'" Then he admitted the unfortunate consequences of being raised with this sense of ethnic identity:

> To tell you the truth, I was kind of ashamed to say that I was Mexican. Mexicans were considered lower class. Most of my friends in Lincoln Heights were Italian, and they bragged about being Italian. They didn't even called themselves "American"; they said they were "Italian." I always wondered how come I wasn't proud to be Mexican.

One of Naunny's nieces (age 69), who was born in Colorado and moved to California when she was a young girl, echoed my uncle's sentiments:

It's so different in Colorado and New Mexico. The people from Mexico are called "Mexicans," and they lived on the other end of town. But if you're born in Colorado or New Mexico, you say you're "Spanish-American." But when you came to California, there's no such thing as Spanish-American. They'd say, who's Spanish and who's American? So you said you're Mexican. But I was ashamed to say that I was Mexican. That prejudice was embedded in us in Colorado.

Sadly, this "prejudice" is one of the enduring legacies of the "Spanish" label that Naunny accepted and passed on to her children, grandchildren, and even great-grandchildren. I certainly do not believe that my grandmother ever held overtly prejudiced attitudes about Mexicans or any other group of people.[3] She was a loving woman who accepted every person as an individual, and no one in the family *ever* heard her make any prejudicial comments about Mexicans. Moreover, she did not decide on her own to use the label "Spanish" to differentiate herself from Mexicans; rather, she was socialized as a child to believe that she was "Spanish" and, thus, different from "Mexicans."

However, as Naunny passed on this label—and its pernicious connotations—to her descendents, we, too, were socialized into believing that we were different—and, in some unstated way, better—than Mexicans were. Thus, most of us disassociated ourselves from Mexican heritage rather than embracing it with pride. For example, when I was growing up in Las Vegas, Nevada, I never told the other kids in school that I was "Mexican"; I *always* said that I was "Spanish." In fact, only in recent years have I started to call myself "Mexican" when asked about my ethnicity, and I have to admit that it still feels a bit strange to use this label. As one of Naunny's granddaughters told me: "Since it was ingrained into my head since the time I can remember, I still consider myself Spanish. I hate to say it, but because of the distinction that was made from my earliest recollection, I almost feel embarrassed about being Mexican. I also have told my daughter that she is Spanish." And so the label—but hopefully not the prejudice—continues.

Fortunately, while Naunny continued to call herself Spanish when asked directly about her ancestry, she did become far more accepting of her Mexican heritage and language later in life.

— — — —

When I attended college in Los Angeles in the 1970s, I visited Naunny and Pete in their little house in East Los Angeles on a regular basis. I remember speaking—actually trying to speak—Spanish with her when I was taking Spanish classes to fulfill my language requirement. I also remember enlisting her help when I was doing a paper on mural art in East Los Angeles. Naunny served as the navigator as I drove around the neighborhoods in my green Volkswagen Beetle, photographing examples of mural art that seemed to be on almost every corner in the area. Although these visits did not completely change my sense of our family's ancestral identity as "Spanish," they did engender at least a limited identification with our Mexican heritage. I only wish that I had spent more time speaking Spanish with Naunny and learning more about her beliefs about our ethnic background.

———

When Naunny Became a Mexican

Naunny's first husband died in a car accident in 1934, and she did not marry again until the mid-1950s. Perhaps it was fitting that she married a Mexican who was born in Mexico, and that they lived most of their life in a predominantly Mexican section of East Los Angeles where he grew up after moving to California with his family. During these years, Naunny spoke Spanish with her neighbors and attended a little church down the street in which Mass was said in Spanish and which served tamales and menudo after Mass. She also listened to Latin music, at least in part because her husband was a piano player in a Latin jazz band.

Many relatives recalled a running joke they shared with Naunny and other relatives around this time. The joke came in the form of a question they asked of her: "When did you become a Mexican?" As her daughter-in-law (age 68) remembered:

Naunny became Hispanic when she moved to East L. A. with Pete. We used to joke, "Hey mom, when did you become Mexican?" That was funny. I think a lot of it had to do with the neighborhood. It was an exclusively Mexican neighborhood, except for the Chinese people who owned the grocery store. But the lady who did her hair was Mexican. And Pete was getting more into his Mexican roots too. So they started changing. She acted totally Mexican there. It was very strange for us. We got a kick out of it.

As her son (age 75) concluded: "When she lived in East L. A., she would even use the term "Mexican" to describe herself sometimes. I don't think the distinction between Spanish and Mexican mattered as much to her anymore."

In sum, while doing this research on Naunny, it has been difficult for me to recognize that she was brought up to hold at least some prejudicial attitudes about Mexicans. However, I am comforted by the fact that she never said a bad word about Mexicans as a group of people and, perhaps more importantly, that she eventually rejected those negative attitudes. It may have taken her 50 years to become a Mexican, but it was an identity that she ultimately embraced with pride. And when she died at age 86 and one of my cousin's hired a Mariachi band to play at her funeral, everyone in attendance could feel the spirit of our little Mexican grandma dancing to the music.

— — — —

My department recently hired an assistant professor that was born in Mexico. Before he arrived this past semester, I mentioned to another colleague that it would be good to have another Mexican on our staff.

"Yeah," my colleague said, "but he's a *real* Mexican."

I did not say anything in response in part because I did not know what to say and in part because I think I ultimately agreed with my colleague. For my entire life I did not call myself Mexican, I grew up in a white middle-class neighborhood, and I do not speak Spanish. Although this study has given me insights into my Mexican heritage that I did not have before, one single study cannot change an ethnic identity that has been constructed over a lifetime.

Notes

1. This area had first been explored by Vasquez de Coronado and his party in 1540 during their search for gold and other riches for the Spanish Empire. However, Coronado and his party did not establish permanent settlements in this area, and the area was not settled by Spanish colonists until Oñate's expedition later in the sixteenth century. As Tushar (1975) summarized:

It has been said repeatedly that the Spaniards were interested only in gold. . . . It is true that they were interested in treasure, but the Spaniards, their leaders and priests, at least, were educated and intellectual men, and they became civilizers as well as explorers. The Conquistadores brought with them agriculturalists, artisans, missionaries, and doctors since their Catholic majesties were anxious, not only to conquer the New World, but to implant culture as well as religion. Thus, they built the first cities, the first churches, the first schools and the first universities as well as wrote the first dictionaries, the first histories and the first geographies in the New World. (p. xiii).

2. Naunny's maternal grandparents had already moved from New Mexico to Colorado a few years earlier and her mother was born in Colorado (in 1871).

3. The only people Naunny ever made negative comments about were people who were overweight. She never discriminated against these people, but made jokes and sarcastic comments about them, such as, "So and so is eight axe handles wide."

References

Abbott, C. (1976). *Colorado: A history of the centennial state*. Boulder, CO: Colorado Associated University Press.

Acuña, R. F. (1996). *Anything but Mexican: Chicanos in contemporary Los Angeles*. London: Verso.

Cole, C. (2001). *African Americans in the workplace: An analysis of voiced experiences*. Master's thesis, California State University, Sacramento.

Communication Studies 298, California State University, Sacramento. (1997). Fragments of self at the postmodern bar. *Journal of Contemporary Ethnography, 26*: 251–292.

Crawford, L. (1996). Personal ethnography. *Communication Monographs, 63*: 158–170.

Denzin, N. K. (1997). *Interpretive ethnography: Ethnographic practices for the 21st century*. Thousand Oaks, CA: Sage Publications, Inc.

Deutsch, S. (1987). *No separate refuge: Culture, class, and gender on an Anglo-Hispanic frontier in the American Southwest, 1880–1940*. New York: Oxford University Press, 1987.

Ellis, C. (1997). Evocative autoethnography: Writing emotionally about our lives. In W. G. Tierney and Y. S. Lincoln (Eds.), *Representation and the text* (pp. 115–142). Albany, NY: State University of New York Press.

Facio, E. (1996). *Understanding older Chicanos*. Thousand Oaks, CA: Sage Publications, Inc.

Fairchild, H. H. (1985). Black, Negro, or Afro-American? The differences are crucial! *Journal of Black Studies, 16*: 47–55.

Fairchild, H. H., and Cozens, J. A. (1981). Chicano, Hispanic, or Mexican-American: What's in a name? *Hispanic Journal of Behavioral Sciences, 3*: 191–198.

Gans, H. (1979). Symolic ethnicity: The future of ethnic groups and cultures in America. *Ethnic and Racial Studies, 2*: 1–20.

González, N. (1967). *The Spanish-Americans of New Mexico: A heritage of pride*. Albuquerque, NM: University of New Mexico Press.

Gutmann, D. (1985). Deculturation and the American grandparent. In V. L. Bengston and J. F. Robertson (Eds.), *Grandparenthood* (pp. 173–181). Beverly Hills, CA: Sage Publications, Inc.

Hecht, M. L., Collier, M. J., and Ribeau, S. A. (1993). *African American communication: Ethnic identity and cultural interpretation*. Newbury Park, CA: Sage Publications, Inc.

Lozano, A. G. (1976). The Spanish language of the San Luis Valley. In J. de Onis (Ed.), *The Hispanic contribution to the state of Colorado* (pp. 191–207). Boulder, CO: Westview.

Nostrand, R. L. (1992). *The Hispano homeland*. Norman, OK: University of Oklahoma Press.

Tinsley, B. J., and Parke, R. D. (1984). Grandparents as support and socialization agents. In M. Lewis (Ed.), *Beyond the dyad* (pp. 161–194). New York: Plenum.

Trujillo, N. (1998). In search of Naunny's grave. *Text and Performance Quarterly*, 18: 344–368.

— — —. (forthcoming 2002). In search of Naunny's history: Reproducing gender ideology in family stories. Women's Studies in Communication.

Tushar, O. L. (1975). *The people of "El Valle": A history of the Spanish colonials in the San Luis Valley*. Denver: Olibama Lopez Tushar

Waters, M. C. (1990). *Ethnic options: Choosing identities in America*. Berkeley: University of California Press.

CHAPTER 24

Rhythms of Dis-Location

Family History, Ethnographic Spaces, and Reflexivity

DEVIKA CHAWLA

To me ethnography embodies a rhythmic cultural process that we sometimes accomplish, but always continue over a period of time and space. As ethnographers, we come to our sites, fields and places with assumptions, presumptions, and beliefs about our own cultural reality (Agar, 1996; Clifford and Marcus, 1986). Accordingly, discussions about ethnography and ethnographers are not only discussions about culture, but also serve as conversations about postmodern and, now, postcolonial identities. After all, there are no ethnographies without ethnographers.

I like to think that my beginnings as an ethnographer occurred much before I knew what the words "ethnography" and "culture" meant. I am, by no means, suggesting that I was born to be an ethnographer. Rather, cultural movements, transitions, periods, and experiences in my family history have made me embrace a reflexive ethnographic and autoethnographic stance to my research. This is a stance in which ambivalences over location and dislocation have gained salience over other areas. In this paper, I interrogate through storytelling how my struggle to find a place in my research about the Indian arranged marriage has its roots in a family history of dislocation. I reflect upon my family's displaced history, both colonial and postcolonial, and argue that my concerns about researcher positionality are a legacy of inhabiting "in-between" times and spaces—between nations, between states, between religions, between homes, between family and between school.

271

Dislocation as a Way of Being

In 1947, when Pakistan and India were declared two independent nations by the British, my paternal grandparents were forced to move to India as refugees. They had been born and raised in Pakistan, but were unfortunate to have been born Hindus in a Pakistan which would come to be declared an Islamic state after the 1947 partition. Just across the border the new India was declared a secular nation, yet there was also a mass exodus of Muslims from her land. The Partition was a separation of lands and an exchange of people.

I grew up listening to stories about my family's escape from Pakistan to India. I remember feeling a sense of awe and humility when my grandmother, whom we called Bibiji, would tell us how she and her three children (my father, his sister and brother) had fled from Deraghazikhan in Pakistan by train. Unlike a few of their relatives, they had to leave in a rush. I don't recall Bibiji's explanations for this, but I do remember her telling us that the only belongings they were able to take with them were a few trunks and a few pieces of gold in wealth. My Bibiji and her husband belonged to families of proud landowners. All their land, property, homes, and wealth were left behind. Bibiji and her generation spoke of witnessing mass executions on the train, of people being pulled out and killed because of their religion. Luckily, my Bibiji and her three children arrived safely in New Delhi, India.

Bibiji always told us, albeit with a sense of drama, that the only real wealth they still had left was their education. My grandparents and my extended family, which included my grandfather's brothers, sisters and their families, moved into what were called "refugee colonies." The government of India at the time had designated massive areas that would serve as refugee quarters for people who had been displaced by the Partition. My family spent many years in these colonies. My father had just turned seven during this time and his childhood memories of school are all related to the refugee colonies.

When my father remembers life in those quarters he never speaks of a "home," rather he refers to the names of the places where they lived—Mata Sundari Place, Bengali Market, Gol Dakhana. In fact, as I write, I cannot recall a single time when my grandmother spoke of any place as a home. Her home and sense of place were left behind in Pakistan. I don't believe she ever recovered a sense of place. Even so, the search for a sense of place came to some completion after my grandfather bought his first house in New Delhi. Yet, the success of this purchase was attributed to education. Education was what helped us to survive as refugees in India.

Education and the need to own property soon became organizing principles (Hardy and Laszloffy, 1995) of our family life. No amount of money in the bank or material wealth could replace these. I believe that education was more important because property followed from it. My Bibiji used all her gold to educate her children. Even when money was tight, she would always find some for a child who wanted to study. She was even able to send my uncle to study in Germany. Money needed for education was never refused, because education, as the cliché goes, was a wealth that could not be surpassed by anything.

My father's stories about growing up were stories about a multilayered dislocated consciousness. He and his siblings had been dislocated and displaced in numerous ways. As I remember and reinterpret his reminiscences, I find myself charting an informal typology. My own memories of his memories have taken a new shape, because I have recontextualized them in light of my own sense of dislocation (Hacking, 1995).

My father, born in 1940, was born into a colonized India. That was his first "othering"—being othered in an India ruled by the British. After 1947, this "othering" came in the shape of the religious riots that drove my family from Pakistan to India. As refugees in their own country, they were further "othered" by being attributed a refugee identity, which became their postcolonial reality. Like in all postcolonial realities, in this one, too, "location" became a distant dream (Anzaldua, 1987; Bhabha, 1994; Das Gupta, 1995; Narayan, 1997). Home became, simply a roof over the head. Dislocation became a way of being.

The refugee reality was a source of much humiliation, and I often heard my father tell us in passing that the British should have stayed on for a few years to tutor Indians on how to reorganize the nation without the imperialist rulers. I remember telling him that he sounded antinationalistic, but, now in retrospect, I know that he was angry about the refugee identity that had been forced upon him in his own country. He had become an other with no sense of place. This anger made us, as my father's children, spend a childhood being in awe of the British who we thought had at least known how to rule. At that time we did not have the intellect or the maturity to understand that India's struggles to maintain a stable political, social, and economic environment was a postcolonial wound. In addition to my family's displacement, it was a legacy we inherited from British India.

Losing one's moorings once breaks one in for a future without location. My father inherited a sense of "disloyalty to place" from his family history. This irreverent search for a place took different shapes and forms. When he began his career as a human resource professional, he was not scared of taking risks and changing jobs that required him to move from one state to another within India. In turn, my brother and I, privy and witness to these discontinuities, inherited dislocation as a rhythm of our everyday lives. We never questioned any of my father's moves. We became used to making new friends as we went along. Schools and teachers remained a concept, not continuities. Discontinuity became our normalcy.

We did not grow up in any single home and/or house. When I think of my childhood, I, too, like my father think of places and not homes. This dislocation took an ironic and fascinating twist when my parents decided to send my brother and myself to boarding schools in the Himalayan region. There were two reasons for this decision. First, we were living in Punjab, a state that was unsettled by religious unrest among Sikhs, who were the religious majority, and the Hindus. My brother and I were being discriminated against and harassed by other school children because we were Hindus. Second, these schools, Waverly for girls and Bishop Cotton for Boys, were single sex schools that had been established by Catholic priests a century before the partition of India. These schools were expensive private schools that turned out ladies and gentleman. I think the schools became a source of pride for my father because they helped him reclaim a little bit of the pride that he had lost in his family's refugee status.

Like our father's before us, our dislocation too became multilayered—physical, emotional, and cultural. We were both away from home for nine months of the year. That was a tremendous loss of place for each of us as adolescents. Our differentiation from the family lifecycle was accelerated and premature. I was ten and my brother was seven when we left home. We came home for three months in the winter. Almost each time we went home we went to a different home in a different place for our holidays. School became a constant and home became a place we visited during the holidays. Yet, we were both fairly normal children in our parents' eyes. We were normal because dislocation no longer represented chaos in our own and the extended family unit.

Waverly is where my own preoccupations with dislocation took serious shape. In Waverly, dislocation came in various forms. Dislocation became a bifurcation between the East and the West. In a regimented Roman Catholic environment with Irish nuns, I found myself forgetting what it meant to be Indian. We barely ate Indian food, we wore western school uniforms, we studied Shakespeare, we called napkins—serviettes, bedspreads—counterpanes, and bras—brassieres. Each time I went home, I relearned the rules and norms of what was considered "Indian." I became adept at shifting between saying two different types of prayers—Catholic and Hindu, eating two different cuisines—continental and North Indian, speaking two languages—English in school and Hindi at home. I remember my parents laughing at me when I made the sign of the cross after a Hindu prayer at home. In school, I would go to the chapel and whisper my Sanskrit prayers. I remember bringing a rosary home and placing it in my mother's Hindu temple. I recall my mother being angry with me for preferring to eat white sliced bread instead of the traditional North Indian bread called "*chapati*." I also remember my father scolding us for talking in English most of the time, yet at the same time he was very proud that we spoke good British English. I was desperate to bridge these two cultures and was searching for answers. Surprisingly, my brother and I never exchanged these stories, but I think we both knew what was happening to us. We were being recolonized in a postcolonial reality. We were just too young to have a name for the process.

In Waverly, I acquired many of the skills needed to live as an "in-between." I was juggling cultures only as a child knows how to juggle. I felt a skewed sense of pride in being so English, yet I felt like an outsider among my cousins and friends from home. I also felt pride in having acquired British social niceties, but was embarrassed to use them at home. Home had never been traditionally Indian, but neither was it English. In retrospect, I think, home had become a site which represented a love-hate relationship with the colonizers which is, perhaps, experienced by most postcolonial peoples (Anzaldua, 1987; Das Gupta, 1995).

Outsidedness became my legacy of dislocation. I did not feel shunned or separated, just "apart." My life before Waverly is a blur. I think that life for me really began in and after Waverly. There was another blurred period between coming home from Waverly and moving to America to study. It was blurred because coming home was always temporary. I always anticipated a *movement*. Therefore, moving to graduate school in America was not a surprise displacement, yet I was scared. This time, home would be almost 14,000 miles away. But my parents scolded me for feeling anxious about being away. After all, my father said, "you're used to living alone." I was going to America for education and that in itself was a source of immense pride for my parents; therefore the pangs of displacement were not given much importance. Discontinuity had become the *everyday* and would always be reinforced as a norm.

(Dis)Locating Myself in Research (about dislocation)

Graduate school in America brought with it new discontinuities. I found myself juggling more cultural realities than I had imagined. As I journeyed through school, I found myself reevaluating my past to understand what and who had influenced my reality. My in-betweeness was beginning to get magnified as I was fascinated with my own struggles to find a sense of self in this new culture. Being in a new setting had distanced me from home, India and Indianness; yet, in and through this physical, emotional and social distance I found myself becoming more reflective and introspective about the past that I carried with me, the present that was influenced by my past, and the future that was being made in my present (Carr, 1986; Crites, 1986). I began to get intrigued with the idea of identity negotiation and wrote my Master's thesis on how other Asian Indian female students *similar* to me negotiated gender identities in American graduate school.

I started by writing my own story in which I interrogated the various selves which were emerging and emerged as I was growing up. It was a story about transformations, contradictions, interruptions, and displacements. With my own story in the background, I proceeded to listen to other women. As I listened, I was literally *located* as an ongoing participant in the research process. I was comfortable in the doing of the research because of my honest involvement. Even though all my participants were experiencing the pangs of dislocation, during the ethnography I experienced a *sense of place*. This sense of place came with knowing where I (thought I) was in that moment.

After the narrative ethnography was written, I found myself in a reflexive quandary which I think is related to my penchant for dislocation. I began to question my positionality in the research. I began to ask myself why I wrote my story before I listened to my participants. I wondered if I had imposed my story on them by writing it first. I wondered if my own story should have emerged in the research process with those of my participants. I was concerned about where I had placed myself, and how that might have affected the research. I even asked myself if I had somehow made the narrative ethnography more deductive by imposing my own story, textually and conceptually, before the stories of my coparticipants. I felt immense conflict about how I might have been unfair to my participants. I wondered if I had located myself too comfortably in the writing down and writing up of the ethnography. These ruminations made me lose my comfortable "sense of place" in the study.

I have carried over these concerns about location and dislocation into my dissertation project in which I will study identity negotiation within the Indian arranged marriage. I am always concerned about why I chose this subject and what is driving me to study it. These concerns are primarily both concerns about position.

In my M.A. thesis, I was an involved participant in the research, but in my current project, I am uninvolved because I have not experienced the arranged marriage. I am not living the arranged marriage reality. Yes, I have experienced a history of such arrangements among women in my family. For example, my Bibiji was married at the age of nine and had a fairly successful arranged marriage. Her daughter, my aunt, was married to man chosen by Bibiji, and even though the marriage was an unhappy one, my aunt was forced to stay in it by her mother. Her story is one of marital abuse. My father's older brother's children were both married to spouses chosen by their parents. They both seem happy and satisfied. My best friend was married at the age of twenty to a man she had met only once before she was engaged. Yet, my own parents did not have an arranged marriage.

Each of these marriages is a different story that I have experienced only partially. However, my experiences of these relationships stem from a history of incomplete memories. These memories are incomplete because we were physically displaced too often to remember constants and to experience those storied relationships for a sustained period of time. They are incomplete also because they were never talked about. These are stories about interruptions and they are interrupted stories.

My dilemma about the location of my position in my research is an autoethnographic dilemma. It is a dilemma that stems from the search for a place and space for my *self* in the research. While I do have incomplete stories from my memories of the different arranged marriages that surround me, these are stories about other people in these marriages, and not stories about *myself*. In these memories, I remain an observer, albeit an observer to myself. My lack of a direct involvement in the reality of an arranged marriage makes me question my legitimacy to do this research. I am still worried that I am too much on the *outside* in this existential and intellectual displacement.

My displacement makes me ask myself numerous reflexive questions. Since I have no direct story of an arranged marriage experience, can I tell the story of my memories about the arranged marriage before I begin the project? And, should I? If yes, then where textually in the process should I tell these stories? In the beginning of the process, all through the process, or at the completion? Are my stories an imposition? Are they at all important to the realities that I will coconstruct? Can I just be an ethnographer without an autoethnographic stance? Is that even possible?

My locational, spatial, and positional dilemma is heightened by the present events that surround me. As I write in this moment, I am conscious of the threat or inevitability of my own marriage being arranged. So, while I feel too much on the "outside," I also fear that I am too personally *occupied* and *preoccupied* by the various *locales*, involving an arranged marriage in which I find myself intertwined. Just as I carry with me a history of these marriages within my family, I also carry a present in which my parents consistently and continuously present me with the option of them making a conjugal choice for me. Therefore, I am forced to ask myself if it is fear that makes me want to delve into this study. I worry that I may be interested in this study to assuage my fears about an impending arranged marriage. I constantly ask myself if the primary reader of this study is really going to be me? Am I being self-indulgent? Or is it another search for belonging? To what extent should I belong to the research and to what extent must it belong to me for me to find a comfortable sense of place in it?

As I write, this participatory dilemma is being further heightened by my knowledge and experience of my parents' search for a bride for my brother. I am, unconsciously, a coconspirator in the search process because I listen to what my family tells me about the prospective brides. I have become witness, though indirectly, to the process of women being rejected by my brother and parents on the basis of their height, weight, skin color, education and/or lack of social status, and so forth. I find it difficult to reconcile the reality of my brother's impending arranged marriage with my own reality of studying it. Each time my parents tell me about the women that my brother has met, I find myself imagining *me* in these women's places. Recently, my brother grumbled about one girl being too short. I responded by reminding him that I, too, am just five feet tall. As he and my family reject people, I almost feel the pain of the rejections because, after all, I could very well be these women. As I find myself becoming a reluctant observer, participant, and victim to the process of my family's search for my brother's bride, I ask myself if I am being disloyal to my own beliefs and my own study? Perhaps I am, yet perhaps I am also adding more layers of dislocation to my own search for a location in the research.

My ambivalence and vulnerability to the positional quandary in my research arises from the reality of my being raised in a semitraditional Indian environment and my transcendence beyond that environment because of the contingencies, displacements, and discontinuities of my life. Ironically, as I search for a location, I find myself more displaced. I find myself shifting between more in-betweens. Am I the reader, writer, researcher, experiencer, ethnographer, or autoethnographer, spectator, victim, or observer? Are these discontinuities my continuity?

Belonging in Reflexivity

My concerns about postionality in the arranged marriage are, therefore, concerns about dislocation. Just as my father normalized physical displacement, I have normalized reflexive positional contingencies in my research. They have become a way of being for me as an ethnographer. I have just shifted the site of dislocation from a physical space to an intellectual space.

My story of dislocation is unique because my discontinuities, my past, my family, history, and my cultural experiences are uniquely my own. My experience of reflexive displacement has, perhaps, been heightened by my overt lived experience of the juxtaposition of colonial and postcolonial realities. An externalization of this juxtaposition is my *in-betweeness*. This in-between space is conceptual, textual, spatial, emotional, and physical; it is a space that shifts with the rhythms of my dislocations.

References

Agar, M. H. (1996). *The professional stranger*. San Diego, CA: Academic Press.

Anzaldua, G. (1987). *Borderlands/la frontera:* The new mestiza. San Francisco, CA: Aunt Lutes.

Bhabha, H. K. (1994). *The location of culture*. New York, NY: Routledge and Kegan Paul.

Carr, D. (1986). *Time, narrative and history*. Bloomington, IN: Indiana University Press.

Clifford, J., and Marcus, G. E. (1986). *Writing culture: The poetics and politics of ethnography*. Berkley, CA: University of California Press.

Crites, S. (1986). Storytime: Recollecting the past and projecting the future. In. Sarbin, T. R. (Eds.), *Narrative Psychology: The storied nature of human conduct*. New York, NY: Praeger.

Das Gupta, M. (1995). "What is Indian about you?" A gendered, transnational approach to ethnicity. *Gender and Society, 11 (5)*: 572–596.

Hacking, I. (1995). *Rewriting the soul: Multiple personality and the sciences of memory*. Princeton, NJ: Princeton University Press.

Hardy, K. V., and Laszloffy, T. A. (1995). The cultural genogram: Key to training culturally competent family therapists. *Journal of Marriage and Family Therapy, 21 (3)*: 227–237.

Narayan, U. (1997). *Dislocating cultures: Identities, traditions, and Third World Feminism*. New York, NY: Routledge and Kegan Paul.

CHAPTER 25

Starvin' Marvin's Got an Injun

A Visit to the Homeland

ROBIN PATRIC CLAIR[1]

O'Siyo, the wind whispered through the mountain pines.
O'Siyo, I silently responded.

As a tired traveler who had finally arrived in the Blue Ridge Mountains, I appreciated nature's welcome. My friend, Cat, who had driven us, seemed to appreciate the ability to loosen her grip from the steering wheel after long hours of traversing winding mountain roads. We arrived later than expected; and so, we gently shut the car doors behind us. Cat and I stretched, breathed in the late night air, and looked toward the star-speckled, sable-colored sky. I inhaled again, more deeply this time. The scent of magnolias blended with a hint of sage and mingled exotically with the fresh smell of autumn leaves decaying on the moist ground. Before intruding on the lodge owner's sleep, I stretched again, as if to touch *nunda*—the light that dwells in the night—the moon—with my fingertips. Cat yawned and waited by the car.

"I'll be right back," I assured her.

Without opening her eyes, she nodded.

I knocked on the door of the rustic lodge where the proprietor lived; then, I waited with both a sense of anticipation and hesitation. We had, after all, rented the cabin sight unseen. Within moments, I was greeted by the sleepy-eyed owner. We exchanged introductions. She handed me the keys to our cabin, stepped outside onto the porch and indicated with an outstretched arm and extended index finger that our cabin waited farther up the mountain side, nestled in a grove of hemlock trees.

"I'll show you the way," she added.

I smiled in appreciation.

Despite the darkness, I noticed that her profile was familiar to me. Moonlight highlighted her features. The chiaroscuro offered up a rich profile of intense highlights and deep shadows.

Incredible, I thought, the similarity is absolutely striking. By the light of *nunda*, I could see her face quite clearly and was struck by the resemblance of her looks to my late grandmother, who, I am told, I take after. Black hair, pale skin, dark eyes, and high cheek bones. They could have been sisters, Cherokee sisters. I had come to visit the birthplace of my mother's grandmothers, the homeland of the ancestors, the Qualla Boundary. This woman was an uncanny reminder of my connection to the Cherokee Nation.

Cat and I drove to a cabin meant for tourists. This seemed both appropriate and inappropriate to me, outsider and insider that I am. My mother's ancestors left the Qualla Boundary after the Civil War. They made their way to Tennessee. My grandparents left Tennessee during the Great Depression in search of factory work in the north. Although my grandparents returned to the mountains and valleys, my mother left the comfort of her parents' home and travelled farther north. She settled in Ohio near the shores of Lake Erie. Each generation of my family drifted further from my own and their Cherokee roots. Each generation had fewer tales to tell of the homeland. I hoped to take a few stories back home with me.

Stairs led to a wide front porch that was draped in honeysuckle vines. After fumbling with the keys, we made our way into the cabin. The wooden-framed screen door banged behind us.

"I just put a new sink in the bathroom," the tiny woman said with pride.

Cat and I both nodded and smiled.

"Oh, yes. It looks nice," I said as she held the door open, allowing me to peer in at the recently installed sink and its artificial marble counter top.

The cabin was more than comfortable. It included a kitchen, bathroom, livingroom, and bedroom. The bed and roll away were covered with handmade quilts. The owner, like a docent in the night, gave us a guided tour before leaving. Cat slept in the bedroom. I took the roll away into the livingroom.

In the morning, I awoke to a panoramic view of the Smoky Mountains. Massive hills rolled out in soft layers of blue-green haze with swirls of autumn-colored leaves. The hemlock, the poplar, the elm, and the birch trees blended into a warm pastel brilliance. The misty mountain fog swirled languidly amidst the autumn hues. I lazily sat back and absorbed the soft hazy world around me. It was a moment suspended in time. Later, I went for a walk and breathed the smells of the autumn woods—dried leaves and moist soil. As the day grew warmer, I decided to explore beyond the cabin. Cat stayed behind to relax in a rocker on the front porch. She had a good book to read. I took off for the shopping district.

There, shop after shop, meant to lure the tourist, provided colorful commentaries on a culture with a rich historical past and a present still torn by the effects of early colonization. Kiosks accented the walkways between the larger stores. The stores and kiosks offered a variety of goods from cheap trinkets to expensive double-woven baskets and handmade smoked pottery. Mini museums, which provided brief overviews of the Cherokee culture and history through artifacts, were interspersed between the shops. One such mini museum/store offered both the traditional and the avant garde. Masks and figurines decorated the walls. Artifacts sat hermetically sealed in glass cases. Tape recorded histories played repetitiously in the background. Plastic mementos, which were for sale at the end of the mini museum tour, waited conveniently close to the cash register. Posters of contemporary artwork graced one wall. Racks of magazines about current Native American artists and their work caught my eye; I bought a couple of these magazines.

With all the festive colorful commercialization it was easy to get lost in the commodification of a people. Identities bought and sold. No example portrayed this more succinctly than the photogenic Smiling Chiefs. Like Santa Clauses at Christmas time, several Chiefs worked at different locations. They greeted tourists. For a small sum of money tourists may have their picture taken with a Chief. The Chiefs dress in the traditional attire of Plains Indians, not in Cherokee regalia. Tourists, the Cherokee believe, like to see a Chief dressed in buckskin and ornamented with a grand feather headdress that encircles the Chief's face and trails down his back to the ground. A colleague told me that when he visited the Qualla Boundary (actually he called it the "Cherokee Reservation" not the Qualla Boundary) the saddest sight for him was when he saw one of these Chiefs punching a time clock at the back of a store. Defeated by colonization, capitalization, and corporatization, the Chief removed his headdress and swung it over a hook as he simultaneously removed his time card from the slot and inserted it into the machine—ka-chink. He left it all behind for another day.

I saw several Chiefs while I was there, but one stood out among the others as he wore the finest full regalia of a Plains Indian. He chatted with a vendor at the candle shop and leaned against the park bench. The Chief must have been weary from a day of smiling that great big Chief Wahoo smile and tired of pretending to be the image of Indian-ness. But a sudden surge of energy brought him about face as a couple of tourists and their children asked him to pose for some pictures. He put his arms around the white family—like the wings of an eagle embracing them. Click, click—a Kodak moment; Click, click—a photo opportunity. Unfolding his wallet, the tourist-father pulled out a couple of bills and paid the Chief. My gut reaction was that the Chief was selling himself and prostituting his culture. Worse yet, he did this after he had corrupted it by confounding it with another Native culture. After all, he was dressed like a Plains Indian, not a traditional Cherokee. I shook my head at the sight. But the Smiling Chief saw me shake my head. He stopped smiling. He gave me a pointed and pedantic stare. I had been caught judging one of my elders, and I suddenly felt ashamed.

Who was I to judge this man's behavior? Who was I to say that this was not acceptable? Did I live on the reservation, a place where salaries are less than half of the poorest salaries in America? Did I have children to feed under such circumstances? Did I even know the history of how the headdress was accepted by many Native Americans as a symbol of Indian-ness to be worn with pride, even by those whose ancestors never wore them? He spoke no words. His eyes said all of this to me. But there was something else deep inside his dark eyes. There was a sorrow and a shame, which my judgmental attitude had forced to rupture like an ugly scab torn from the skin. I felt ashamed. I left the shopping district wanting to leave the reservation. But I had several days left within the homeland and I would have to learn to live with myself.

In the days that followed, I hiked through the mountains with my companion. We attended the living history museum. A much more accurate portrayal of my grandmother's people and early indigenous culture was presented at Oconaluftee Indian village. I learned much about the old ways. We chatted with a man who demonstrated the art of making and using a blow gun. We talked to Cherokee High School students about current linguistics programs. Later, that evening, I attended the fall festival. I felt at home.

I watched the dancing and laughed at the Navajo comedian who said that he was surprised to see so many dark-haired, dark-eyed Cherokee. They had heard in Oklahoma that all those Cherokees on the Qualla Boundary had blonde hair and blue eyes. That's okay, I thought, because we had heard that the Navajo have no sense of humor. I ate fry bread and wandered from booth to booth. I laughed with others as a Cherokee woman made oohing and aahing sounds as she sold calendars of handsome Native American men. These men represented each of the months, and several of the different Indian Nations. The vendor told the women they should, "Buy now," for the calendars were selling quickly. And she was telling the truth. "Ooh, very handsome, don't you think?" I heard her say to the next woman coming along behind me. I smiled again. Her voice and the giggling trailed away as I wound through the throng.

Cheap carnival rides framed the eastern edge of the fairgrounds. Twister and a small Ferris Wheel competed with Scrambler and Moonwalk for the attention of teenagers, who seemed only interested in flirting with each other. The rides were never full. I stepped over the thick, black, snake-like cables that gave the mechanical rides their life and circled around past the bleachers where the Navajo comedian had performed earlier that evening, where the jingle dancers had moved about to rhythmic chants in colorful regalia, where a call for donations had been taken up for a family with a sick child. Past the bleachers, I made my way to a series of small booths near the food stands. Fry bread aroma filled the air.

An elementary school teacher sat on a folding chair behind a card table. "Three for a dollar," she said. Her sleek black hair framed her face neatly and curved under her chin. I asked her what cause the raffle supported. Following her explanation, I bought raffle tickets in support of the Cherokee Elementary School's efforts to raise money so that fourth graders might attend space camp. Space camp. Shaking my head, I thought to myself, here I am reaching for my past as these children are reaching for their future. But the next few displays acknowledged that the past was not forgotten.

After entering the brightly lit community hall, I perused the displays of children's artwork, beadwork, and basketwork. Pieces of white, 8 1/2 x 11 inch sheets of paper hung on the portable bulletin boards. Various roots, plants, and nuts had been scotch taped to the papers. Simple descriptions of what color dye came from which of the various vegetation had been handprinted along the side of the root, plant, or seedling—yellowroot, bloodroot, or walnut. The dyes would be applied to the reeds that were used in basket weaving. The bulletin boards and cafeteria-style tables held many crafts and a variety of artwork. Teenagers submitted ancestral-style paintings sometimes marked by modern identity as well as contemporary-style still life paintings. Children entered colorful crayon work. Adults contributed sophisticated watercolors. First prize, second prize, third prize! Best of show! Oh, and there were pies!

After leaving the brightly lit community hall, I found comfort in the soothing autumn moon. Moths fluttered high above the grease and the grills in the stadium light that lit the food stands. Carnival rides flickered with neon—red, blue, and green. I closed my eyes and took in a deep breath, as deep as I could breathe. I held it tight. The fall festival was like being home. It was comfortable. I breathed it in and made it a part of me. Actually, I don't remember exhaling.

Cat called out my name from somewhere in the crowd. I glanced around and caught a glimpse of her hand waving me toward her. She arrived late, after having fallen asleep at the cabin. I bought her some fry bread and showed her around. She laughed aloud at the vendor selling the sexy calendars, and she enjoyed the children's artwork. Vendors began packing up and we returned to our cabin. I slept well that night. Deep and undisturbed. Dreams, filled with the warmth of autumn, drifted luxuriously through my mind. An Indian Summer night's dream.

In the morning, I looked out over the valleys and mountains and was reminded of a poem that I had written, for the novel, *Echoes of Silence*, that I was currently writing. Based on Cherokee legend, the poem speaks of the homeland:

A Homeland

In search of a homeland,
they sent birds to find dry land,
so that some might leave Galunlati—
A heaven that had become too crowded.
But each of the birds returned exhausted
from flying over expansive oceans.
At last, they sent the Great Buzzard,
Who flew with strength and pride,
But he too became weary in his search.

The earth was dark and wet.
It seemed that no homeland would be found.
The Great Buzzard searched in the darkness.
He flew steadily, his wings rhythmically
moved through a vacuous
silence.

Darkness gave way only to the blackness of his wings.
Slowly, swooping downward, exhausted
by his search, Great Buzzard's
mammoth wings
struck wet
earth.
He arched
his weary back
and struggled skyward, soaring once again,

Bringing earth and soil and clay to heights unfathomable. Mountains!
Yet, Great Buzzard's strength could not hold.
His head drooped; His wings gave out;
He dove downward.
Dipping his wings into damp dirt,
Great Buzzard scooped up
the rich moist clay
leaving behind
valleys.

The once flat, wet, earth heaved and reeled
under the flapping of his wings
Upward and downward,
again and again
all this—
motion—existed without a murmur.
In the dark silence, in the shadow of the Creator,
the great flapping wings
brought mountains and valleys—
A homeland.

I packed slowly the day we left the Qualla Boundary. The television news-
caster's voice droned in the background as I filled my suitcase. Suddenly his
words caught my attention. He reported on the Columbus Day events that had
taken place the day before. I had not realized it was Columbus Day. I smiled to

think that I had passed through a Columbus day unscathed by stories of his hero-
ics. Yes, it warmed my heart to realize that I had spent Columbus Day as an
insider on the Qualla Boundary eating fry bread, instead of hearing about
Christopher Columbus, the hero-explorer, and inundated with parades in his
honor. But I also felt like an *outsider*, one who did not know how to relate to the
Smiling Chiefs, one who was surprised to find the children seeking money for
space camp, one who found the museums tacky, but the baskets and pottery col-
lectible by western standards. I was/am as torn as the place itself.

Images of the richness of the land and the poverty of the housing stood out
as Cat and I began our homeward trip. Decrepit trailers, old buses, junk of every
type and a billboard for Herrod's gambling casino set against the lush green and
autumn-colored mountain foliage attested to the tormented character of the
Cherokee reservation. A future trapped by the past; a past trapped by the present.
Nevertheless, I knew that I would miss the homeland.

I felt the car slowing. My reverie was interrupted. We were just on the other
side of the reservation, when my companion pulled into the local Starvin'
Marvin's mini-market to fill up on gas. As I turned back to see the reservation
behind me, I noticed the wooden sign that welcomed people to the Qualla Boundary. I crossed the street, took a final photo, then entered Starvin' Marvin's to buy
a soda for the road. I passed my friend, Cat, in the doorway of the mini-mart. The
bell above the door jingled. She returned to the car to wait for me.

A freckled-faced, red-haired man wearing coke-bottle thick glasses stood
behind the counter. I'll call him Marvin. I gave him the money for the diet pepsi
I had taken from the cooler. He said to me, "You want an Injun?" I looked confused. He pointed behind me as he repeated, "You want an Injun? I got a couple
of Injuns right here." I turned and looked. There sat two Cherokee men. Obviously, Marvin intended to get a good belly laugh by embarrassing them and me.
I said, "These men don't want me. They are much too handsome. They must
already have girlfriends of their own." One of the Cherokee men smiled at me as
if to say that I could not have made a better response.

Marvin grew angry. He pushed his face in front of me. He took off his coke-
bottle glasses.

"You think they're handsome? You need some glasses!" he said nearly spit-
ting on me in the process.

He tried to force the glasses on to my face. I cut his gesture short with a
quick move of my forearm against his wrist. I turned around to the Cherokee man
who had smiled at me. I made eyes with him and he made eyes with me. Then, I
brushed Marvin aside and left Starvin' Marvin's. I wish that I would have turned
around one last time and said to the Cherokee man, loud enough for Marvin to
hear, "*Donvdagohvi*, cousin" (till we meet again).

I looked back over my shoulder before getting into the car. The Cherokee
man with the expressive eyes stood at the doorway and looked at me. He smiled
and nodded. As we drove down the mountain road, I nodded, too.[2]

Note

1. I would like to thank Cat Warren for being my companion on the trip to the Qualla Boundary. Her efforts helped to make my trip possible. I also would like thank Timothy Hack, my husband, who also made this trip possible in many ways. In addition, I am grateful to Shirley Simpson, Peggy Rowe, Lisa Tillman-Healy, Devika Chawla, and Timothy Hack for their editorial comments. Finally, Purdue University supported my sabbatical research which allowed me to travel not only to the Qualla Boundary, but also to several other important cites in relation to Cherokee history. An earlier version of this story was presented at the National Communication Association's annual meeting in New York City (November, 1998).

Future Directions

ROBIN PATRIC CLAIR

Ethnography, a way of engaging and expressing cultural phenomenon, holds rich possibilities for contributing to cultural awareness despite its checkered past. At times, ethnographers have unveiled cultural mysteries; and at other times, they have disguised or oppressed cultural distinctions with colonial biases. The long history of ethnography provides moments of glory and moments of shame. However, recognizing our own cultural biases should help us to create alternatives that will allow us to approach cultural studies with "a good heart and a good mind."

Alternative approaches to cultural studies do more than wake up ethnographers to their own cultural prejudice; they open the door to new possibilities. This book is just the tip of the proverbial iceberg. The number of performance studies, documentary, virtual ethnography and multimedia ethnographies are growing. Not only are varied forms of representation achieving acceptance, but also varied theoretical perspectives are gaining momentum, as well. New theories, new methods, new practices and new expressions of ethnography are on the horizon. All of this adds up to new questions that by necessity call for new definitions of culture.

Cultures are neither static nor isolated. In today's world, cultures are woven together by social, political, and organizational threads that tie one culture to another. Ethnographers no longer have the luxury of studying a culture as if it is a simple job of isolating an *exotic* people and describing their existence. Instead, ethnographers need to look at the connecting and disconnecting discourses, the expressions that represent the betwixt and the between, and the communication that co-opts as well as the communication that confronts co-optation. For too long we have isolated a culture and then compared it to another culture. Today, cultures are colliding, slipping, and sliding into one another, sometimes in exciting,

289

novel ways; other times, in violent or repressive ways. To put it simply, culture is complex and ethnographers must acknowledge it is so.

Accepting complexity in ethnographic studies may raise more complicated questions both about cultures and about the methods and representation of culture. For example, research questions may grapple with the following kinds of questions: How does the economic discourse of one culture impact upon the religious discourse of another culture? How do patriarchal expressions of sexism create countercultures of feminism that live within a variety of ethnic cultures? How does the expression of one culture constitute another culture? How does one's identity shift as one passes from one cultural experience to another? New questions may require new methods. New methods may lead to unique forms of expression.

Taken together, researchers who advocate categorizing cultures according to certain variables may revise what they have offered in the past as organizational typologies. Previous labeling of cultures has been grounded in a myopic view. That is, categories like masculine or feminine, cooperative or competitive are derived from a European cultural foundation. Thus, the category system encourages the old colonial bias. For ethnography to step beyond its own inherent prejudice of the Other; its own inherent privileging of the Self, the ethnographer must engage in serious reflective critique with a considerably open mind. This will be challenging, to say the least.

And it is with this challenge to undertake alternative ethnographies of expression that I will end this epilogue. This appended commentary is meant not as a conclusion or a summary, but as a point of departure for future work in cultural studies. After all, an afterward is nothing more than the next forward.

Contributors

Catherine Becker (Ph.D., State University of New York at Buffalo) is an Associate Professor in the Communication Department at the University of Hawaii, Hilo. Her research interests focus on intersection of communication, cultural reproduction and transformation, boundaries, diversity, and healthy systems. Publications include book chapters and articles in the *Organization-Communication Emerging Perspective Series*, *International and Intercultural Communication Annual*, *Organizational Communication and Change*, and *The Huddled Masses*.

Mary Helen Brown (Ph.D., University of Texas) is an Associate Professor in the Department of Communication and Journalism at Auburn University. Research and teaching interests include organizational communication, health communication, and narrative. Publications include articles in *Research in Language and Social Interaction*, *Journal of Applied Communication Research*, *Journal of Health Communication*, *International Listening Journal*, *American Journalism*, among others. She has written chapters in *Communication Yearbook*, *Studies in Language and Social Interaction*, *Case Studies in Organizational Communication*, and *Qualitative Research: Applications in Organizational Life,* to name a few.

Devika Chawla (M.A., Central Michigan University) is a doctoral candidate in the Department of Communication at Purdue University. Research interests include relational and cultural approaches to interpersonal communication, and post-colonial approaches to the family. Her dissertation examines identity co-construction among women in India Hindu arranged marriages. Publications include articles in *Qualitative Inquiry* and *Radical Pedagogy*.

Robin Patric Clair (Ph.D., Kent State University) is an Associate Professor in the Department of Communication at Purdue University. Research and teaching interests include organizational communication, culture and ethnography, narrative, and film studies. Professor Clair has also written extensively on the topics of sexual harassment, socialization, and ethnic identity. Publications include articles in *Communication Monographs, Journal of Applied Communication, Management Communication Quarterly, Western Journal of Communication* and *Southern Journal of Communication* and numerous book chapters. Books include *Organizing Silence: A World of Possibilities* (SUNY, 1998). Professor Clair is a founding member of the Ethnography Division of the National Communication Association (NCA). She sits on numerous editorial boards and has received the "Outstanding Book of the Year" award as well as the "Golden Anniversary" award from NCA for her scholarship.

Jason E. Combs (M.A., University of Dayton) is a doctoral candidate in the Department of Communication at Purdue University. Research and teaching interests focus upon the intersections of power, identity, and discourse as these processes both condition possibilities for organization and communication and are conditioned by them, especially in relation to being family.

Frederick C. Corey (Ph.D., University of Arizona) is an Associate Dean of the College of Public Programs at Arizona State University. Research interests are performance studies and gay culture. Publications include articles in *Text and Performance Quarterly, Journal of Homosexuality, Western Journal of Communication,* and *Communication Quarterly*.

Julie M. Crandall (M.A., Auburn University) is a catcher in the Women's Professional Softball League. In the off-season, she lives and teaches in California.

Sarah Amira De la Garza (formerly Maria Cristina González) (Ph.D., University of Texas at Austin, D.Min., University of Creation Spirituality) is an Associate Professor and Southwest Borderlands Scholar in the Hugh Downs School of Human Communication at Arizona State University. She has held two Fulbright senior scholar awards to Mexico, where her fieldwork has contributed to the development of *The Four Seasons of Ethnography*, and her book, *Maria Speaks: Journeys into the Mysteries of the Mother in My Life as a Chicana,* an autoethnographic examination of culture and expression (in revision process, Peter Lang, 2003/2004).

Patricia Geist-Martin (Ph.D., Purdue University) is a Full Professor in the School of Communication at San Diego State University. Her research interests focus on negotiating identity, ideology, and control in organizations, particularly in health and illness. Geist-Martin has published over 40 articles and book chapters covering a wide range of topics. She just completed her third book, *Commu-*

nicating Health: Personal, cultural, and political complexities, (co-authored with Eileen Berlin Ray and Barbara Sharf) (Wadsworth, 2003). Her second book, co-edited with Linda A. M. Perry, is entitled *Courage of Conviction: Women's Words, Women's Wisdom*, (Mayfield, 1997). Her first book, *Negotiating the Crisis: DRGs and the Transformation of Hospitals* (with Monica Hardesty), was published in 1992 by Erlbaum. Her work appears in regional, national, and international journals such as *Communication Monographs*, *Management Communication Quarterly*, *Health Communication*, *Western Journal of Communication*, *Southern States Speech Journal*, and *Small Group Behavior*.

Harold Lloyd Goodall, Jr. (Ph.D., Penn State) is a Full Professor and Head in the Communication Department at the University of North Carolina at Greensboro. Research interests are in the intersections of ethnography, organizational, and family studies. Publications include articles in *Communication Theory*, *Qualitative Inquiry*, *American Communication Journal*, *Quarterly Journal of Speech*, *Communication Quarterly*, and *Southern Communication Journal*. Books include *Writing the New Ethnography*; *Casing a Promised Land: The Autobiography of an Organizational Detective as Cultural Ethnographer*; *Living in the Rock n Roll Mystery: Reading Context, Self, and Others as Clues*; and *Divine Signs: Connecting Spirit to Community*.

Elaine Bass Jenks, (Ph.D., Pennsylvania State University) is an Associate Professor in the Department of Communication Studies at West Chester University. Research interests focus on interpersonal communication between and among the blind, the sighted, and the visually impaired.

Christine E. Kiesinger, (Ph.D., University of South Florida), is an Assistant Professor and Chair of the Communication Studies Department at Southwestern University. Research interests include an exploration into the emotional and relational worlds of anorexic and bulimic women, autoethnography, and narrative inquiry. Publications include articles and book chapters in *Qualitative Inquiry*, *Fiction and Social Research*, *The Emotional Nature of Qualitative Research*, *Ethnographically Speaking: Autoethnography, Literature, and Aesthetics*, and the *American Communication Journal*.

Robert L. Krizek (Ph.D., Arizona State University), is an Associate Professor and Director of Graduate Studies in the Department of Communication at Saint Louis University. Teaching and research interests include organizational culture, ethnographic methodologies, sport communication, communication in third places, and, most recently, the examination of the personal and cultural significance of non-routine public events through the excavation of the personal narratives of those in attendance. Publications include chapters in five recent anthologies as well as articles in the *Quarterly Journal of Speech*, *Management Communication Quarterly*, *Journal of Applied Communication Research*, *Journal of Sport and Social Issues*, *Adolescence*, and other journals.

Marifran Mattson (Ph.D., Arizona State University) is an Associate Professor in the Department of Communication at Purdue University. Research and teaching interests explore the intersection of health communication and organizational communication by considering the relationship between communication processes and problems related to health and human safety. Publications include articles in *Communication Monographs*, *Journal of Applied Communication Research*, *Health Communication*, *Journal of Health Communication*, *Communication Studies*, *Management Communication Quarterly*, *American Journal of Health Behavior*, and *American Journal of Pharmaceutical Education*, a chapter in the *Handbook of Health Communication*, and other book chapters.

William K. Rawlins (Ph.D., Temple University) is a Full Professor in the Department of Communication at Purdue University. His research and teaching interests address interpersonal and relational communication, dialogue and experience, communication and narrative, interpretive and ethnographic inquiry, Gregory Bateson and communication theory, and communication in friendships across the life course. His publications include articles in *Communication Theory*, *Journal of Social and Personal Relationships*, *Western Journal of Communication*, and *Studies in Symbolic Interaction*. He is author of the book, *Friendship Matters: Communication, Dialectics, and the Life Course*.

Amardo Rodriguez (Ph.D., Howard University) is an Associate Professor in the Communication Department at Syracuse University. Research and teaching interests explore the potentiality of emergent conceptions of communication that foreground moral, existential, and spiritual assumptions about the human condition to redefine and enlarge current understandings of democracy, diversity, and community. Publications include articles in *Journal of Intercultural Communication*, *Journal of Intergroup Relations*, *Journal of Religion and Society*, *Qualitative Report*, *Journal of Rural Community Psychology*, *Southern Communication Journal*, and elsewhere. Books include *On Matters of Liberation (I): The Case Against Hierarchy*, *Diversity as Liberation (II): Introducing a New Understanding of Diversity*, and *Essays on Communication and Spirituality: Contributions to a New Discourse on Communication*.

Pamela Chapman Sanger (M.A., Purdue University) is the mother of two boys and a lecturer at California State University, Sacramento. Research interests include: issues of organization and gender and the intersection of work and family life. Publications include articles in *Qualitative Inquiry* and the *Journal of*

Applied Communication Research, and book chapters in *Rethinking Organizational and Managerial Communication from a Feminist Perspective* and the *Handbook of Organizational Studies.*

Dean Scheibel (Ph.D., Arizona State University) is an Associate Professor in the Communication Studies Department at Loyola Marymount University. His work has been published in *Communication Monographs, Communication Studies, Journal of Applied Communication Research, Southern Communication Journal, Text and Performance Quarterly,* and *Western Journal of Communication.* He plays bass guitar in Back Pages, a "cover" band that works frequently in Los Angeles.

Christina W. Stage (Ph.D., Arizona State University) is the Director of the Interdisciplinary Studies Program at Arizona State University. Research and teaching interests explore the intersection of organizational communication and intercultural communication. Publications include articles in *Management Communication Quarterly,* a chapter in *Whiteness: The Communication of Social Identity* and contributions to other organizational and intercultural publications.

Bryan C. Taylor (Ph.D., University of Utah) is an Associate Professor in the Department of Communication at the University of Colorado, Boulder. His research specializes in qualitative methods, and in cultural, organizational, and technology studies. His qualitative research has been published in *Communication Research; Journal of Applied Communication Research; Journal of Contemporary Ethnography; Journal of Organizational Change Management; Studies in Cultures, Organizations, and Societies;* and *Western Journal of Communication.* He is co-author with Thomas R. Lindlof of *Qualitative Communication Research Methods* (2nd ed.) (Sage, 2002).

Jim Thomas (Ph.D., Michigan State University), is a Full Professor of Sociology/Criminal Justice at Northern Illinois University. He specializes in prison research, research ethics and methods, social theory, and computer culture. His journal articles have appeared in *Social Problems, Criminology, Justice Quarterly,* and *Symbolic Interaction,* among others. In addition to numerous book chapters, he is author of several books, including *Doing Critical Ethnography* (Sage, 1993).

Lisa M. Tillmann-Healy (Ph.D., University of South Florida) is an Assistant Professor in the Communication Department at Rollins College. Her research interests center around qualitative and narrative approaches to the study of relationships, gender, and sexualities. Publications include articles in *The Journal of Personal and Interpersonal Loss* and chapters in *Composing Ethnography* and

Ethnographically Speaking. Between Gay and Straight: Understanding Friendship Across Sexual Orientation (AltaMira Press, 2001) is her first book.

Sarah J. Tracy (Ph.D., University of Colorado, Boulder) is an Assistant Professor in The Hugh Downs School of Human Communication at Arizona State University. Research interests focus upon the qualitative study of emotion, identity and burnout in organizations. Her work has appeared in the *Journal of Applied Communication Research*, *Management Communication Quarterly*, *Human Communication Research* and *The Western Journal of Communication*, as well as in edited books and trade magazines. She is coauthor with Stan Deetz and Lyn Simpson of the book *Leading Organizations through Transition: Communication and Cultural Change* (Sage, 2000).

Nick Trujillo (Ph.D., University of Utah) is a Full Professor in the Department of Communication Studies at California State University, Sacramento. His research and teaching interests include organizational culture, media sports culture, family culture, and, most recently, dog culture. Publications include articles in *Communication Monographs*, *Quarterly Journal of Speech*, *Critical Studies in Mass Communication*, *Text and Performance Quarterly*, *Management Communication Quarterly*, *Journal of Contemporary Ethnography*, *Qualitative Inquiry*, *Journal of Sport and Social Issues*, *Sociology of Sport Journal* and others. His books include *Organizational Life on Television* (with Leah Vande Berg), *The Meaning of Nolan Ryan*, and *In Search of Naunny's Grave: The Meaning of Grandmother in American Culture*.

Paaige K. Turner (Ph.D., Purdue University) is an Assistant Professor in the Communication Department at Saint Louis University. She teaches and conducts research in the general areas of organizational communication, feminist theory, and health communication. Her research has looked at the creation and negotiation of contradiction, specifically within the topics of organizational socialization, midwifery and birth, and the body in the workplace. Publications include articles in *Communication Monographs*, *Qualitative Inquiry*, *Women and Language*, *Argumentation and Advocacy*, and *Midwifery Today*.

Index